A
Golden Harvest

Kelsang Pawo

Table of Contents

Introduction 1

Part one: The East End 3

Part Two: A Life on the Ocean Waves... 87

Part Three: India and the Himalayas...208

Part Four: London and new friends.Good food, film stars and a Princess 261

Part 4: Back to the Himalayas. 298

Conclusion 354

Acknowledgements 357

Introduction

This is a story of an East London boy, who left his roots to travel the world, to finally become a Buddhist monk in the Himalayan Kingdom of Bhutan.

Along the way, he rubbed shoulders with many individuals, from the infamous Kray Twins, to Princess Diana, to stars of stage and screen.

He tells of these experiences and his eventual friendship with the Dalia Lama and the Royal family of Bhutan. All were to play their part in helping him reach his ultimate goal of indomitable happiness.

It is quite remarkable to meet a man, who claims that every moment of his life has born fruit. There is no doubt that the reader of this book will be inspired, to plant healthy seeds, that inevitably lead to a *Golden Harvest*.

Through past karma, you have gained a rare and precious human life.

Do not fall asleep now.

H.H the 14th Dalai Lama

Part one

The East End

Birth to Fifteen

I was still in short trousers when Mum bought me a wrist watch. I don't know how old I was, maybe I was eight, or perhaps I was nine or ten. She waited until the house was empty. There was just Mum and I, we were alone. Her face was lit by pleasure and excitement, that made me wary as to what was to come. Mum was up to a something, a conspiracy she was about to share with me.

"I have something very special for you" she said, then in a whisper she added "but don't tell your father. He'll go up the wall" With those few words, she took my elbow and half pushed and half led me up the wooden hill, as she called our stairs.

Mum led me to her bedroom. I wondered when I would ever tell Dad a secret. "We would need to have a conversation first," I thought. Chats with Dad did not happen in our house. Mum's room was rare turf for me, I had only been in there on a few previous occasions, it was usually out of bounds.

Reaching up, stretching on tip toe, Mum felt around on the top shelf of the built-in pine cupboard. Whilst watching her with one eye, I looked with the other, at the lino under the window. I wondered, just as I did the last time I was in her room, why it had been cut so badly? It had been trimmed in an uneven gagged line, perhaps even torn with a hope and a prayer. Part went under the skirting board and another part did not. Perhaps the workman was inexperienced, may be Dad did the work himself and made a mess of it. The lino was clean, as was the room, but I could see ends of floorboards and thought it un-necessary. Whoever did the work, with a little care and attention, could have made a better job of it. Or maybe it was me, maybe I had an eye for detail, or maybe I was a perfectionist.

The gift that Mum produced from its hiding place came as a great disappointment to me. It sent me into a silence, that I now associate with having been *struck dumb*. I don't know why, but I felt a deep sense of foreboding. I wished Mum had not bought it for me. I did not want to be in this position and I did not want to look at the lino either. *Heart Break Hotel* played on the radio. Fitting in a way. Mum usually sang along with Elvis, she danced to his music too, but she was not singing or dancing now.

I did not want a watch and I know Mum saw this written on my face. I only wore it once and that was for twenty minutes on the day that I received it. I could hear the disappointment in Mums voice and saw it in her demeanour. For days to come she would ask where the watch was. She could see it was not on my wrist. She would ask. *"Had I lost it?" "Had it broken?"* I did not wish to hurt her feelings, but I felt strongly against ever wearing a time piece and had in the end to tell her so. I did not understand the need or necessity to be encumbered by unnecessary weight. By weight, I do not mean the physical weight, but I did see it as a form of burden. Like negative thoughts, they do not actually weigh anything, they are just thoughts, but they are still in themselves heavy and therefore a burden. Strange thoughts for a kid to have. But truly I did not like the watch and did not like it in my bedroom either. It was like the crocodile I thought to be under my bed, the one that I was secretly afraid of, on every evening of my young years, I thought of Captain Hook, I thought the crocodile would bite me, only it would be my foot it would eat and not my hand. The watch even had a crocodile strap, artificial but none the less it was crocodile, so why would I wish to wear it? I had no intention to ever be late for anything in life. I had been taught to be respectful of the time people gave to me, therefore through good manners, if I agreed to meet with others, or gave my word to them, then I would always be on time. Why would things change? I was too young to think these things through, but I suppose that's what confidence is. It helps you make up your mind and to follow instincts and to make decisions. That's its job! Certainly, I was a confident young man. I had a strong sense that, not only my childhood, but my life potential would be hampered, or redirected if I was to adopt this alien thing as being an appropriate addition to my body weight. I described my feelings to Mum with the kindest words I could muster. "A watch is the first step to becoming a slave," I told her. I do not think she really understood my reasons for such strong and heartfelt rejection. I told her that I would keep the watch safe, that maybe I would see things differently one day and we both left it at that, though Mum did add, that she was pleased I had not made a promise to her. "The braking of a promise is a person's undoing and eventually the inability to keep a vow will bring about the end of the world" she foretold. It is short statements of this nature that I have remembered from my childhood. Not because I ever thought these words would ever help me, or at the time, that the world would ever come to an end through a lack of moral discipline, but more because the circumstances of their delivery embedded them into my mind. It was several weeks later that my grandpop told me that Mum had gone to the extra expense of having my name engraved on the back of the watch. It was beautifully done, written in italics and I had not noticed.

My parents were the best in the world. I received undiluted love and true affection from Mum and no guidance or encouragement from Dad, but that suited me right down to the ground. That's why I thought him to be the best dad in the world, because he did not interfere, nag or drag me off anywhere for bonding purposes. I was a happy kid with a good life and I had no wish to be like him. He was my dad and I left it at that. He was never one to say much. In fact, he rarely spoke to anybody at all. The general opinion seemed to be, that he lived and fed from a diet of misery. I do remember him telling me once, that he would have made something of his life, if it had not have been for Adolf Hitler and his antics. I could not believe he would say something like that. I told him that we all had Mum and that should be enough for all of us.

I was always confident, that I was going to have a good and fruitful life, free of fear, no doubts and no confusion. I believed that my success would likely be despite anyone else and not necessarily because of them. I did not want conversation with Dad, he always brought me down. I felt, that I was born and then placed into storage, waiting for my day or time to arrive and then my life would begin. I knew nothing outside of the East End but I did know that life could be better than this. Mum had a fear of the future and advised me not to be so cock-sure about my own, that I should be watchful for pitfall's. "They're everywhere and mostly appear out from the blue," she would warn. Life can change in a single moment, just like that," she would say, clicking her thumb and index finger.

I listened but kept most of my thoughts to myself, not because there was no person for me to talk to, or that there was no person who would listen, but because I was unable to express myself clearly. I did not want for my confidence to be misunderstood. It was an under-laying knowledge of prosperity that I had for my future, rather than a conscious thought or vision of its certainty. I always felt fortunate and therefore always believed myself to be so. If I had tried to express myself, I am certain that my tongue would have become knotted, and Mum would have carted me off to the doctors. I later read in the library, that when Brunel told his father that iron would float, his father told him to keep his thoughts to himself and not to tell the neighbours. I felt the same instincts, to keep my thoughts to myself too. I did not believe that everything would go my way on a daily basis, indeed, they rarely did. There were times when it rained and times when Arsenal lost. But I did believe that whatever low blow that life would bestow upon me, I would be of a mind to understand it and therefore, there would be no need to overcome it.

Dad was a great teacher. I had a living example, right under my nose, of what I did not want to be like. I was desperately sad for him but I was Okay with it. I was learning lessons right from the off and most of them from him. I would often defend Dad when need be. I was never comfortable when *outsiders* so to speak, took delight in telling me how crass he was. If anyone had a hard time with him, then it was of no use coming to me as a mediator. Despite everything he was my dad. His way was his own business and definitely not any of mine, and who were these people, that thought it okay to run someone down via that person's son? Always there were lessons to be learnt. It's not that I dismissed everything I heard, I logged everything that was said. But I did learn early that a gossip was an unhappy person and one to be very wary of. Grandpop told me stories of how gossips had a poisonous and wicked tongue. His stories made great sense to me. *Beware a gossip!*

Dad always worked. He never harmed me with his dower moods and though there was no evidence, I somehow knew he was always there to keep an eye over me. Though, it is a possibility that he kept me in sight, so to speak, as he knew I was fully aware of his secret. I knew he gambled and he knew I knew. Therefore, he knew that I was aware of why Mum had to struggle financially at times.

My relationship with Dad was contradictory. I loved him but did not like him. His company was always awkward and never comfortable, as much as I tried to ignore it, it still brought with it a thick air that was definitely unpleasant. There was little oxygen to breath when we were alone together. The atmosphere was draining. Like being under water. If I had been wearing a neck tie, I would have wanted to loosen it, or take it off all together. I felt strangled in Dads company. I would often avoid him, particularly if I saw him with his mates over at the Arsenal. He was happy there, especially when the Gunners won, which they usually did at home, and that seemed odd to me. How could he jump up and down celebrating a football victory and then come home a totally different person? I thought it very strange! I realise now, that I did not approach dad at the football, I would not even say hello to him, or even wave to attract his attention because I did not want to see his mood change at the sight of me. I suppose I felt that the responsibility of his family was the source of his deep discontent. But I did love him dearly, in a sad sort of a way. I learnt to become grateful to him for my birth. Much later in life, at his funeral, he taught me one of life's greatest lessons. *Never to assume!* Never think we know everything about everyone and everything. Family members and close friends told me snippets of Dad's difficult history and if those stories were true, then there is no doubt, he was a good man, if somewhat damaged.

I did not need a bossy or over powering father who told me to do things his way and I saw it as a blessing that I did not get one. It would have led, most likely, to conflict. I was my own person. Life as it was prepared me for the future. When I look back now that I have some experience to weigh things up by, I can see that Dad lived in pain, that he suffered mental anguish. Not a physical pain, but unable to express his love and affection. He was scarred by his past and hurting at the thought of the future. He did not feel secure. He could visualise, that at any given moment, his world could collapse around his ears. Therefore, he held all that he cherished at a distance. Nothing and nobody could enter in through his defence systems. He held up strong walls, as solid and impregnable as a bullet proof shield. I have spoken to him several times since his death. I know that most people would think this to be nonsense. But whether he has heard me, or not, does not matter. I feel that we reconciled, and that's good enough for me.

Everybody thought Dad was a tough nut to crack, but again, looking back, I can see signs, flashes that he definitely did care about all manner of things. He had solid opinions and would have liked to change the world for the better. He was a bright, and I think intelligent man. He had high and very clear standards. There was much more to him than immediately met the eye. Too often we are quick to judge! I recall when a condemned murderer was hung in Wandsworth jail. We youngsters were not supposed to know about these things but of course we did. The radio on execution days would go to Big Ben and the countdown to the trap door dropping was heard in every household. All went deathly quiet. The only sound in our house was the clunk of Big Bens hands turning toward the hour mark. I waited by the stairs for the BBC announcement that the condemned prisoner had been hung by the neck until dead. Years later I was to meet Georgie Ellis, the daughter of Ruth Ellis, the last woman in England to have been hanged for murder. I wondered how Georgie dealt with this. Sometimes she seemed to deal with it well and other times she seemed to not be dealing with it at all. Bless her heart, I liked Georgie.

Execution times were difficult for Dad to stomach, he had compassion and he had vivid memories too. It was written on his face. At his funeral, his brothers told me that Dad was forced, whilst in the military, to be a prosecution witness in a treason trial. Dad was a driver to a senior officer in Egypt. The officer was accused of colluding with the enemy. He was found guilty and hung by the neck until dead. This gave me great cause to think. We don't always know the contents of other people's lives, the things that affect them deeply, those events that have a profound effect upon them. It is not always big things but often an accumulation of smaller things that gather together and hit them hard. In retrospect there were signs of Dad's better nature in many things that he did. Sundays he would often go off to Hyde Park, *Speakers Corner*. Where, not every week, but occasionally, he would speak from a soap box. I would go ahead of him and watch from a distance, just like I did at the Arsenal. I learnt a great deal watching him in this way. People would shout at him whilst others cheered and clapped. He was steadfast against the taunting and always said his piece but always came home defeated, never elated. He was a labour man and wanted fare play and was never slow in sharing his political views.

Speaker's corner was very well known as the place where anyone with something to say, could stand up and say it without fear of being arrested. It was very political and I am certain there would have been national security officials mingling in the crowd. I thought, that this would make sense, if you give a person an opportunity to speak, then he or she will, and when they do you can hear what they say and keep record of it, if controversial. Karl Marx, the communist spoke at Speakers corner in his day. I am sure government would have sent an agent to listen to him! I would scan the crowd looking for the secret service. I would check out those in trilby hats and rain macs. I wondered if the spies had spotted me, I know Dad was not aware of my occasional presence. I would arrive early and leave late. It was a secret game for me, like being in a John le Carre novel.

The tradition of Speaker's Corner dates back to the Victorian times when all protest marches would end at Hyde Park, even Emily Pankhurst and other Suffragettes spoke at Speakers Corner. Whether the marchers came to London from the North, South, East or West, Hyde Park was their destination. It is to be found near Marble Arch, a land mark, that was built on the site of Tyburn village. Tyburn was most noted for the gallows that took the lives of many highway men and local scoundrels. The end of Tyburn as a village was linked to the gallows being taken to Newgate prison where those in debt were incarcerated, often with their families until there debt was paid.

London has a fascination history. I discovered much of it whilst pretending as a youth, to be an undercover agent. This is when I discovered the museums and the art galleries of the

West End. Dad was working class and proud of it too. He believed in ruling classes. He believed the ordinary person was not equipped to run a country. He was proud to be British and felt few people were capable of looking after themselves, let alone the affairs of fifty-two million people. For this reason, he was content to see his employer buy a bigger house and a bigger car, as to him this meant, he would keep his job and would likely mean a pay rise due to the company doing well. That is all he wanted, safety and security. He had no interest in risk or aspiring to anything more.

I did not know my father's father. I never did hear any stories of him either. I had no proof and I did not seek any but I had grown up always believing that he was a scoundrel. He knocked on doors and bought suits and fur coats from those who needed money to pay rent or buy groceries. Nan and he had six children. They all closely resembled each other, all having what I always saw as an East End jaw line, so without having to ask or wonder, I knew they all had the same dad. No need to ask questions if what you see supplies the answer I would think. My dad was the eldest of the six children, then came three younger sisters. All three married career villains and then came the two youngest, two inseparable brothers born less than a year apart. Children in those days were not permitted to listen to adult conversation. "It's not for your ears" Mum would say. But I saw the company my uncles kept and how they stood in corners, eyes looking everywhere, ever watchful whilst talking in deep whispers as they chatted, listened and nodded with some of the most unlikely looking characters. Often, I saw them with the Kray twins who later were to become notorious and eventually they, along with several others were convicted of gangland murders.

The Kray family lived along the road from us. This was another place where I often saw my uncles, standing in the street chatting, but more often with the twin's elder brother, Charlie Kray. I stood in the back ground and watched from the corner of my eye, watching the body language. I suppose if you lived in that world of villainy, then those of a kind, were bound to know each other. "Birds of a feather," Mum would have said. But better to not be seen. I kept my head down, still pretending to be a secret agent. This was my game and I was good at it.

The chaps, as they were known, always had their shoes shone to a mirror finish. Their suits were always stitched by hand by their chosen tailor. Just what the gangsters ordered! Wives would starch shirt collars and cuffs and buy their men golden cufflinks. This it seemed to be the trade mark for those who moved in that world of dodginess. These men were adored by their families, their wives spoke of them with enormous love and respect, their children hugged them and sat on their lap to tell them excitedly about their day. Friends were loyal, integrity was total. It was good to see. This style of dress was not limited to the few. There were many dodgy characters and many dressed in the same immaculate way. Of course, I did not know the full extent of my uncle's activities. I am not certain anybody knew exactly what they did, apart from have some connection, or at least some influence over the unlicensed drinking clubs and card dens in Whitechapel, Shoreditch, Hackney, Bethnal Green and Stepney. Certainly, these establishments were common knowledge. They had to be for people to know about them and use them. This naturally meant that my uncles were both connected and therefore protected. Something else for Dad to be depressed about, but it was none of my business. It was best that way! Even though I was called upon to run an occasional errand. An envelope from here to there, it was still none of my business.

Mum, her family and background were a completely different kettle of fish altogether. Goodness me, what a beautiful woman my mother was. Completely selfless! There to serve her family without question or waiver. I loved her so very much! I always complimented her. She had a figure to die for. I remember her slim waist. She was so warm, not hard but not soft either. She was perfect! I remember she told me of how she and her sisters-in-laws, Dads sisters, would draw an ink line down the back of their legs during the war. This would give the impression they were wearing nylon stockings. There was no money to buy the real thing when in their youth, so they faked it. I was surprised at this attempt to appear beautiful. As nice as Mums legs were, it was her smile, her beautiful face and the graceful manner in which she moved that caught the eye. Mum told me that young ladies in those days drank vinegar, not too much, but a sip a day would keep them slim. Everything it seemed, boiled down to money and image.

Without Mum in the house, the atmosphere was very bleak. When she came home, she brought sunshine, joy and optimism with her. The house lit up and came to life with her presence. The house even smelt differently when she was out. It's as though her perfume, her very essence was missing. If I knew where she was, then I would go and meet her, often I would see her walking along the road, heavily laden with her bags. Anything was better than waiting for her in the house. I sometimes thought, that she may not come home. That she may have had enough of the life she was living. She could not read or write very well but I knew she could always do well for herself. She was a worker and had a solid work ethic. It was circumstances that led her to remain near illiterate. Her brothers kept a very close eye on her when she was young and would not allow her out of their sight, this included school. They would not let her attend. They kept her home, where they knew where she was. Often, I would help carry her shopping. It really hurt me to the core of my being, to see how she would struggle with several bags of groceries. One or even two bags in each hand and others hanging from her wrist, cutting off the blood flow it seemed, leaving deep welts, marks that showed her efforts on our behalf. But as usual, never a moan left her lips. The hurtful thing was, as I mentioned earlier, that I knew Dad gambled and he knew I knew, therefore I realised he was keeping mum financially short, but she always managed and there was always food in the house. Always a clean house. Always patience from her and loving kindness. Dad would disappear over to Hackney dog stadium, White City or Wimbledon, whilst mum always had time for troubled neighbours, who would call round on a regular basis to express their hardships. Mum always found time for them. Her response to them was always the same. "Put the kettle on," she would say. "We'll have a nice cup of tea, then you can tell me all about it." I was never told what their troubles were. It was not for my ears, so I was sent out. That always suited me.

I did not think much about girls or of having a girlfriend. I liked girls of course and certainly had a favourite, but I always knew, that were I to settle down, so to speak, to a married life, then my chosen one would have to share the same qualities as my mother. I'm afraid to say that my tolerance levels were not too high. I tried going shopping with a few girls in those early years but soon I made up my mind that I was not going to spend too much of my life going from one stall to another, dithering and unable to make up my mind, as to whether to buy this dress or another. I simply could not be bothered with grey areas. To me it was simple. If you like a garment, then buy it. No point in dithering. In fact, better if you know what you're going out to purchase, head straight for it, buy it and then get on with your day. Later in life, I was to realise that confidence in one self is a good thing but it is healthy, if that confidence is tempered with a good dose of humility. A bit of give and take. I am sure that I displayed too much impatience and a lack of understanding with the ways and habits of others. Without humility, confidence can soon come across as bossy, uncaring or even arrogant. But again, that is how I was. I had my own speed, my own time table and any girl who was going to last the distance with me was going to have her own life and interest besides me. Strange thing to realise before the age of fifteen, but that's how it was, I did not ever stand still, my life had a forward momentum and certainly I had no intention to hover for long periods, or to go backward.

Jennifer was my only serious girl friend from school days. She was perfect and came from a good family. Her mum was home all day and kept a spotless house. Her father was a bus conductor. He was always whistling a happy tune. I liked her parents a lot and her two elder brothers soon became mates. They were a very kind family and encouraged me in many ways. We lost touch after school. I went to sea and that was that. I often think of how Jenny faired. She was a twin. I wondered if we may have had twins too. *Please!* Not boy's! and not in the East End! And definitely not named Reg and Ron!

Boyfriends and girlfriends were not encouraged among youngsters in our part of the world. "Plenty enough time for all of that" Mum would say. She made it clear that she was not happy about my having a girlfriend, so I never took Jenny home. Mum met her on a few occasions, when she called at the door, but Mum never invited her over the threshold. I can only be grateful at the Victorian values held by Mum, as involvement or commitment at such a young age would definitely have altered the outcome of my life, so I have no regrets. Mum as always was right! I have no idea of how mum would have taken to my brief association with Linda, who lived in Mare Street. Linda knew my mum; she was a good-looking woman in her forties. Her husband did not come home from the war, He was lost in action. Linda would often flash her bits in front of me, she knew I was looking and I never pretended I wasn't. As time went by, she got more and more daring. After all, said and done, I definitely wasn't going to call the police. Linda was lonely and I hoped life worked out well for her. I think Jenny and I worked because we did not actually need each other. She functioned, as I did, perfectly well, whether we were together or not. I truly believe we would have eventually married but how many other couples are there of the same mind as me? Millions no doubt. The first love being the deepest! But it's true. We did not try and get along, we just did. We did not bicker. We were both adults by the age of ten. It was natural to be with her.

The East End was made up by very close communities. Whether directly or indirectly, everybody knew each other. If us children made a nuisance of ourselves, there was always somebody who would warn us that they Knew our mum, or called out, that they knew where we lived. Nothing got past our mothers. This is why most of us attended school. Our mothers would know if we did not. There was a watch system that had built up among women that kept a social order. An East End woman was not a person to mess with. If you gave one any lip, they were not slow to clip your ear, or worst still, you would have their sons chasing after you. Women held homes together. They were the back bone of our existence. Our mothers knew everything. It was a safe place to live for us youngsters. There were eyes everywhere. The streets were lined with prams. They were outside each house on the pavement, while mothers did their house work. This of course is something that would not happen today, as the communities no longer exist. This is just one example of the difference between a real community and a supposed one. Children were safe. I believe this because mothers would not have left their babies outside in the street, if there was even a hint of danger. I don't know if I actually remember, or whether I think I do, but I seem to recall laying in a pram, looking at the sky, while parked in the street, where all infants spend an hour or two in the afternoons.

School was exciting for me. I did not adore it, in the sense that I found it easy or exhilarating, but I did recognise its uses. I figured that if my teachers were dedicated to their career, as they obviously were, then they might have something useful to teach me, so naturally I listened, absorbed and learnt. Why would I not? Mathematics itself was never an easy subject for me, try as I may, even to this day, I do not know what algebra means but I grew up certainly knowing how much change I was given in shops and the value of a pound note. Mum had always been fugal and I decided that this would do for me too. There was no sense in wastage, whether it be money or time. By listening and watching closely, I learnt how to sum up the character of people and situations and whether there was a good agenda or not. This was to become my form of mathematics, what actions added up in life and what actions certainly did not. My time spent pretending to be a spy were certainly well spent, I learnt what not to do by noting the mistakes and fool hardiness of others, whilst understanding that kindness would always have its own rewards.

My teachers had no ulterior motives. They were good people who cared about their profession. Why would I make life difficult for them, when it was me who was so fortunate? I could imagine them as young students, I want to be a teacher when I grow up, they would tell their parents. It was not for me, to cause them to regret such a dream. I learnt a great deal at school. Mostly what I did not want from life rather than what would be useful, but none the less, my time at school was of great value. For instance, I somehow knew, that I was not to become a nine to five factory worker, but I thrived at metal work and could make a wrought iron gate, if ever that was to prove useful. It was good to use my hands, to visualise, to measure things and to develop eye to hand coordination. Teaching was once seen as a lifelong dedication. Our female teachers often remained unmarried, as indeed nurses did also. It was considered the thing to do. To marry ones dedicated profession. It must have been hard for them at times as so many children were wayward. Fathers came home from the war as different people. Relationships changed within the home and traditionally the East End was known to be trying, to say the very least.

One of my teachers, Mr Wilson, was a particularly good man. I took to him the moment I met him. He was an open book and easy to read. I would see how his eyebrows would travel up and down on his forehead. They told a story. They revealed his caring nature. None of my class mates ever mentioned his eyebrows and nor did I, it would have been disrespectful to do so. It would be unfair to describe them as caterpillars, but they were rather like that, as if they had a life of their own. They would come together and kiss when he frowned and separate to opposite sides of his head when he felt surprise. He did not look like Groucho Marks but he did make me think of him.

Mr Wilson watched with a careful unobtrusive eye over all his students, I am certain he understood every one of us and was somehow aware of our individual background and the homes we each came from. He would treat us all the same whilst recognising us as individuals, always encouraging where he was able and leaving us be where he felt he could not. Certainly, he encouraged me in every interest I had. I watched him deal with sticky situations. He cared about people. It was clear to see. I was very fortunate! I remember once he told me to not groan. He said it would make me old before my time. "Making sounds like that will not encourage others" he used to say. He said that moaning is not a good example to set within any community as it never helps a situation to improve. I listened to him and put his advice to the test. The truth is, I have only occasionally moaned since. He was right! Who is ever inspired by a groaner? On occasion I have let half a groan out of my mouth, then thought of Mr Wilson, smiled and let the rest of the negative sound remain unexpressed. Bless his heart, such a little teaching but none the less, immense in terms of life enhancing.

I stored these words in my mind, in the same place as I stored mums advise, of never making a promise I cannot keep. I was accumulating a useful list of good advice. On my leaving school, Mr Wilson became my confidant. On a few occasions I went back to school after hours and caught him before he headed for home. I talked to him about Dad making arrangement, behind my back, to send me off to sea. I was shocked by Dads decision and could not make neither head nor tail of it. I thought he simply wanted rid of me. Mr Wilson and I spoke about all manner of things. I told him of my interest in the meaning of life. "What is the meaning of life" I asked, "if someone can make decisions on your behalf, that can make us so deeply unhappy?". He told me he had heard about my interest, from Miss Hobart, whilst taking tea in the staff room, and believed that one day I would gain the knowledge I sought. We became very close and discussed things that might have been considered private, or should have been kept in house so to speak. He told me of how he was placed in jail during the war. That he was a conscientious objector. He refuted violence and was severely punished for his stance. Just by listening to him, I realised how noble, brave and completely sincere he was. In my eyes, he was a true hero. I will always be thankful to dear old Mr Wilson. On account of going to sea, he suggested I obey my father. He said with eyes and ears as sharp as mine, I would surely discover a world far beyond the restrictions of East London. He told me the world would become my oyster. "Try it and see" he said. "You can always come back here. And who knows, you may even discover the meaning of life," he added.

During the course of our lives, there are times, if we are truly fortunate, when we meet a person with our interest truly at their heart. When this happens, we must recognise our good fortune and put their advice to the litmus test. I did just this with Mr Wilson's advice, I truly believed that our meeting each other in life had a very real purpose. I went many times to the library over the coming few weeks and looked at the pictures in travel books, whilst reading snippets from here and there. I saw mud huts, vast oceans and great lakes. Whales, penguins and great apes. Elephants and kangaroos. Places and wild life that most would never see. It was the mountains that caught my imagination most. Not the Alps or the Pyrenes nor the Andes but the Himalayas. Twelve hundred miles of immense stone structures, often with the most extreme weather conditions that felt truly familiar to me. I had a strong sense of certainty that one day, I would feel their magnificence beneath my feet again. I did not say, but I believed I had been there before. The region was very real to me. Combing through the books I felt I had a knowledge of the place, that I would know my way around when I eventually find myself there. I felt that my period in storage was coming to an end, that life was about to begin, that Mr Wilson was right, that I would find all my answers and find complete contentment. I did not read any of the library books from cover to cover. There were too many that attracted my attention, but I took something from all of them. Books are so very important. They have the power to truly help us, maybe not the whole book, but just a phrase, or a few words within each of them.

On several occasions during my life I have thanked authors for the words they wrote for us, whether that be Charles Dickens or any other great writer who expressed themselves for the benefit of the reader. I learnt to listen and not dismiss the views of those who are considered to be of dim wit, for instance. Charles Dickens character, Mr Dicks, like a child, would always have words of wisdom to offer. It was a great teaching to realise at such a young age, that answers are found in the simplicity of things and rarely in the complexity of an issue.

I made up my mind that I would not groan or show any apprehension of going to sea, but look forward with great optimism to a life beyond the limited horizons of my birth place. Maybe, I smiled to myself, I may get to meet Robinson Crusoe. You may not be too surprised to hear, that I did not meet Mr Crusoe, but I certainly went to islands, particularly in the Pacific Ocean and the Caribbean Sea, that could easily have been his habitat. I was certain, that I would find my answers to the meaning of life when free in the world of wonder. If I had been asked about my life prior to this date, I would have compared it to living in a windowless, though very comfortable hut, on a mountain top. I had been very happy to live in the hut, but now the walls were to slip away. I was excited to see what the greater view held for me. I was on the brink of something exhilarating and with thanks for my father's decision, I was set to see the bigger picture.

English, history and geography were my favourite subjects. English, because I truly believed that if I learnt my own language well, then I would be able to express myself without generating conflict. I figured that the art of give and take, negotiation, was of great importance. Throughout my life to date, I have not once been in a physical dispute. Not once been in a fisty-cuffs. This is definitely because I was able to calm a heated situation down with the use of words and measured humour. Very important! Language was always important to me. It made no sense to use swear words like so many people did. Mum used to call women that swore *fish wives*. Where she got that saying from, I do not know. This is something that Dad and I had in common, a respectful tongue. He would not allow visitors to stay in the house, if they used bad language. Without any pre-amble he would tell them to leave. "On your way. You don't use words like that in my house" he would say. I followed in Dads footsteps in this regard. Nothing cheapens a person more in my eyes than choosing to be foul mouthed. It is the one action that I am barely able to tolerate. It simply is not clever and clearly displays a complete disregard for women and children that may be within ear shot, it is not helpful, and it gets us nowhere. From my observations, I arrived at the conclusion that a man who spits his words out with venom and bitter frustration was not to be befriended. Why would we trust any person that cannot trust themselves to be decent and of a respectful character? If you have something to complain about and start to use foul language, then the other party has no obligation to listen. They are free and entitled to walk away, therefore your complaint does not get heard and nothing is resolved. That's what I do, even to this day. If anyone swears in my company, then I stop listening and walk away. What else would I do? Try to reason with an unreasonable person who has, if only temporarily, lost their marbles? Better to sort things out at a later date, when the heat has died down. This advice was given by Sun Tzu, centuries ago in his book *The Art of War*. And still we have not learnt our lesson. Sun Tzu wrote his work during the time of Confucius, 750 B.C, and it's relevance still applies to this day.

His advice was so solid, that it was used by Napoleon, Field Marshall Montgomery and many others. But Sun Tzu did not only talk about outside enemy forces. He also spoke of the enemy within and how to deal with disturbing emotions. This advice is not obvious. It is written between the lines. It is for the seeker to decipher. When I first took an interest in reading, I realised the shear importance of words. So often we use them without thought, when if we are or a mind to, we can paint pictures with them, just as the great poets do. Hemmingway to my mind was a dedicated artist, a true wordsmith. I read and reread his works whilst at sea. I was first attracted by his wonderful story entitled, *The Old Man and the Sea*. Thomas Hardy was another author who had mastered the art of words. There are so many examples of this.

Few people throughout the world understand the true value of language. Few understand the true value of eloquence. Many houses, and all the pubs in my youth had a piano in them. Many people played these wonderful instruments with their black and white keys, but how many were true *pianist* I wondered. It's the same with words. We can all say them, but how many say them well? How many among us, are wordsmiths? I soon realised, that the spoken and written word, house the power to transport us to far off places. They are able to transport us to both bliss and reflection and all places in between. Words are wonderful things that have a history all of their own. They were born somewhere and have a distinct meaning, a life of their own. They have roots in history and a part to play in the present and the future. We must never throw them away and we must be careful how we use them. Once a word leaves our tongue it can never be taken back. Cruel words have the ability to destroy people, particularly children or those who are weak in spirit. They can, when negative, stab in the heart, or bruise deep in the mind. People are affected by our words and the tone we use to project them. Even a dog will cowl, if our tone is threatening.

Robinson Crusoe was my favourite story book as a young man, and he definitely did not swear. What a character! I lost myself for a while every day in his world. His story, so beautifully written by Daniel Defoe was the only book that I actually owned. It was always on my bed and every day I looked at the pictures. When Mum changed my bed sheets, she would always be careful to leave my book in the centre of my pillow. It was never askew. It was always laid square. She knew my affection for this tale and respected my love for it.

I had no idea at the time of how my own life, in some respects, would be like Mr Crusoe's. In more recent times, though I am not marooned on a desert island, I do live alone in a hut overlooking the ocean. I have started to make those things I need for my use, cups, bowls and plates. They are not perfect. They are a little rough at the edges because I am not very skilled with wood work as yet, so with great humour, I call my home-made items, my Robinson Crusoe collection. As long as it functions, then it's good enough for now! Things will improve as I learn a new art and iron out imperfections!

I am surprised that there was never a Robinson Crusoe song, Like Robin Hood or Davie Crocket. Talking of Davie Crocket. My son and I met an aid worker, again in more recent years, whilst in Nepal. She came from Tennessee with a church group. We asked her to sing the Crocket song for us, which she did, with her fellow travelling companions. They formed a choir and sang in true authentic hillbilly fashion. Lots of foot stomping and plenty of knee slapping, a wonderful memory!

Robin Hood as a hero made me question the meaning of thief. To me a thief could never be a hero. They chose the wrong title for Robin, I think. How on earth could anyone be a king of thieves and be proud of it? There are many words, that we are so familiar with, that we let the meaning go over our head. Butcher is one of these words. How can we sleep easily if we are a butcher? Butchers butcher. Wow! That is not nice and certainly it can be no reason to feel proud of ourselves. Who on earth would ever aspire to be a butcher? Should we investigate words such as this, then we will recognise something about ourselves, that we are content to associate with killing, disfigurement, aggression and the ultimate level of thoughtlessness toward life itself, which is sacred.

History was of great interest to me. But I was always fully aware of the present becoming history with every moment that passed us by. I had seen the giant statues, erect in the streets and great squares of London. I wondered if the stone carved figure on the plinth, ever did anything with long term fore thought. If they were in deed, perfect examples to the wellbeing of society and should be remembered, as should be a great saint. Decisions of the past have led to our lives today and still there is social injustice. I wondered what the future held for these statues. Would future generations continue to revere them? When things change and move on, would we still, as a nation, believe them still to be such great historical figures? It was thoughts of this nature that made me think about my life and the purpose of it. Life I believed was not worth a dot unless used well and if I did not use it well, then I should not deserve to be remembered, certainly not by a whole nation, let alone the world and certainly not for eternity. Much better to be remembered as a useful character, I thought, rather than a tyrant. Both have an effect on the world but in a way, a life is like a word, it can be misused. What a waste of an opportunity!

Geography fascinated me too. I have often wondered, if I knew, that I would grow up and travel the world. Place names were not unfamiliar to me. I somehow, on some level, had heard them before. There was a strange familiarity between myself and the world. When I first went to the Middle East, Persia was Persia, but then it was gone, broken and dismantled. Rhodesia was on its last legs in Africa. Bombay was waiting to become Mombie, and what a shame we got rid of Constantinople. Just to hear the name was enough to make me want to go visit there. What about Sri Lanka, it was once Ceylon and Tai land was once the most exotic place ever, Old Siam. Do you remember the film, *The King and I?* Later in life, I was to go alone to explore all those places that seemed so familiar to me as a boy.

The one subject I soon became a little fed up with, was religious education. I found the whole subject, or how it was taught, to be very tiresome. Our teacher, Miss Hobart, could not, or would not answer my questions. I could tell she was a little fed up with me, thinking me *awkward* or just a plain nuisance. I suppose she was not used to young men asking *why* all the time. I tried to explain, that I had a deep interest in this subject and that I sought answers. I wished to live a good and useful life and did not welcome confusion, though in the end, I asked her *"why am I at school?"* What was the point, if I was not allowed to ask questions? It didn't add up. You did not have to be Einstein, to realise that there had to be a message within the bible, but I needed aspects of it to be explained. Spiritual realisation is supposed to free us from miscomprehension but Miss Hobart was not free, that was plain to see. She was stiff and clipped, with pinched lips, that made me think twice before approaching her. I know it sounds rude but she walked with a tight bum. She had this way of throwing herself a lengthy step backwards if you said something to her that was in any way a challenge to her very firmly fixed view. Looking back now I wish I had had the maturity to suggest, that we investigate these matters together. But instead I was in effect left high and dry by her pinched lips and set jaw. Of course, I had no proof or knowledge of such matters, but instinct told me that our experiences were not limited to one lifetime. The idea of being funnelled off to either heaven or hell at death did not add up on the grounds that there would be no ultimate justice, if that were the case. No body, not even murderers, would have the opportunity to suffer their worldly consequences or redeem themselves, if it all ended at death. Mum always told me to not gossip for instance, she said it would come back on me and I would create a form of hell for myself. Nobody would trust me and I would be perceived, quite rightly, as being of dubious character. This she said would be the start of whispering and lead to my not having true friends. I told Miss Hobart that most people I know gossiped and asked if those who did so would be allowed into heaven. Her answer was, in short, that god is merciful. She was not a happy bunny, when I suggested that sharing eternity with back stabbers did not sound like heaven to me. That comment pretty well ended our relationship. I lost respect for her and I think she was pleased. It shut me up and rendered me silent! I asked the same question of our local vicar. We were not a family of church goers, so I did not know him as such. A family wedding seemed to be an ideal opportunity to introduce myself, much it transpired to his discomfort. I asked him about the odds of going to heaven on the basis that the good book stated us to be sinners. His answer was, that god worked in mysterious ways. He said that mere man has free will on day to day decisions, but when it comes to heaven and hell, these decisions are made by the almighty. The idea of us being *mere* human beings did not sit right with me and I told the vicar so. The definition of *mere,* is to be almost nothing, or at least of very little account, something small, something insignificant, something that we need not be too bothered about, something not to stress over. If all we human beings looked at others as being mere, then how would this sit with our innate sense of compassion, or why did we mourn our dead? This *'mere'* business I refused to believe. If life is sacred then how could it be mere? Basic reasoning told me that all things, including the nature of existence are within our understanding. Can you tell me of any subject that is beyond us, if we take the trouble to explore it to its full and boundless depth I asked?

What I wanted, was a starting point for my investigation into the meaning of life. I was a kid, who genuinely wished to know the meaning of existence. The subject inspired me and I was driving myself around the bend, in trying to work it out. Why would a kid like me be encouraged to reach my limits by Mr Wilson and my grandfather, if in truth the church thought me to be limited? Where was I to get my inspiration? Spiritual realisation was not a phrase that I was familiar with as a child but those supposedly in the know, did not appear to actually know at all. There were several gangsters at the wedding. The vicar seemed to give them more attention than me. I know they were charismatic characters that drew the eye, but it did not make me feel any better, to be afforded less attention than the subject demanded.

I decided to give up on religion, in as much as I would rely more on personal responsibility. Religiously mindful of my intentions! Best I thought! Blind faith seemed a bit touch and go to me. Actions, to my mind were going to prove more beneficial than prayer. If there was a heaven and I was to find myself there, then it would be because I was a decent person, through and through, and not because some degree of mercy was applied or was judged on the day to be applicable. If the world's population made wholesome choices, then there would be no need for prayer, as all in every corner would be well, everyone would be in heaven before they died. No need for a day of judgement! This was my thinking. I do not wish to sound as though I was anti-Christian. That would not be true. Live and let live, was and still is, one of my several mottos'. What others believe in is not my business, just as my father's silence or my mothers' tolerance, was not my business either. How the gangsters earnt their living. Whether someone drank away their wages or smoked themselves to death. None of this was my business. My interest was in the reasons why one person would believe *this* and another would believe *that*. It's a free world, but I did wonder where the Christians were coming from. What could they see or perceive that I was missing? Did I have limited vision? I have much to thank Miss Hobart and the vicar for. Their inability to answer my questions gave me the momentum to find out for myself, to use my intellect and powers of deduction. I was certain I would recognise the answers I sought, when I had investigated enough to eventually discover them. It would be like a dawning I thought; the coming on of a light, a final realisation! The meaning of truth from how I understood it, meant arrow straight, as in true and not bent or distorted. We would all recognise the truth, if we are fortunate enough to discover it.

I told my Grandpop about my conversations with Miss Hobart and our vicar. He mentioned how he was baffled during the war. He said both we and the Germans asked god for victory and a safe return home to our families and loved ones. "Didn't add up" he said "as we were both doing our very best to wipe each other of the face of the earth." If god answered all prayers, then to his mind the war would have ended then and there. "God," he said "would not have a preference, one nation over another." Then he added that he hoped he was not blaspheming. Fear of god, even if you are not certain he is there? I know things are not as simple as I have laid them out here but I did not feel inspired, whilst being considered an upstart.

I went to the library to investigate the word *mere*. Whilst there, I read a brief account on the life of Brunel. The book had been returned to the wrong shelf, but after browsing through it, I believed it had been misplaced for me to find. Why else would it be there? I thought! The passage, I noted, was highly meaningful to me. Brunel was twelve years of age when he first thought he might build a metal ship. It's a good job someone encouraged him. His father patted him on the head and asked him to promise, to not tell the neighbours about his plan. That's what I needed. A pat of encouragement and I would promise to not tell the neighbours of my vision either, few would understand.

Mum suggested that I should not push for answers. She said I would become obsessed and they would take me around the bend. Mental hospitals in those days were always set back off the road. There was always a bend in the driveway from the gate. This was so the main house, the hospital itself, was not visible from the road. Hence the common saying of being driven crazy and going around the bend. But I was happy to let others think how they chose to think. It made good sense to avoid the subject in a way. It caused less hassle and no headway was gained on the god front, when none of us at home understood the subject. To me it was all hopeful speculation or fear based. No footing, I thought, to base my future upon, let alone eternity. It just did not add up to me, that there were those who tried to make god the foundation of my life and yet could not introduce me to him, or her, black or white, on any realistic level.

In those post war years, there was no abundance in terms of what you could spend your money on. It took a long time for any real signs of prosperity to establish themselves. Raw materials were still in short supply following the end of the world conflicts. Mum told me that some foods were still rationed when I was born and there were very few raw materials to make new things with. Industry was yet to spark. Parents managed with what they had. The most important thing to me was my mum. I had her and as far as I was concerned, I therefore had everything in the world. How could life go wrong, when I had a mum like mine? She always worried over my happiness and safety. I told her not to, but she always did. It was written on her face. The strain. I tried to put her mind at ease. I told her one day, that I would live to be one hundred and two. Where that came from, I have no idea, but I did believe it then and I still believe it now. Why would I say it if it was not on my mind to do just that? Mum asked me why I seemed so sure and I said, that I did not know.

I did what I could to help Mum. She sent me to the barbers once to have a trim but I thought I would save her some long-term money by having a crew cut. The bus driver, a friend of Jenny's dad, who cut hair on the side, for a little added income, called it a two penny all off. I always thought of Mum. There were always small ways that I could help her. Put all those small efforts together and there would be quite a big saving. That's how I thought. The result was, that Mum nick named me Yanky Doodle. She said I looked like an American soldier. With a broad smile upon her face, while making the sound of a low flying airplane, she continually swiped the palm of her hand across my scalp. Grandpop reverted to Cockney rhyming slang and called me Fish Tank meaning Yank. This he soon shortened to Fish. My friends called me Hedgehog, but pronounced it as Edge, as East Enders rarely pronounced an H. Hackney was 'ackney and hood was 'ood. Of course, Dad did not notice my hair, so continued to call me by no name at all. I waved my head in front of his face a few times but he had no humour. He kept his head in the *Racing Post*.

Grandpop told me to never have regrets. He said when we are young, we have the energy to bury or push away thoughts that make us cringe. But as we become older, that same force of life energy is no longer available and we have to live with our past. "It catches up on us and becomes our present" he would say.

"It stays with us and won't go away." He did not say that he was talking about Dad but I thought that he was. This reminded me of Mum saying on more than one occasion. "You can't sweep your history under the carpet. One day, the good and the bad will all have to come out." I wonder what kind of father Grandpop had been. He seems to have taught Mum well and her absolute affection for him showed like a flood light at the Arsenal. Mum loved her dad, and so did I.

It was common place to worry about what the neighbours thought. We as a family had little other than our standards. Mums kept their doorsteps clean. This was a matter of pride but also there was a secret, hidden message in it. A clean doorstep told strangers to not bring their dirty business into the house. If your intentions are not clean, then do not enter. It was the same with the brass door knockers. Shone to a mirror finish, whether the door was in good shape or not told my uncles to not visit. They never came to the house or my cousins either. Neither Mum or Dad wanted any favours from them, not even cloths for us children when my cousins were always so smart in their brand-new shoes and warm winter coats. As previously mentioned, we lived down the road from the Kray family. Ten houses away to be exact. The twins were older than me, so I can say that I saw them pretty well every day, but I never knew them as such. Just being around, watching points and listening, I knew they were something to avoid. Not my cup of tea. Friendship with them didn't add up.

They would not have the interest that I had and certainly, I had no interest in what they found so interesting about fights and battles. I could see, there was no fruit in any association and when face to face with them, I would pretend to be dim. I don't think they were bad boys by purpose, just victims of circumstances. They were born into a set of conditions that was always going to lead to a major problem. Mum would never suggest that I kept clear of them, just in case she was overheard or repeated, she knew she had to be careful, but I knew by her facial expressions, that she foresaw an eventual nightmare for the Kray boys, as she called them.

The fact was, that each manor had its tough guys and each of these groups, or gangs, had leaders who were the toughest among them. Gangs would visit the turf of another gang for the sole purpose of a brawl. In the main, these clashes were pretty fair as they had unspoken rules and the ordinary public were left alone and not directly involved. Things did not change much until knives and other weapons replaced fist but those who rose superior in all of this, were the Kray brothers, Ron and Reg. They were both fierce and fearless, nothing ever fazed them. They were always ready for a challenge. They set out to defeat all comers and their reputation naturally grew. They revelled in their dubious status. Their Grandpop, old Grandpa Lee. A fighting man himself, taught the twins to box from a young age and I was told that they could well have had a professional career. I have no first-hand knowledge of this, as I did not wish to show any interest. Showing interest could have led to involvement and involvement could have led to entanglement. As the years passed by, their activities developed from those of tough, dangerous but fun-loving kids, to something far more sinister, if not organised.

I don't think anybody would claim that the twins were good business men. They had a reputation of squandering their money, draining their business interest and never reinvesting. They were lavish entertainers and lived the high life, surrounded by celebrities, business people and politicians of the day. Mum told me of the day when a crowd of people filled the street around the Kray house. Later she discovered that George Raft, and American film star had visited.

The twins were not like the Richardson brothers for instance, who ruled the roost on the other side of the Thames, in South London. Charlie and his younger brother Eddie, were well known for the scrap yards they owned and their criminal activities throughout their turf. These activities included large scale frauds, lorry high jacking and the financing of cash robberies and other large-scale scams, but few people at the time knew that they owned a diamond mine in South Africa. They kept a lower profile and shied away from fame, they also invested well. I did not meet the Richardson brothers or any of their associates, the likes of Mad Frankie Fraser were strangers to me but like I said, I always had my ears open and I listened a lot.

The twins did not have to learn the art of terrorisation, they were born with that factor in abundance. They became associated with crooked business men who, through terror, they further corrupted. They took over the turf of older established gangsters who were unwilling to take on the new comers, but it would be wrong to assume that they had a business plan as such. If they had been born in Surrey and been attracted to golf, then things may well have been different for them. But they were not, they were born in Bethnal Green, All the conditions were there to draw out their negative aspects. I don't believe that the twins ever thought there was an alternative to their life style. They were born to it. It's a very sad story. Locking them up saved them from themselves as much as the world from them. It is my guess, that due to how dangerous and unpredictable they had become, it is likely that they would have been tucked up in the end by fellow gangsters, who wished to carry on with their activities without drawing unwanted attention. More business minded gangsters, would no doubt see the end of the twins as being good business. The East End changed following the convictions of Ron and Reg Kray. The old terrace houses were demolished around that time and tower blocks were erected. Communities were torn apart and other gangs started to pop up. New outfits looked to fill the void and ordinary everyday hard-working people started to feel the effect of street crime.

I had my own tight group of friends. None of us had a childhood as such. Not that this was denied us, we did not think to have one. If it snowed, we didn't play snowballs. There were other things to do, like earning a few bob or two, by shovelling snow away from market stalls, so the trader could trade. If the sun shone, then we would sell sun glasses on the street corners. There were four of us in the main, Vicky Green, Paul Skalski, Chippy Woods and myself. Vicky! What a great guy! I can't say enough about his character. He was the only kid that I knew who was shorter in height than me, but as a person he was immense, without a second thought, he would drag me from a fire and ask for no thanks for it. He was always there, always willing to go that extra mile. Vicky was my trusted friend, a true companion and I loved him for it. We were always together, but he would never come along to the public bath house with me. I liked to keep clean, it helped me to move about with greater ease. I'm sure Vic did bath on occasion but he did not look dirty, unless he washed his face. His neck was black, just like his shirt cuffs and his shirt collar. A washed face showed up the grimy bits like painting a ceiling and leaving the walls un touched. One highlighted the other and made the over-all effect look worse.

Nothing ever defeated our Vic. Mum liked him too. She used to say, "that they could make glue out of you two," she would tell her friends that we were like two planks nailed together. Very difficult to pull apart. Paul was a different kettle of fish. Silent but wide awake. His eyes were everywhere. He knew what was going on and where. Nothing escaped Paul. His dad won a large amount of money on the football pools and disappeared out of his life, leaving his mum and elder brother to fend for themselves. Paul didn't have an opinion on this. He said nothing about it. Why would he? He didn't say anything about anything, so nothing changed. Chippy? Well Chippy was Chippy. He wound up earning a living in the markets as a stall holder. I can remember how shocked I was when I once saw him in the Hackney bath house. His skin was as white as lard. It looked exactly the same as the fat that his mum cooked her chips in. They say you are what you eat and dear old Chippy was in distinct danger of turning into a fry up, that was for certain. He was whiter than milk yet as grey as death, but he was bred on chips, so what else could you expect? I was to use the memory of Chippies skin a few years later. I became interested in longevity when in Japan and knew that if a bad diet can ruin you, then a good diet could be the making of you. *Adds up eh!* The four of us did not have to talk about loyalty. We thought along the same lines and mates in our world were always unquestionably loyal. We didn't question our friendship's. We were just mates and that was it. If we needed an extra hand or a favour done, then we turned to each other first. One example of this was when Vicky was playing truant from school on a regular basis. His parents were going through a bad time. Nobody knew exactly where his dad was, but Vicky thought he had a good idea, so he took time out and went and waited behind a lamp post in Whitechapel. He wanted to see his dad. Who can blame him for that? As a close friend of his I was called to see our headmaster and questioned about the whole affair. Vicky knew this might happen, so kept the details from me, to protect me from having to tell lies in covering for him. In turn I told the headmaster, that I was not certain if I knew the Victor Green he was talking about, knowing that this statement would be enough for the headmaster to know he would not get anywhere by asking me any further questions. I was a good student myself and allowed back to my class with a nod, and a knowing smile from the headmaster. He would have known that this was not cunning or some sort of a conspiracy. He knew we were not bad youths. We were products of an environment and without being really aware of it we followed an age-old code. It was not seen as fit to poke your nose into another person's business. Vicky's business was nothing to do with me unless we agreed to make it so. If I had told my mum about the incident, she would have said the same thing *'keep your nose out'*. Vicky and I were particularly close as I have mentioned. Most Saturday's we would use his uncles hand cart, to go pick up the horse droppings from around the busy street market's. It wasn't hard to find; horses were commonly used by the traders. Horse manure was left all over the streets by the police horses too, even the milkman and the coalman had horse drawn vehicles, there were small piles of golden, steaming horse poo, that were to be found in regular places. We came to know where carts were regularly parked, where horses were left to feed from their nose bags, awaiting their next command. To us boys, this was a valuable commodity. These days we hear about the gold market, copper prices, along with oil and other minerals. In those days there was only one market for us boys and it came out of the rear end of every horse that ever stepped into Petticoat lane. Or at least that's where we mined it. There and Ridley Road and Dalston Lane in the main. We did not earn a fortune of course but it did give a sense of independence and gave us a good working ethic. Time on a Saturday was always limited so we had an early start. It was not unusual to meet with Vic as early as five thirty in the morning. Neither of us were ever late. We had a clock in our head, we would tap our head on our pillow five times before going to sleep on the Friday evening and sure enough we would wake at five o'clock on the Saturday morning, this habit would never fail us. It was a habit I became familiar with and found it a reliable method to employ throughout my life. Where ever I was in this world of ours, there would be no need to check the time upon waking, I knew the time in the mornings, it was dependant on how many times I tapped my head on my pillow, on the evening before.

It was not easy to over fill a large market barrow with horse droppings and between us heave its heavy and smelly cargo over to Hampstead so we could sell our product to those who owned their houses and who had a tendency to grow roses, rhubarb and vegetables. We built a healthy customer base with those who had gardeners and green houses. It was definitely a business of sorts, and I think our customers enjoyed dealing with us. We thought they admired us in a sense, and being good people, they wished to encourage us. We would get tea and biscuits offered and would accept them if we had time to stop, but often we were in a bit of a rush. Saturdays were important to us. We wanted to use it well and not idle our time away in lazy chit chat, so we often said no to the tea and put the biscuits in our pockets.

A mug of tea to this day reminds me of Grandpop. He came home from his military service with his army issue green and cream enamelled mug. He never drank tea from anything else. In the morning he made his first cup of the day, drank half of it and used the rest for a hot shave. It was a habit from his time in the trenches and saved him boiling more water. This was a habit I was to copy later in life, when I found myself in some of the world's most remote regions. Mostly we would collect our few pounds profit and rush our empty barrow and heavy metal shovels over to a scrap iron merchant who my uncles introduced us to. It was hard work pushing the cart empty. We had to work harder in a way to control it. It went off on tangents, as if it had a mind of its own. It was easier and more straight forward, to have a bit of weight on it. A bit of weight stopped it from bouncing here there and everywhere.

We had to be careful. One wrong move would hurt our back. The scrap merchant had a very scary air of no nonsense about him, there was something about his manner that told us not to mess him around. He made me think of the bare fist fighting men, that fought to a bloody end in the secluded yards and warehouses of the East End. These men were notorious and earnt extra money from the betting that went on around them. The events themselves were well organised and though un-licenced were enormously profitable to all involved, with fighters coming from all parts of the British Isles, there were miners from the north, steel workers from Wales and gypsies from here, there and everywhere. I did not know any of them, but it was the whisper I had overheard.

I once heard a story, that an East End man deserted the army. He sold his tank for its scrap value to this yard, before going off to live in Newcastle, until the heat from his desertion and crime cooled down. Word had it, that he was captured a few weeks later, when he went to St James Park to see the Arsenal play against Newcastle United. The military knew of his love of Arsenal football Club and that he had gone to ground in Newcastle. They sent a squadron of military police, his photograph in hand, to await his arrival for the match. They arrested him on sight but he still asked if he could watch the football before they carted him off in handcuffs. No doubt he too, had been a fun-loving kid and probably saw no real harm, in what he had done.

The scrap man was happy to let us park our barrow in his yard for a few hours, as like us, we all had to get across to the Arsenal, it was match day and we all had a common interest. Arsenal was our social life. All us boys thought we were going to play for the mighty Gunners one day. My Grandpop gave me an old Arsenal shirt with a number nine on the back. He told me he had been saving it for me, that he had stored it in a draw for years. "It was once worn by the great Arsenal legend Alex James" he said. I was the envy of all the kids. I used to wear it to bed, clean or not, like a treasure that must be kept in sight at all times. To have lost it would have been devastating, like a young bride losing her wedding ring on her wedding day, she would be distraught too. Imagine my disappointment, when years later, Grandpop told me that the story was not true. He told me how he had got the jersey from one of his mates and thought he would spin me a line because he had nothing else to give me. Bless his heart. I loved him so much and I know he loved me. We were mates. I would play cribbage with him in the evenings and often I would buy him a small bottle of rum. Why not? He had little else to cheer him up. He lived with us all his life from my earliest memory. I cannot remember a time before, when things were different. It was years later, that I discovered that our house was actually his house and that it was us who lived with him.

It was Grandpop, during one of our evenings, who first told me that the world was my oyster. I asked him what that meant but he said "that he did not know for certain but thought it meant that I will crack it, find the pearl so to speak." Later when Mr Wilson, my old school teacher said the same thing to me, I did not have to ask him what he meant. I had already grasped the picture. Positive people plant positive seeds in your head. How fortunate was I to have such a wonderful grandpop? Grandpops life was typical of many from that era. He had had it tough for all of his life, as did, it seems, millions of working-class men and women nationwide, His friends called him Georgie boy and sometimes with affection they would call him the "Tack." To call a man boy after his name was common place. Charlie boy, Billy boy, Harry boy and so on, but the nick name *Tack* came from Grandpops appearance. He always wore a wide brimmed flat cap, his suits were made with heavily padded shoulders and the trousers tapered down to his shoes, almost to a point. Hence the tag *Tack*. He joined the army at sixteen and fought through the first and second world wars. When playing cards, or sometimes Ludo, I would ask him about his past and he would mention the odd story, if I brought the subject up with enough subtlety. The old boys did not talk of their war experiences. They mentioned the war years often. It was a big part of their lives but they did not talk easily about any particular instance. I think the memories must have been horrific and they buried them deep within themselves. He did say that he was at the battle for Casino and thought the whole world was on fire. I asked him why he went to war, why he told lies about his age to become a soldier. He said that posters were going up on walls. People told of how the *Hun* was going to take our women, jobs and houses. In those days the Germans were called square heads, This was due to the shape of the helmet they were issued with. "Well" he said. "I don't care how he spells his name or what shape his head is. "He ain't going to take a future wife, job or house from me. He can stay at home" That was his attitude. Many men did think like that. In essence, other than a way of life and a national pride, they had nothing to fight for, but to them, very little was all they had and they had no intentions to surrender it, or let go of it under any circumstances. On another occasion he told me, that he shot as many bullets as the next man in battle but never at another person. He came to realise, that the ordinary German did not want to kill him either. They just wanted to go home. He told me that he and his fellow soldiers used to shout at their enemy, whether they could hear them, or understand them or not. "No good coming this way mate" they would shout. "All the frankfurters you'll ever see are behind you." I got Grandpop in trouble once. He told me how he got his belt. He stole it from a dead German. Not as a trophy, or that he was a thief, he wasn't, but because he needed it to keep his strides in place, meaning his trousers up. I shared his secret with Mum and she went ballistic at him. She said that he was teaching me that stealing is an okay thing to do. Grandpops argument was that the guy was brown bread, meaning that he was dead, and did not know whether his belt was gone or not. "I don't care what you say Dad" she said. "It was still his belt and definitely was not yours to bring home and wear for the rest of your life. Stealing from a corpse. What next!" Then she went on to say. "Suppose his Mum wanted it back or it belonged to his dad." I could see Mums point, but poor old Grandpop, she would not leave him alone. "What doesn't belong to you, isn't yours, so keep your mitts off of it." "It's simply then." "No arguments!" I apologised to Grandpop for getting him in hot water. He asked me if I had learnt anything by it. Before I could answer, he answered for me and said, "Never repeat what someone tells you. It may get you, and them in trouble." Grandpop married an Irish girl who came to London at age fourteen, to be a house maid in Kensington, she came here to avoid the Irish famine that was devastating at the time, thousands lost their lives. It was something to do with a potato blight. Grandpop said, that the problem with the potato was a terrible thing but it was his good fortune, as it brought him his wife. The only problem with that was, due to spuds being rare, the price of chips went up. He was very light hearted and always had something funny to add, he made me smile and he always ruffled my hair. Between them they had twelve children but only seven survived, six boys and one girl, my mother. Mum was the youngest and spoilt terribly by her older brothers. They held her so close, they would not allow her even to go to school.

Weird eh? Her eldest brother, Tommy, was married with two children before Mum was born and one of the middle brothers brought Dad home on leave whilst in the army. This is how Mum and Dad first met. Years later, after Dad had died, Mum said something to me that, in itself was quite innocent but from her tone I then knew that Mum did not choose Dad as a husband. It was expected of her to marry him. And she did! But no matter. We were a family and we got on with things. Mum and Dad never did have a cross word in my presence and I'm very thankful to them for that. It would have affected me. I would have taken Mum's side and trouble would have ensued.

At the time of this conversation, I was a Buddhist monk and Mum asked many questions about my life choice and what I believed the future held for me. She wanted to know what her son had gotten himself involved in. She took great interest in our discussions but asked me never to tell her the Buddhist view on the death process and on any afterlife theories. She said that she believed in vows. "Vows should never be broken," she reminded me. "Vows are sacred. A promise must always be kept. She was firm on this. Then she went on to explain that she stayed with Dad because she had taken lifelong vows to do so. 'Until death do us part' Then she went on to say, that when she passes away, she had no intention to go seek Dad in the after world. She said, "I am going to sit on a pure white cloud and swing my feet and there is no room on the cloud for two, she was determined to spend eternity alone and at peace."

Mum was a spiritualist, in as much as she would take herself off on occasion to sit with a medium that she trusted and had great respect for. Mum missed my grandpop after his passing and when troubled she would always ask him for guidance, even if she was sitting on a bus. Mum took comfort, that he was there to help her. "Even if it is not true," she had said. "The thought of him being there, was a great comfort." Whether he was present or not, she still received her answers.

Grandpop, I think was a pagan, or maybe wicker in belief. He said nothing directly on this subject but indirectly he gave me the indication. "Come home when the temperature drops" he would say. "When a chill suddenly runs through you and the leaves on the trees shake, it's the Green man, telling all the youngsters to go home before it gets dark." One of Mums brothers, Georgie, went down with TB as a child and as a result, did not grow to more than four feet tall. He mated up with a giant of a man, as wide as a double bed. Grandpop told me, that if sat on the flat bed of a lorry, the mud guards would come down low and touch the tires. He was covered from head to foot in tattoos, including a tattooed face. Between them they became a street double act. Georgie would stand with one foot on his mates' hand with the other foot on his shoulder. Holding out a tin can, they would collect coins from people passing through the markets or in the evenings from those who were in the queue for the cinema. Grandpop had embellished this story by telling of how paving slabs would crack as they stomped across London. "If ever you see a broken paving slab, then you know your uncle had been there" He had said. I understand they did quite well. On other occasions Georgie's mate would sit in a tent, wearing nothing but his shorts, while Georgie would draw the crowd by calling out. *"Roll up!" "Roll up!" "Come on and see the tattooed man."* George would wear a heavily checked suit that he called his bookmakers outfit, cravat, white gloves, spats and a straw boater, that made him look like he was from the music hall, or should be at Epsom races. The two became very well-known and mum kept, with great pride an old copy of *The London Evening Standard*, that had a photograph of the pair performing whilst leading the procession at the Lord Mayor's Show. I remember her telling me about her memories of Georgie. She did not have many as her brother was a sick man and was never going to live a long life. He died when she was young and much of what she knew of him came from the stories that others had told her. I can still recall that old newspaper though. It was brittle and brown, as though stained by damp and then dried like thin toast. It was as dry as a biscuit. Mum and I were very careful with the unfolding of it, the creases had cracked and we made them worse. The Lord Mayor's Show was a big event in those days. The paper was full of it. The centre page was one big photograph of finery. Horses with plumes and fine carriages full of men with high hats and women with broad ones, with flowers and all sorts planted on them, they looked like Covent garden.

Grandpop was an honest, straight forward gentle person. I could not help notice how his strength was housed in his quiet nature. Not religious but religiously decent. He had principles and he held them dear. He worked hard all of his life. Even when there were no jobs, he still got up from bed early and went to the docks looking for a day's labour. I can see him now. Flat cap, belt loose around his waist holding up nothing, as well as braces that held up everything, no collar on his shirt and shining boots. Having shaved of course in half a mug of tea. We kids were not supposed to listen to adult conversation but, though he never voiced it, I think he disapproved of mum marrying dad and therefore, it was obvious to me as his facial expressions showed his attitude often. He didn't like my father's family. He was fully aware that they were villains.

Saturday, as I have mentioned was a great day for us all. Grandpop would meet his old buddies down at their favourite pub. Without fail, he would always come home singing *'It's a long way to Tipperary'*. He would go straight to bed and nothing would be loud enough to wake him, until morning. Dad would work in the morning, up until lunch time, then go for a pint with his mates before heading for the Arsenal, whilst Vicky and I would have a pound or two in our pocket from a mornings dung shifting. We would rush to drop off our cart making certain we did not leave it in anybody's way. We would then run, laughing all the way to meet up with Paul and Chippy. Full of innocent and youthful joy we would dance through the streets playing imaginary football all the way to Highbury. We would pretend we had a ball, kicking it and heading it to each other all the way to the Arsenal's stadium. The closer we got, the more the atmosphere built. I remember being waste high to the adults, being crushed as we jostled our way through the crowd. I was able to smell the manure from the police horse droppings, while thinking about how much money I was stepping over. I can still see the dancing legs of the police horses, visible to us boys from the saddle stirrups down. We could hear the cries of the programme sellers but only see their feet. *"Get your programmes here."* The hub bub was thrilling. The smell from the fast food barrows and carts filled the air, everything was red and white. The scarves, hats, gloves and shirts. All for sale and all sought after by a vast and loyal fan base.

As we approached the famous old ground, where our heroes and legends had played on the sacred turf, the four of us gathered closer together, all headed for the same turnstile. It was like a military move that we had practised many times. We dropped to our knees, then fell on our tummies and without a moment's hesitation we crawled in commando fashion over the boots and shoes of people and straight under the turnstile. No one stopped us. We were just fun-loving kids. We would get lost in the crowd and head for the front, singing at the top of our voices. " *Arsenal! Arsenal! Arsenal!*" And there we waited, full of energy, waiting for our heroes to appear.

There was one occasion, when an official grabbed my shirt collar as I crawled under the turnstile. It was not the usual man. I did not look him in the face but I could tell by his tight grip and grunting that he was not a happy bunny. I wriggled out of my shirt leaving the official holding it in his hand with his mouth wide open. The trouble was that it was my number nine shirt. The one Grandpop had given me. The one that once belonged to Alex James. Being stripped to the waist was no problem, Vicky immediately took off his jacket and gave it to me but what about my shirt? Mum would ask after it and what was I going to say? On our way home, Arsenal won by the way, we called into Vicky's place, where he lent to me his Arsenal shirt that we thought would cover us until we sorted the answer out. The only trouble was that Vicky's shirt had a number four on the back. But Vicky being Vicky, said, "I'd be ok if I keep a coat on." *What a guy*! We both knew that this had to be sorted before wash day, that was only one full day away. Mum will find us out for certain! *Mum's knew everything!* We need not have been concerned, as Mum came home, unknowing to me, with my shirt in her shopping bag. Arsenal officials had hung it outside the doors at the Marble Hall entrance, with a note asking who the shirt belonged to. Mum of course recognised it in the same way a drinking man would know his own pint in a crowded pub. She had left her name and address with the club along with the promise that she would deal with the matter. "Where is your Arsenal shirt" she called out, as soon as she came in the door? *"Blimey!"* I thought! *Trouble*! "Don't know Mum" I called back. "You've lied to your Mother" she said. "Come on! You're coming with me!" The long and the short of it was, that she took me back to Arsenal stadium, where I apologised for all the trouble caused but, in the end, it worked out wonderfully well, as we met Jack Kelsey, our Welsh international goal keeper. He gave me his autograph and Mum told me not to get caught sneaking in again, or there will be trouble! Kids eh? What would you do with them! I did not tell her that I was following in Grandpops footsteps, as that is how he got to see all the home games, when he was a kid. It did not cross our mind, that what we did each week was wrong, though in truth, we knew it was not right either. It was just part of our childhood, it's what we did. Another boy from our road, a thin sickly kid named Jimmy Watts used to stand on his dad's feet. He would hug him around the waist as the pair of them waddled as one through the turn stiles, smothered by a giant army over coat. People eh! They had their act practised to perfection and sailed through the turn style, like a well drilled circus act. Jimmy would not come out and mix with us boy's, not even to play football, he was a loner, even though our goal post were painted onto the side wall of his house along with the cricket stumps that were painted dead centre between the post. His dad was a grave digger and during the school holidays, Jimmy would go off to help him dig holes in the local cemetery's. I saw them once sitting on a tomb stone, eating their lunch. Jimmy was a double for his father, Mum thought they both looked like *Dr Death*, whoever he might be.

Only once did I think I might miss an Arsenal home match. It was the day I first saw two men cry. Vicky and I were unable to use his uncle's old market cart, his new one needed repair so he needed the old. This meant our usual manure run was out of the question. Instead we popped down the market, crawled in under the fruit stalls to pick up any bruised apples the traders had discarded. They made their display look bad and were no advertisement, so they dropped them in the curb. It did not take long for the two of us to half fill quite a large discarded box. We took the apples around the corner and knocked on the first door of the first terrace we came to, to ask if they wanted an apple pie to follow their Sunday dinner. This wasn't a great earner, in fact it was virtually a waste of our time but we picked up a few pennies and one of the green grocers, Billy Stack, gave us some Bramley apples because he liked our gumption. Billy was a good man, we knew his young nephew, Billy boy, he was a bit tough and we had to be careful what we said to him. If he mis understood you, he would not hesitate, he would throw a punch. With these apples, we started knocking doors again. One was answered by a polish man, I asked him if he was a Pole. In his thick accent he asked me who I was and why did I want to know his business? I replied that I had a mate, "Paul Skalski, his father Stefan came from Poland" I said. With this, the man gripped my coat to prevent my escape. He demanded I take him to Stefan Skalski. Again, the thick accent, but this time it seemed threatening, with an edge of urgency about it. I can remember his breath; he was right up against my face. I felt no fear but I was thankful that he had no dental problem. Of course, I refused to take him anywhere. I wondered what lessons I was going to learn from this turn of events. Probably to keep my mouth shut as Grandpop had told me, but my comment seemed so harmless, how careful we had to be. I made a deal with him. I promised I would tell Stefan where he lived if he gave me his name and details. I had a very strong feeling that this was a very important matte,r so I left the apples with Vicky, whilst I shot as quick as I could to Pauls house. Stefan, his father listened to my message before reaching for his coat and bounding with one single stride out of the door like someone had just run off with his only golden nugget. Again, there was that sense of urgency, a feeling of something very meaningful that was about to happen, it was in the air. It was odd to watch Stefan running. He was a heavy lumbering man who earnt his living on the end of a shovel, digging holes and clearing bomb site rubble. I remember clearly, his hands; they were more like club hammers. They were clumsy with the fingers that were abnormally short, thick beyond balance and therefore, truly stumpy. I used to stare at them, wondering if the short digits ever bent further than a very slight curl. Paul, like me, was intrigued by his father's sense of urgency, our interest went far beyond any usual level of curiosity. He jumped into a pair of shoes and keeping a distance, we followed to see what was about to happen. Certainly, we were about to witness an event. We watched Stefan, first asking for street directions from a postman and then minutes later looking at the door numbers to make sure he was going to approach the right house. There were no front gates or garden paths, just doors directly on the street. Several houses were missing due to the war time bombing. The whole area had no colour, it was like a charcoal drawing, highlighted only by the occasional gawdy garment that flapped from a washing line. Stefan knocked the right door and without any delay, like the whole thing had been synchronised, the man answered it. There was no time span, as though the man was standing directly behind it waiting for his caller. Immediately without any preamble the two men on recognition embraced each other. They beat each other on the back with hammer like thumps that would drown out the sound of the Bow bells. Both, too emotional to speak, they had been friends in Poland from childhood. They played football together and called each other brother. Both men believed the other to be dead. They had heard stories, false stories and rumours about what had happened to them at the hands of the occupying forces.

Strange, they should both wind up in London living two miles apart. Paul and I stood silently and watched the two men crying like small children, not just tears but real and uncontrolled sobs that caused them to wipe their faces with their coat cuffs. They disappeared eventually into the house and at that point I turned toward Vicky who was watching with his mouth wide open. He still had some apples in the box but we left them on the curb and all three of us set off heading for the Arsenal. It was time. Women were heading towards the market and the men were heading north, towards the football. I don't know what happened after that, I heard a few rumours but Paul never said another word about it, perhaps his dad said nothing either, so I didn't ask. Knowledge can sometimes get you into trouble.

There were many foreigners in our part of London. I didn't know too much about the rest of the city or the rest of the country for that matter. We did not have a television so there was little or no news about who was where. Everybody it seemed was reliant on the grapevine. The East End was our world and there was nothing outside of what we knew. There were times when I wandered over West. I loved to visit the museums. Not often but sometimes, when Arsenal were not playing at Highbury. The Victoria and Albert museum was my favourite along with the National Portrait Gallery. But this was a private thing. I just liked the occasional time on my own, and I felt that I was intelligent, having a fascination of art that none of my piers thought to be of interest. I loved the subway. Mum told me she used to sleep down there during the blitz. They even had a piano down there on the platform and had a sing song. As soon as the air raid sirens sounded, everyone would head below ground until the all clear was given. Except apparently, Mum's brother Georgie. He said he was not going to live a long life due to his TB so refused to leave his bed. In the end it was TB that took his life, and not the bombs.

One old lady, a Russian Jew, would stand in the market in Ridley Road, over in Dalston. Her and her husband roasted and sold hot chestnuts. They roasted them over an open fire they had burning in an old oil drum. Old man Malkovich, we called her husband. I have a lot to thank Mrs Malkovich for, whenever she saw me, she would wave me over and give me a bag of hot chestnuts. I remember her clearly, wrapped up so heavily in clothing, her scarf so long it went around her head and neck at least six times and an overcoat which appeared to have at least two other coats underneath it. In short, she looked like a face appearing from inside a hollow tree trunk, like someone from pantomime. Like Stefan, she had short fat fingers too. They were always red or blue or a mixture of the two colours leaving them a veiny mauve colour. Funny how some images remain with us throughout our lives! They stuck out from fingerless gloves but my most striking memory was how she always danced from one foot to the other, to save the cold from coming up through her fur lined zip boots. She was not blessed with the longest arms in the world with all that clothing to restrict her movements but she would always pull me tight and hug me and tell me how handsome I was. It was strange, I would think of her, when later in life I watched spy films. It was the accent. To me, she was a character, created by John le Carre.

Everyone seemed to look after Vic and I. We would eat in cafes and the owner would say "don't worry about paying, I'll see your mum!" Wow! What a life we had, nobody told us what to do, we just knew what to do and we did it. We had no idea as to what happened to Mr and Mrs Markavich during the summer. They just disappeared when the cold weather came to an end. Mum called them *"The Pair of Chestnut"*. Mum told us that they were probably seasonal, that they came out as the chestnuts appeared. East End humour eh? I just thought that I may not recognise them in the warmer months without all their layers on. I had no doubt they would look totally different…who knows?

Life went bandy on Vicky, the day when he threw an egg at a local butcher, who had cheated his mum. He had sold her some older meat, that had started to smell. The egg Vicky aimed at him came from the butchers' own display. It hit him right on the temple and exploded like a yellow hand grenade. I was with Vic at the time. He gave me no warning, of what he was about to do. Spontaneously, I ran off with him. We ducked and ran. Being quite short, we hopped from one foot to the other, waist high through the crowds, until we got to Dalston lane, where at last, exhausted but laughing, we felt safe. Vicky had already forgotten about the butcher and asked if we could call in on my aunt Mary. She lived in the Peabody Trust flats right on the corner and made the best bread pudding in the whole entire world. Vicky loved aunt Marys bread pudding! It weighed like a house brick in your hand. Literally! Each piece cut in a square from a large baking tray, must have weighed a pound or more. Moist, sweet and delicious! Stacked full with fruit. We picked out the sultanas and saved them to last. Aunt Mary was uncle Tom's wife. They were the ones that were married with two children, before Mum was born. Aunt Mary was short and dumpy. Well over weight! Uncle Tom had really bad arthritis. His neck, shoulders, elbows and wrist were swollen, as well as his knees and ankles. He was always grumpy. I think that is why I never knew my cousins. They left home as soon as they were able, never to contact their parents again. I don't know what happened to young Mary but young Tom did what I was to do. He joined the merchant navy. He eventually jumped ship in Australia, where he made a life for himself. I remember thinking that Uncle Toms disability would not be so crippling, if he learnt to relax. He was very uptight! Very stiff, strict and stern!

Thoughts of bread pudding left my mind, when over my shoulder, I heard heavy breathing, heavy foot falls, and then saw an angry, gasping for air, red faced butcher come into view. He was swinging over his head, a dead, half frozen game bird by its neck. He slammed it from side on into the rear of Vicky's head. Vicky went down like a wet sack of sand, dropped from height. I thought a hole had opened up in the ground and he went down into it. Vic just sank as though his bones had suddenly melted and his skin was empty. How something so stupid could change the course of a person's life. It was a terrifying sight to see, I was truly shocked and rendered speechless, just as I lost words and thoughts, when Mum presented me with the watch. I could not believe my eyes. I went dumb. Everything went silent and distant, dreamlike and hazy. I cannot remember hearing voices. Truly I went into shock! The butcher stood over Vic, swearing at him and pointing out to the crowd, the egg all over his face, shirt and apron. Vicky was never the same after that. He developed a stammer and dribbled a bit, and his left shoulder, arm and leg didn't quite function right. He didn't complain, he just got on with it. It was unbelievable! Vicky was taken off in an ambulance, whilst I was overlooked, shoved and told to move on. Alone, hands in pockets and not knowing what to think, I went for pie and mash, not because I was hungry, I would rather have had bread pudding, but to settle down and think of what I should do.

Entering the shop, I was surprised to see Dad's brothers in there. Both uncles were together, joined at the hip, as they always were. Always together. Inseparable. It was not usual to see them out during the day and not usual to see them eating pie and mash. *Something was up*! They called me to join them and asked why I was so glum. "Not like you boy, to look so miserable." I told them about the Vicky incident, as I thought somehow inside of me, instinct probably, that they ought to know what had happened to my mate. I asked them, "what should I do?" I couldn't just leave it. "Something ought to be done. Somebody must know about it." As I told the story, I noticed how my uncles glanced at each other with that knowing look they both had. No words spoken but plenty said none the less. They both had the same facial expressions and made them at the same time. It was like one face in a mirror. It was uncanny how alike they were.

I knew they knew the butcher. I had dropped a note off for them once, maybe to tell him that he had winnings due, or maybe to let him know he had lost. He used to bet with them. Both listened to my story, then said that it was not their business and that I should not get involved. I said I would obey them but I was troubled by this loyalty thing, that Vic and I shared.

A few days later I heard from Vicky's mum, that the butcher had taken meat around to her house. He had said. "Anything you want, just come and get it." Nobody can say for certain where this sudden display of charity arose from but I knew he had been spoken to, there was no other conclusion. My aunties were seen using the same butchers following this nightmare episode. Mum was told where she could go get free meat too but did not take up on the offer. Everything was sorted it seems. The East End way! It was some months later, that the butcher went bankrupt. The new owners kept him on as their manager, having taken over the business with barely enough money to cover his debts. It was only me, that knew who the new owners were, my uncles were now in the meat trade. The business started going from strength to strength under the new ownership. It started to supply local cafes and boarding houses with all their needs but no suppliers were ever paid, nothing went back into the business, there was no reinvestment and the inevitable happened, the business caved in, with the butchers' name still over the door. I do not know what became of him but he certainly was left with many debts to clear. When I next saw my uncles, I nodded towards them. "*What*," they said, in a tone that warned me, to say no more.

In those post war days, every street had at least one amputee living in it. Men who came home from the war with one or more body part missing. We had a near neighbour, Albie Banks. He had returned home with only one leg, along with a permanently closed eye. He was injured whilst serving in Egypt. Vicky asked him one day, having been injured himself, what was it like to live with a leg missing? Albie told him, he wished he could have it off again. He said everyday he can still feel it. He had an itch under his foot but the foot wasn't there. Then he offered Vicky some advice. "Whatever happens to you in life son, remember, "you just gotta get on with it." And he went on to say, "that's what I'm doing son, I'm just getting on with it." And that's what Vicky did after the game bird incident, but that was our Vicky, it's how he dealt with things. He always said, that normal was what he got used to. That's how he was. He broke his pelvis one time and went home to change his under pants, before going to the hospital in agony. He was more troubled about his mother's reputation of keeping him in fresh socks and pants, than he was of his own pain. I know I keep saying it, but that was our Vicky! He used to sing that old Delta blues number. *Good job I get some bad luck, else I would not get any luck at all. John Lee Hooker,* I think. We learnt our lesson after the pelvis episode, Vicky and I. We figured it was better to find a new way to earn a few pounds, than spend our time jumping between roofs of bombed out buildings, particularly with Vicky's body not being in such good condition. Our manure business days were numbered. Vicky could not hold his end up physically so we both called an end to it. It was a sad good bye to it all really. I know we worked hard but we only took on what we knew we could manage and we were young. When you're young you're supposed to be able to manage, that's what we believed. It was the by products to our business, that we looked to build upon. We were often given unwanted items. This is where Vic and I got our first bicycle from. We shared it for a while but it soon became an incumbrance. I did not want it and nor did he, so we sold it. This is how I was able to give a sowing machine to Mum, Vicky and I agreed to make it a gift to her, and not sell it, she truly cherished it and our customer was very happy to receive from Mum, a message of gratitude. Everybody was happy. Times like this brought about a great sense of joy and achievement. We felt like we were Kings. Mum would proudly tell her friends, that we were going to be millionaires. Before getting rid of unwanted items, our customers, few as they were, would always ask us if we could find a home for their throw outs. We were good kids and people rewarded us for our spirit and enterprise but it was of no use, we had no choice, we had to put an end to our dung run business. Anything that involved lifting was now beyond my dear and cherished friend. Vic simply was not up to it. It still makes me shudder, as I remember watching Vicky trip and go down between two, three storied buildings and, of course, how he got whacked with the half-frozen game bird. He landed in a heap of leaves gathered in the basement steps, that led down to a cellar. How fortunate he was! He was fortunate to survive. He could easily have impaled himself on the rusty old spiked iron railings, that surrounded them, like a decorative row of spears, upright, standing patiently to attention for some poor sole to trip and befall their fate by them, I have no idea whoever designed those awful things but what is worse in my eyes, is that authorities throughout the land it seems, authorised them.

Mum was a seamstress. she worked in a small machine shop in Brick Lane, making fighter pilot jackets during the war, then afterwards, she took on piece work, knocking out ladies' dresses at ten to the dozen. Her boss was a Jew, which went hand in hand in those days with the East End rag trade. I had a similar relationship with him as I did my father. I would wait outside the small factory workshop for mum to leave at the end of the day. He would stand at the exit door, wringing his hands, to show fake anxiety, thanking his workers for their days labour and begging them not to be late in the morning, as he was under pressure to fulfil his orders. I looked at him and he looked at me. I knew, he knew, that I knew better. Just the way dad and I looked at each other about his gambling. What is it about these guys? Who on earth did they think they were kidding? It's so easy to detect deceit. It's in the sound, the tone, of the words. Theirs an insincerity about them. It's in the body language. I found this guy to be weak. In my eyes, he was not a man at all. I could see nothing noble or courageous about his demeaner. He wanted only money and if Mum had become sick, he would, without a second thought, simply replace her. I wanted to tell mum, that he was a liberty taker but I think she knew and it was not my business to interfere. It's very easy to express an opinion but what is the point in causing discontent when you don't have the answer? I felt shame that mum worked so hard. I would never tell anybody that mum was a peace worker. It was, to my mind, no different to telling people that my mum was a slave. Whenever I have read of East End history, it has often been about poverty, but I don't have these memories. In my eyes I was never poor. Leftovers from Sunday dinner saw us through to Wednesday. Friday was traditionally fish and chips and Saturday was beans on toast. Every week was the same, but this wasn't poverty. It was how it was. Anyone can be miserable if they wish, but most of my memories are of really happy, superb times. I remember Dads sisters. They would come around home on a Sunday morning. Each could sing loud and clear, like song bird they were. They sounded great together and would sing in perfect harmony. I loved it and looked forward to it every week, to hear them sing with the radio. Perry Como, Ray Charles *I can't stop loving you* Nat King Col, Paul Anchor, Danny Kaye. The whole house sang out loud. Everybody shouted out, me included, 'wakey wakeheee' at the start of the Billy Cotton Band show. From home everybody left for the pub. The men in their shiny shoes, well cut suits, brylcreamed hair and starched collars and cuffs. They would all stand at the bar while the girls sat at the tables, where they would pod their peas and peel their potatoes. The men had their conversation and girls had theirs. Even then I could see that Dad stood in no man's land. Neither was he with the men or with the women. He took centre ground and stood somewhere in the middle. Aunt Rosie, she wasn't really an aunty but close family friend. She would bring me out a glass of lemonade, where I sat with it on the curb, leaning against the dark green tiles on the pub wall and under the window from where I could over hear all the chatter before the sing song started once more. It always led to eventually, to a drunken rendition of *Roll out the Barre,l* but Rosie herself used to take the lead when it came to *"Daisy, Daisy, Give Me Your Answer Do"*. Dear old Rosie. She always put a sixpence in my lemonade glass." It will take the fizz out" she would say. Mind you she always came and took the sixpence back before closing time to buy a last cream stout or whatever it was that she drank. Rosie used to come home with us and sleep in Mums bed all afternoon. Mum did mind, but in a way she didn't. Rosie was a war widow and had never really recovered from her loss. Mum told me that all the women used to stand and chat in the street during the war. Often there would be the sound of the telegraph man, on his motorbike, coming around the corner. The women would all rush to get indoors. They didn't want to be the one who was to receive a telegram and certainly not in public. Mum said, there was this particular day when the motor bike appeared and Rosie said. "This is for me!" She Knew in that moment that her Stan was missing and likely dead. She felt it in her bones, as though it was certain and could not be argued with. Call it what we like. Woman's intuition! Whatever it was, Rosie was right. The man came and delivered to her the telegram, that told her that her Stan was dead. Along with Rosie, Mum started to attend a spiritualist church. Rosie at that time gained immense comfort from mediums. She told me all about her experiences, though as per usual, Mum made me promise to not tell Dad. I cannot say that I believed in it, spiritualism I mean, but I did not dismiss it either, I had my own experiences, but I was not ready to discuss them. Anything said, any view expressed on the matter of life and death was of immense interest to me, so I listened intently to any information or comments made, no matter who made them or where. I even asked Paul once, to introduce me to a woman he knew, who claimed to have found God after having seen Jesus in a vision. She saw from across the road, when she was waiting at a bus stop. *Who can be certain she did not?* This is my point, as I tried to explain to Mum, but she did not understand my reasoning and told me to steer clear of what she called dangerous ground. "But Mum," I insisted, "it may well be the majority who has got it wrong, suppose there is a minority who have got it right." I did not mention it to Mum, but Paul and I went to visit the lady, but we were too late. She had been sectioned and that was that. It was fashion in those days for women to pluck out their eye brows and paint them on again higher on their forehead. *"Was this less insane."* I asked "than a good person being able to describe the light and love that surrounded a vision they had seen of a holy being?" I just felt, deep in the marrow of my bones, that due to strong attachments, there could well be a continuum of contact on some level after death, but nobody I knew understood these matters to the extent I wished to discuss them. We all love someone or something deeply, whether it be a family member, friend, pet or even Jesus, so who is to say, that those who had been close to us, would not attend their own funeral, or come to that, attend ours? Certainly, I was not about to discuss these theories with Miss Hobart. She would go up the wall! The air between myself and my RE teacher was a little on the thick side and I did not think it a good idea to make it worse. As for the vicar, he had already given his opinion, that only god knows these things. It was best for me to hold my own council. To gather information as time was to unfold and make my own decisions. Throughout my life, I have felt the distinct presence of my Grandpop following his death, and others, who had been close to me. In the earlier years, it was the spirits of those I had known personally, on what we may call the earth plain, but later in life I was to meet deities, those indomitable spirits that arise in mind in perfect form, transparent and filling the sky in their fine detail. This will to some, be considered as delusional, but when at any cross road in life, so to speak, those trusted friends, in whom I had unlimited trust, have appeared to my mind and given me the answer as to what route I should take. My friends, those who have loved me, have never failed in giving their guidance. "Be patient and wait for some sort of indication, some sort of sign, they would say." This is what I have done, and when direction appeared, I have always said, thank you!"

When I was young, Mum would tell me to stay away from the dockland area, due to drunken sailors spilling from public houses onto the streets. Ships, after a long voyage, would return to port, men would have money and the pubs would thrive. I did not disobey Mum as a rule, but on occasion I would find myself walking, but mostly sprinting, through the area as I made my way from one place to another. There was certainly danger in the air, it was something tangible, I could smell it but still I loved it there. In a strange way, it made me feel grown up, like showing no fear and doing something heroic, something brave. Grandpop on one occasion, met with an old friend as he finished a stevedore working shift. Happy to see each other, they went to have a pint and finished the day very drunk indeed. During this drinking session Grandpop bought a small monkey. He had no recollection of how he managed to get it home, nor that he had left it in the kitchen before going straight to bed. Mum came home from her work to find the house had been destroyed, torn to bits by this frantic monkey. The streets were cobbled and worn by cart wheels, how Grandpop managed to stay upright, let alone carry the monkey has always been a mystery. Mum was right, the docks were no place to be for a child, particularly in the winter evenings, when the smog, yellow and web like, descended like a thread bare disintegrating nicotine curtain. It clung to your face like cob webs that hung from the coal shed ceiling. Jack the Ripper was very much alive and in the air. I swear that I saw him, wearing his black cloak, his tall hat and grasping close to his chest his bulky and battered Gladstone bag. He guarded it just as a mother bear would hold her infant cub. He was in every corner and every hidden place in every street I passed through. It really was a spooky place to be and was the cause of me to hurry towards home as if my life would depend upon it. I was being chased by very real thoughts that existed only in my own imagination. I had to find an urgency, that lay between too fast and too slow. With limited vision there were kerbs to trip over and a multitude of other things to bump into. Even the prostitutes, that stood on the street corners would call to me in a haunting voice, to get on home before danger befell me. This in itself was unsettling, as due to the thick smog I could not always see them. Their voices came at me, sometimes from close by, clear and crisp and sometimes from a distance as though a street away, far and with an echo quality. It was like being in a Hammer Horror movie. The prostitutes were like angels guiding me from the certainty of an unhappy demise.

I asked Mum about the prostitutes once. She was not happy about my interest. She told me, that they were fallen women and I should be certain to keep my distance, but the ones that had spoken to me seemed quite nice and I thought very caring. I chose to not pursue the subject. It was in the air, Mum, with a face of stone and lips that were pinched closed, had ended the conversation with one fierce stare. Mum, when upset, had a face, an expression, that would have stopped a steam train in its tracks. Grandpop told me, that she would have done well on the Western Front. "If the Germans had seen that look," he had said, "then they would not have crossed their lines."

Once or twice a year I would visit and stay over for a week with Mum's mate and her family in Whitechapel. It was the same there. Jack the Ripper, coal fires, smog and heavy coats thrown over us in bed to keep the cold out at night. Ice on the inside of our windows. Grandpop would be at home, so cold he went to bed in his hat and gloves, socks and long john's. I did not need an annual holiday; I had a life and I loved it! Life in the East End was not always full of gloom. We had summers too, just like everybody else in the country. We would go to the wonderful parks we had to hand, all with their wide-open spaces. We would swim in the boating lake in Victoria park and ride on the platform of a steam train, that slowed down for us to jump aboard in Finsbury park. We would ride the train through to Kings Cross. It was some years later when I was at sea, that I realised my mother's fear for my safety and wellbeing had very real foundation. She wished to protect me from the dangers of life and keep me away from the debris filled canals, the railway lines and the drink sodden sailors as she called them.

It's true, that some men, and women too, would brawl and brawl often, but these men also worked hard and, in many cases, they had deep rooted frustrations. This of course was no excuse for their poor behaviour, but they appeared to be very angry, *at everyone and everything*, they lived the only life that they knew. Like the twins, like most of us, our adult years develop from our youth and the examples we have around us. I wondered about the circumstances of their childhood. I don't even think they thought about consequences or survival, they were reckless, but no doubt, they believed themselves to be justified. They lived an unruly existence. A life of rough and tumble. In many cases they broke their backs to earn a living. Those at sea, particularly those who worked in the engine rooms, would labour in the worst conditions imaginable. The heat generated from the fires in that enclosed space was in itself, a form of hell. Working down in the hole, as they called it, was hard enough when in cooler climates like England in winter, but picture the same work, as these guys were shovelling coal to get the ship through the red sea, or across the Caribbean ocean. No matter how hot the weather, or how rough the ocean, these guys toiled on. It was there job to keep the ship moving, and the vessel safe from drifting, so as to get a cargo from one place to another. A whole nation depended upon them. Tea from India, rubber, salt and sugar, wheat, barley, rice and everything else was in demand, and these men more than played their part in delivering these items, to our shores. The whole nation wanted goods and raw materials. The whole economy depended on them. What could we buy without trade? I remember pointing out to mother, to not despise these men. They would die to stay afloat. You *can* depend on them when the chips are down. "It was these guys, among many others, who went in to rescue Dad off the beach in Dunkirk," I reminded her. Despite the heavy artillery, constant bombing, enemy planes in the air and relentless gun fire. Whatever the enemy threw at them, it was not enough to stop them from shovelling coal, to help save the lives of thousands of our men. It was not merchant seaman alone. Some were fisherman for example, but all who went across the English Channel on D Day had at least a little experience of the sea and all liked, most likely, to have a pint of beer or two. I was not one to celebrate war and would not like to see another one, but I was very thankful to have met and lived among men and women who did not have to try and explain what guts meant. They showed this through their actions. I had living examples all around me. Some lived in deep shock, some would not recover from their experiences. Others had limbs missing or had lost one or both eyes, others had been burnt, but from all of this I gleamed a distinct message, that some of them liked to get drunk and I asked Mum to try not to judge them. They were not all bad men, far from it.

During the 1950's, we as a family went to a massive street party over in Highbury. I do not know the exact year. I had already given up on dates as well as time by then. We were celebrating the Arsenal. We had won a trophy. The league or the F A cup maybe. Everyone was joyous and singing along to

My Diane, a Paul Anker song, that I always sang years later when I befriended Princess Di. Mum watched on, as the fans cheered our team's achievement, then told me of the street parties that followed the end of the 2nd world war. "We believed that there would never be another war" she said. She told me how it was, when she heard the announcement on the radio. She ran into the street as neighbours did the same. All the girls held their arms aloft, skipping, shouting and dancing in their aprons and head scarves. All jumped in the air and in one voice they shouted that the war was over. It had come to an end. "Our men are coming home" they screamed. "Never did we ever think that we would ever fight again. That was a party of parties" she said. Then in a solemn tone she added "poor old Rosie, she never did see her Stan again."

As I mentioned earlier, we had many foreigners in the East End but mainly they were white from Poland, some from Russia, others from Ireland and a few other places, so it was a surprise to see my first black man. There were likely to have been others before him but none that I recall. Goodness me he was a giant. It was hard to tell how tall he was because on the top of his head he wore a circus master's hat, or it may have been an undertaker's hat. Over all, he must have been eight feet from top to bottom. Standing head and shoulders above the Sunday market crowd. He would walk through the East End markets with a hand full of envelopes selling his horse racing tips. I've met many people over the years who remember him. He was a great character, who claimed to be an African prince, he called himself Prince Honolulu. Kids being cheeky, I remember my mate Chippy asking him how he got to be that colour. I can still hear the roar of amusement now. Loud and clear, it came from the Prince's belly and echoed out his mouth to fill the street. I'd never heard a laugh like that before in my life. It was like the roar of a lion. Definitely, I thought, this is theatre. Just like Mum's brother Georgie and his tattooed mate, he was an entertainer and wanted to earn a living. I do not know how he was accepted. I do not know where he lived, but in those days, it was not always easy for foreign people to live. I always wished him well. The pubs and boarding houses had signs in the windows, No Blacks, No Gypsies, and No Irish. Unjustified fear! I did not realise the significance of these prejudices until I travelled the world. I then looked back and thought "how sad!" But overall, Community spirit was unquestioned and very real. I remember a lady at the end of Valance Road, who often broke down and went away for a rest. Her five boys, who, like the twins, I avoided like a plague, were to say the least, a living nightmare. The older ones had spent time in reform schools and the younger ones seemed destined to follow suit. They were far too much for her to cope with. I remember Dad came in one evening and said to mum. "I hear the Brompton woman is away again" and mum simply answered by saying "yes, I took up the boys some broth." And that's what people did.

They just helped. They did not question or judge. They did not get involved either. They just did their bit, where they could, or were able!

There is no need for me to keep giving background of my early years. What I've said already, I am sure, gives a basic picture to the springboard, that I and many others of the era, had to life. All in all, I am extremely thankful for my young years. They were the foundation to build a life upon. Without those characters, the loyalty and the friendships, I think I might have been of a mind to collapse at times in my life, but in the words of old Albie Banks. "You just gotta get on with it."

It was much later in life that I started to understand what impermanence meant. All things have to come to an end and my life as an East End boy was cut off and severed on the day I left school, with Dad informing me, that he had arranged for me to go to sea. It was much later in life, that I discovered that this decision had nothing to do with our relationship being wary, but everything to do with his two younger brothers. They had been placing pressure on him to put me in the police force. Life changed. I was to travel the ocean waves.

Part Two

A Life on the Ocean Waves.

Well I must say! The day didn't start too well. I was grateful for morning. *Daylight! Wonderful!* Let's get going. I had a restless sleep. I woke thinking, I had been awake all night. Tension in my neck and shoulders were never my cup of tea. Best to be on my way. As I quickly jumped from my bed and into my freezing cold cloths, that I had folded as usual during winter months and placed under my mattress, I noticed, not for the first time in my life, how the ice had frozen on the inside of the small window that served to bring light into the small room. There were lots of it, ice that is. It must have been a very cold night, which meant I must have slept because I could not remember it. How wonderful to have Grandpops old army coat to, ensure I was warm. He often crept into my room in the winter months and threw it over me as I slept. I think it was probably warmer than the slightly thread bare blankets that Mum placed over my bed, making the whole thing look like a multi coloured layer cake, in the corner of an otherwise pretty empty room. It was certainly a very heavy coat and no doubt, had been with him through some very heavy times. I did not know at the time, or rather I did not have cause to think about it, but I believe Grandpop was rather attached to his old army ware. It brought him some comfort, not like a child that takes comfort from their favourite soft toy but from the memories of friends and battles that it had absorbed into its very fibres. It was to him a trophy of sorts, a sign that he was once young, there to defend his country. I would always return the coat to his room, whenever he left it with me and I was always certain to thank him for his kindness. I smiled, as I thought of Africa. It's unlikely that they have seen very much ice on that continent, let alone seen it inside their window. *Do they have windows in Africa*? I will soon find out. They must have, otherwise wild animals, monkeys or even a lion would come into their home and eat them. A hundred thoughts ran simultaneously through my head. They came multi layered and in an unbroken flow, like dreams stacked upon one and other. Life was changing and I could see it all at once and very clearly.

I slid down the stairs in my usual enthusiastic manner, that was somewhere between running and jumping, and just fast enough to draw a tut and sideways glance of annoyance from Dad. I called for, and then searched for Mum and Grandpop. I wanted to give them both a hug and a see you soon kiss. I was ready to leave the house and I would not be returning for several months. My search did not take too long, as there were only three small rooms and an outhouse in the yard. It was soon clear to see that both my beloveds had chosen to go on the missing list. They were nowhere to be found. The house was empty, apart from the sound of Del Shannon on the radio that Mum rented. He was singing what seemed to me an appropriate song *"Run, Run, Run Away."* To make certain that they were not home I put my head into Mum's bedroom to see if they had hidden in there. Nothing had changed since the day Mum gave me the watch. I noticed the lino was still jagged and I could still see the floorboards.

Dad and his mate, a Jewish fellow by the name of Izzy Isaacs, walked with me, down to Victoria dock, where I was to join a steam ship by the name of The Rhodesia Castle. Maybe it's a good thing that I did not see Mum and Grandpop before I left. It would have been harrowing, I think for all of us! They disappeared deliberately to avoid their feelings. They both loved me more than I can express here in words. They were always hugging me, asking if I was alright, singing songs whilst pretending the words were written about me. Now all of that went to the back burner. It would have to start again another day.

So here I was. The Rhodesia Castle. A ship I was to sign onto as arranged by Dad. The following day we would leave London's Victoria dock destined for Cape Town. There were to be many stops on the way and many stops on the way back. All in all, I was reliably informed that we would be at sea from start to finish for five, or maybe six months. Not that long. I will see Mum and Grandpop on my return. I had to think about something else, to take my thoughts away from them, but I did not know what else I could, at that time think about. It was overwhelming to know that my mother and Grandpop were hiding around a corner somewhere enduring the same emotional agony as me. Nothing added up. The words of Albie Banks, my one-legged neighbour came to mind and gave me the strength to just *"get on with it"*

Oddly I didn't mind how long it took us to sail to Cape Town, or come to that, I was not concerned over how long it would take to sail back again either. It didn't cross my mind to think about time or distance. It was not a conscious thought to ignore these details, it's just how I was in my life, I wasn't about to change any lifelong habit and start counting the days. *Days to what?* The journey would take as long as it took and when it is over, then something else would start! This I was certain would always remain the pattern. I thought of my dear and cherished mate Vicky and how life took a turn following his bout with the butcher. Things change, and though I missed him, we both had to press on and face whatever life had in store for us, just as Mum and Grandpop had to do the same. We all had to get on with change and simply see the good side, that is sometimes secreted in every moving moment, just as everybody in the world must learn to do the same. Dear old Albie, his few words to us, as he sat on his chair in Vallance Road, took on great significance. I hoped others would deal well with change, just as I knew I had to. We will all cope and knowing Vic, like I did; I knew he would just get on with things too. He would have occasional thoughts of me, maybe we may think of each other at the same moment and both smile knowing that the other would always find a way through any difficult times. It's strange how loved ones could be oceans apart in essence, and yet have no distance between them at all. Mum always said that even after death she would stay with me. I suppose, that if we are of a mind to, then we can do anything we choose. But was this through attachment, are we somehow intertwined by love and affection throughout eternity? Maybe it's the loving thoughts of a mother, who is unable to part from the love for her child? One day I would discover the unlimited capacity of the heart and how a closed heart will disable our ability to truly love and fully appreciate each other. With all these thoughts floating through my mind, like a silent screening of a dreamy movie, I made my way up the gangplank, to finally board the 17,000-ton ship, whilst singing *Fly Me to The Moon,* one of Mum's favourite songs. Dean Martin or Sammie Davies Jr, it did not matter to Mum, it was the words she resonated with, but looking back I think I sang this song, on this day, for the benefit of my father. I thought he did not want me at home any longer than necessary and I wanted to show him, that I did not care a single hoot. The truth was that I did give a hoot and I knew that one day, if I was not careful, these feelings of rejection that I felt, would come back and truly hurt me. My feelings held a strong sense of deep potential damage and I had to stop them from taking root. Grandpop was a good man. Look what he had been through. He had lived knee deep in mud from the battle of the Somme and came home from the war with trench feet, whilst many of his friends were now dead and gone. This is all he knew from the tender age of sixteen, so who was I to complain about my present circumstances?

I thought of Robinson Crusoe, of how he lost his sense of resentment for his remote and lonesome condition, once he became grateful to the fact, that he had survived the wild seas, that his fellow shipmen did not. The conversations I had shared with my old teacher, the reliable Mr Wilson appeared to my mind. His advice made sense and though he was not here and physically present with me, in a sense he was, he was very present and very real, I listened to his voice all over again in my head, even when I was at the other side of the world, he sometimes spoke to me. The memories I hold, even to this day of Mr Wilson are a display of the absolute, undiluted power of a caring nature. The ongoing ripples of his kindness have never diminished, the echoes of his words reverberate on, and should I eventually be as kind as him, then they will continue to resonate like the warmth of a rising sun, through to another generation, to inspire them also. The fault lay within my father, if he did not want me. His feelings were not my responsibility. One day this may all change but I was not going to hold my breath.

Mum would appear to mind too; Grandpop was always with me and our neighbour Albie Banks made regular visits, as I have mentioned. There were times when the advice Albie gave Vicky and I, came to my aid more than once during a day. I could see my loved ones in every fine detail and hear their voices too but they always appeared like ghost, like they were made of smoke. Sometimes I would wake up from a dreamy moment and they would be gone. I had received good advice from some loving people and rather than use it in a closed environment, I was about to widen my horizons and use it in the wider world. This is the reasoning, that made sense to me. Every time I thought of my old mate Vic, I would re-live the vision I had of him sinking to the floor at the hand of the butcher. I swore to always avoid violence. I saw its fruitless nature whenever I recalled my dear friend and what happened to him. I could have argued, or at least put my case forward to not go away to sea at all. I had never disobeyed my parents but this would have been a good place to start. But an inner voice told me, that to see the world was far better, than to face the prospects of a working life, in the East End of London. What would I do apart from make a living? I definitely was not going to play football for the Arsenal, that was for certain. Plenty of *will* but no talent! With the right attitude and right approach, I was going to see, in real life, as a living experience, all those weird and wonderful sights depicted in the library books, that I had spent so much time thumbing through. I was not going to just drink tea in future. I was going to know the exotic, far off places, where the tea leaf was harvested. I was setting out, on the sound and trusted advice of Mr Wilson, to gather unknown and varied experiences, that would no doubt assist in my answering those ultimate questions that I had, for so long sought.

May be at some point in the future, I would discuss my findings with Miss Hobart and the vicar too. After all said and done, no person I ever knew, had been gifted the opportunity, that I had so perfectly fall into my lap. I could not recall ever thinking, that when I am older, I would like to follow in the career footsteps of any particular person that I knew from Bethnal Green. In short, and I did not know why, I had no hero's and had little, if any real respect for many of the men around me in my youth. There were those I loved and befriended but when it came down to it, I thought I would be better off having a little peek elsewhere.

There were no hugs from Dad as I left his side, but he did give me a light tap on the jaw from his closed fist, as he handed me my brand spanking new canvas rucksack. With a gentle boot of the back side, he sent me up the gangplank to begin my new life. At the top I was met by the deck hand, who was on watch duty, and whilst speaking to him I was surprised to see, out the corner of my eye, my father still standing at the quay side. He hadn't moved. I was surprised to see him waving and I truly believe he had a lump in his throat. From that distance I saw an air around him, a desperate sadness, and I realised in a single moment, *that he did love me*. He loved me very much. I was about to run down the gangplank to hug him but I hesitated as my attention was drawn elsewhere. I was being given instructions. Moments later, I turned to wave back to Dad. In that instant, I felt that the opportunity to speak with him had arisen, to begin a fresh relationship with him, but both he and Izzy were gone. For the first time in my life I felt that I was, for real, truly alone. I always sought and embraced my own company. Wandering off and doing my own thing, museums and art galleries and what have you, but this episode in my life was a tester, a real examination of my character. I was going to sing *See you later alligator* but it did not seem appropriate. I wanted to show my father respect.

Little did I know at that moment, that within the coming half an hour, I was going to meet two of the lowest people I was ever going to meet in my entire life. I was brought up amongst a mixture of people, some of them villains, some just plain scally wags and others who were simply miss guided, who were best to avoid, but I knew no one intimately who would prepare me for these tow rag Liverpudlian lowlifes. The guy on watch first showed me, from a clip board hanging by his seat, to my cabin. I instantly loved it. Wow! A proper space of my own. Fitted cupboards and a bunk and all in highly polished dark wood. I immediately noticed the beauty of the grain. I ran over the surfaces with the cuff of my coat, with a determination to keep it pristine and always in good order. All the furniture had been shone to a fine, mark free finish. It was sparkling clean, warm and welcoming. A perfect thrill ran through me. "I would definitely settle in here," I thought. Even the brass porthole had a shine on it, not a finger print, or speck of dust in sight. I wanted, Mum and Dad, and Grandpop, to come and see it. I thought of the flower vase that uncle Bill had bought for Mum one Christmas. It was a very heavy glass crystal vase that had been made in Ireland. It was beautiful and Mums only claim to material treasure, but it sadly looked alone and isolated, out of place in our house. It probably weighed more than the furniture it stood on. It only served to bring attention to a lack of quality elsewhere in the room. Just when Vic washed his face. It brought attention to his dirty neck. It was a beautiful rainbow set against a slightly off colour white washed wall. It would look wonderful and be truly at home, sat upon the beautiful polished wood of my cabin. Perhaps one day I may be in a position financially to buy Mum the perfect piece of furniture to enhance the beauty of her vase.

I dropped my bag and followed the watch guy, who told me his name was Steve, I was amused by him. He made me laugh with his easy- going comments and relaxed manner, though I was still distracted by thoughts of my Dad. In truth, I felt a desperate need to be alone, I wanted very much to think things through, clear my thoughts, so as to start my day again, on a new footing. My head was full of tears, I could feel their weight behind my eyes and I could barely swallow. I could feel the mucus in my nose and throat, I wanted to clear it as a man with flu would want to clear their channels and find some air.

It turned out, that Steve was born in Hertfordshire. He had, just like me, first gone to sea as a boy. He fell in love with an Australian girl and got married in Sydney. He told me all this whilst taking me off to meet our boss, the Boatswain. The ship was nearing its sail time. Just another eight hours, and he wanted to check that his crew were gathering and were all on board. He needed to know especially, that I was present, as he had a special obligation toward me. All boy ratings, in this case, only me, were adopted, in a sense, by the Captain. This lasted for the duration of any one voyage. In effect he was now, according to my articles of employment, my legal guardian. I did not mind this arrangement. I did not fore see a problem. I would hold up at my end, therefore he would not have anything to get all parenty about. *Perfect!*

Little did I know, that whilst engaged in an encouraging conversation with these older guys, who had sailed the seven seas and had seen the whole entire world, my cabin was being robbed. These Liverpool chaps were in the double cabin directly next to my single birth. I had to pass there's to get to mine and when doing so, I could not help but notice my bag, my brand spanking new canvas kit bag. It was parked in their space. Thigh high and round enough to drop a football into it, with a white unsoiled rope to pull it tight at the neck. The rope went through brass eyelets and had a leather toggle. It struck me, in the moment, that they had the same canvas bag, that I had. Coincidence? They must have got theirs from where mine had been purchased. I thought they must be very common on ships and all the lads will likely have one. Though, despite my forgiving thoughts, I had no doubt, that the ruck sack I was looking at belonged to me, in the same way that a driver of an old motor car would know their vehicle, even if it was parked in among one hundred other old vehicle that looked the same. That was my bag, and I knew it. Their cabin door was wide open. They weren't hiding anything, so I said hi, and carried on the few steps to my allotted accommodation, my sanctuary, my wonderful polished space but as I entered, I found it bare, empty, not a thing in it, nothing. No bag, no packed lunch from Mum to see me through. Nothing! My feelings were right! My bag was next door! I felt my blood rise and immediately prepared to confront my neighbours, but common-sense halted me in my tracks. What had I been taught about reacting too quickly? Think before you act. This is a bit blatant and needed thinking about. *Who are these guys?* How do I deal with this? I was to sail for several months or more aboard a ship with this pair of low lives and that meant that this business had to be dealt with properly from the beginning. This is not a good start, I thought! But it did have to be resolved, it could not become a feud with winners or losers. There had to be a happy ending. Old habits die hard, to use my grandpops old phrase *"sometimes however hard or difficult a situation is, you have to nip things in the bud."* It's no use thinking that things may improve, often they don't, they are more likely to get worse. I remember him saying, that a gangrenous leg has to come off. No use dithering, it has to be severed.

With a few deep breaths to settle my rapid breathing, I went next door. I knocked politely, though the door remained open, it was held back by a wooden wedge. Before they had a chance to speak, I thanked them for looking after my belongings while I was gone. I assured them, that in future I will lock my door, so they don't have to worry about my welfare. "Nothing worse than tempting a thief eh!" I said. Would you believe it? they denied that any of the stuff in their cabin was mine. They said it all belonged to them. While they were speaking, I was counting the floor tiles, it was compulsive and I could not draw my eye from them, but I did not have the time to finish. It was obvious to me, that these guys were really cheap characters, the kind I'd heard of, but not met, they would rob their own mother, so I apologised for making a mistake, told them to enjoy their windfall and on leaving, told them of my good fortune. 'If I haven't got anything to steal, then I can't be robbed, can I?" I said. The terrible thing was, that I was fifteen, and I knew that I had to deal with these guys, both I guessed to be in their middle to late twenties. This business wasn't going to continue, that was for certain, but I needed to think a plan of action through. I'd never been in a physical fight in my life. Never had to be, but these guys looked and sounded aggressive. They lacked conversational skills and I knew there would be no reasoning with this pair. I looked at their knuckles, uneven and looking twisted and lumpy. There were signs on their faces, that they had taken a punch or two in their time. Not that I was surprised by that. They were obviously real roughie's. Mum would call them, *cheap stock*. But one thing was for absolute certain. They were not going to keep my watch. The one thing I had never worn but the one thing that was precious to me. *Mum bought me that!* I packed it into my sack that very morning. Where ever I was to go in life, it was my intention, with my name engraved upon it, to take the watch with me. These guys made me feel ill but unbeknowing to them, they were to become great teachers to me. For years, I mistrusted all those with a scouse accent. Whenever I met a Liverpudlian, I immediately checked my pockets and stood with my back to a wall. Whilst talking with them, I would keep alert, with one eye looking all around me, whilst reminding myself that I should do well to not believe a word they spoke. It sounds extreme but that is how deeply I was affected by this experience. I was truly, to the bone, sickened by these two so called ship mates. I removed the wedge that held their door open and felt relieved to close their door behind me. I felt this action had left a message, by shutting them in, I had also shut them out. There was fresh air in the gangway corridor. These guys had only been in their cabin for a matter of a few hours and already it stank of dirty socks.

The following day, as the light was starting to turn to dusk, the Rhodesia Castle with us upon her was about to enter into the Bay of Biscay. I'd been told by Steve and the other descent guys that I had to be prepared for some rough seas. Of course, in my innocence, having never been on water before, apart from the boating lake in Victoria park, I brushed their warnings to one side, thinking, *so what*, a bit of rough water won't hurt you. The Rhodesia castle, as I have mentioned, was seventeen thousand tonnes, big enough to hold a bit of water at bay, I thought, but I was wrong. The Bay of Biscay was a big lesson to me. Seventeen thousand tonnes of steel were being thrown around like it was weightless and had no control over its destiny. The ocean was tossing us around like we were a mere cork. The sounds, the creaking and straining of metal, the shaking and shuddering, was mixed with the deafening howl of the wind and the mighty thud of waves that landed constantly, one after the other, upon us. Blows were coming at us from every direction, sometimes from two directions at once, we were being bombarded by weather, so far out of control, that I thought that any prayer, strong and heart felt, would be of no use what so ever. The spray that broke over us was forceful to the extreme. When hitting us straight on, I swear, for a moment the ship stopped its forward momentum, like a boxer who takes a jab in the face, that stops him in his tracks.

The ocean housed an unforgiving power that was truly awesome. It was relentless. The sea had no conscience for our wellbeing. We were either going to survive it or we were not. This was no time to think about a mere kit bag, so for the time being I shelved any idea of sorting out the scoundrels next door. Good thing really, it gave me time to think about a strategy that would work and not cause further conflict. I swear we went under water and came up sideways at times, sometimes *this way* and sometimes *that way*. Never easy, always violent! The whole experience I can only liken to an eighteen-hour fairground ride, that beg as I may, it would not end until its own wrath had abated. I made the decision, sensibly I thought, that throughout the storm's duration, I would not leave the sanctuary of my bunk.

Apart, that is, for one thirty-minute spell, when I felt I would be better off on deck. Being thrown from one bulkhead to another, unable to keep my feet and banging my head, elbows and knees, I tried to make my way, upright and stable, toward fresh air and I hoped relief of my plight. The storm door, that led onto deck, had six levers to keep it water tight. It was made in very heavy steel. There were two levers at the top, two at the bottom and two on the side, opposite the heavy, reinforced hinges. I swung all six levers, the door swung back like a bullet blast in the gail and a wave immediately broke into our accommodation. Water poured down the stairs, leaving the corridor awash. *But never mind.* I will deal with that later, along with the flak I would no doubt receive. For now, I had to get some air. It's the only time in my life, when I seriously thought that suicide was a viable option to my circumstances. Death was definitely a thought that brought great comfort to my very being. I'd never felt so ill in my life.

I managed despite the winds, the waves, the ups and the downs, to step out beyond the storm door, as the ship rolled from port to starboard, the door swung violently closed under its own weight and from there, I was able to quickly lock it. I hung on tight with my arm wrapped desperately around a heavy cable, that ran from top mast to desk. I was certainly in both a state of desperation, equalled only by my confusion. One thing was for certain, I was not a reincarnation of admiral Nelson, or any other sea faring fellow come to that. Across the deck, he had not seen me, was one of the Liverpudlians. He was vomiting. I could see his position was precarious. *Dangerous!* He was extremely foolish to be exposed as he was. He was standing as best he could, gripping the hand rail. He was far too close to going overboard and overboard meant certain death. One moment his feet were forty feet above water and then he was knee deep in it.

My own discomfort eased as it struck me that I had the opportunity to grab him by the ankles, place my forehead under his backside, then lift and tip him over board. *Job done! Finished and over with!* All I would have to do then, is handle his reprobate mate. Where on earth that thought came from, I just did not know. It was a shameful and shocking thought that frightened me to later recall, but at that moment it appeared in my mind as a clear and viable plan. I wondered later. What are we capable of in this life, given a reason or the circumstances? But none the less, to end the life of another person arose from somewhere in my mind. I did not act upon it, for which I am eternally grateful, but I learnt something of immense value. I now knew, that no matter what, these guys weren't going to hold any threat over me. Sometimes I think, that I did not go on deck for air at all, the ultimate reason being, to understand something about myself, these guys were not scary at all. They were sad and pitiful. They did not have the power to hurt me. They only held the power to destroy themselves. I did not need a plan to come through my dilemma. The answer was in my keeping my dignity. I was without a change of clothing but only, I decided, until tomorrow. Tomorrow I was going to politely take my belongings back. I hoped that neither of these wretched men was wearing my watch. I prayed, to whom I was not certain, that all that was mine would be within my sack or within reach, from where I may easily take back ownership of it.

Back on my bunk and still feeling distinctly green about my face, I heard and saw my cabin door swing open. It opened so quickly and with such force, that I immediately thought the door frame had twisted through force of movement from the violet rise and crash of seventeen thousand tonnes of metal moving, each component part of the ship grinding and straining against the next. But to my instant relief, it was the boatswain! We were not sinking and it wasn't the guys from next door. He staggered into the cabin, doing his best to stay upright, feet wide apart and swaying from shoulders to waist like a man on rubber legs. He had come to tell me, my four to eight watch would start in half an hour, and I promise you, never before had I been rude to an adult, but on this occasion, without hesitation, or a second thought, I told the boatswain, in no uncertain terms, to go find someone else to do my shift, but I still retained my sense of humour. He was one of those guys, that would never manage to look smart. He could put on a fresh shirt and wear a tailored suit, but he would not look ready, not even for his daughter's wedding. He always had a distressed look about him, and his boots looked like he had bought them, in the far too big shop. His trousers were no better. They barely reached his ankles and yet there was so much room in the seat, that they looked like they were tailored for a horse, but I let these observations pass, though they brought me some cheer, as I made it clear I was going no-where. I was going to stay flat out on my bunk, where at least I could get some idea of the rhythm of the ocean and therefore be able to prepare myself for the next up, or down, or sideways movement or whatever was to come next. I was so ill. All I could do was wait for things to change, to calm down and become normal, if ever there was to be a normal in nautical terms. I was firmly set to do my waiting on my back, on my bunk. I had no doubts about that. Wild horses were not going to shift me! And wild horses would not get me on deck again during any storm conditions, whether I needed air or not. I saw how foolish the Liverpudlian had been and knew I had acted in a similar way. It wasn't going to happen again. One day out from London and I could well have died from my own hand of ignorance!

My respect for dear old Bos, as he was to become known to me, started there and then. He laughed and as he was leaving the cabin said "you'll get used to it son," I shouted after him "I don't want to get used to it, but I'm just going to have to get on with it." That started me thinking of Albie Banks again. I wondered how he would have managed on board with one leg. I thought of Admiral Nelson and how he managed it. I also thought, that if I had brought Mums vase to compliment my wonderful wooden surfaces, then it would certainly have broken by now. It would have been thrown from its place and smashed on the floor. Some things are better off in Bethnal Green! I then called after Bos and told him to hang on, I was going to join him on watch. Everything about my past and upbringing told me to get up off my back and get on with it. I had ahead of me a test of character and it was time to take the examination and I am pleased to this day that I did. My decision earnt me great respect and many slaps on the back from my fellow crewmen. I was part of a team and I had to live with myself. Further to this, I realised that well-chosen words were not always the answer to a dilemma, sometimes we had to face the eye of the storm so to speak.

Once through the Bay of Biscay, we came to beautiful waters, wonderful weather, salt in the air and breakfast with the other lads, all of them fantastic guys, all with a story to tell. Some of the crew came down from the Orkney Isles, former fisherman who were looking for deep sea employment to feed their families. Fishing, they informed me, in an accent I could barely understand, was hard going and very dangerous. High seas and big nets to get your feet caught up in were no laughing matter. Many islanders had lost their lives at sea. This made my neck and shoulders become tight, as I thought of a certain scouse who nearly lost his life yesterday at my hand. Where ever that thought had come from was in need of attention. I must not have that thought, ever again. Fishing it seemed was not an occupation for the faint hearted. One of the guys, Peter, was an orphan, brought up by the local council in Southampton. He came to sea in search of a roof and somewhere safe to be when he reached an age to be expelled from council care. He told me he did not think he would cope, having been turfed out of his orphanage. He was a frightened sort of guy who laughed nervously at almost everything that was ever said. Other guys were just plain attracted to the romantic idea of being at sea. *Nothing romantic about the Bay of Biscay!* I was famished. Vomiting and the salt air had both emptied me and given me an appetite. The only thing that made me sick now was the thought I had to tip another human being to his certain death. I recalled when my friend Paul had been cheated out of a minor investment proposed by some local boys. I asked him what he was going to do about it. Paul did not answer straight away and I wondered what he was thinking, or whether he had heard me at all. Then he simply said, almost talking to himself. "Maybe I will dig a hole for them in Epping Forest." Wow! What was it about us boys? Were we a product of an environment? Was this truly how we would act? Were we really so damaged and by what?

I thought of how local men would go to seek council with my uncles. They would tell them their wows, of the hardships they faced. They would ask for a recommendation, so they may find work, some sort of employment. These men would always be given a few pounds to place food on their tables, to help their wives cope and to feed their children. This cash was always a gift and never a loan. These acts of so-called kindness generated a respect toward the villain's, but in the long term would often prove to have terrible consequences. There always came a time, when a kindness had to be returned. I thought of the wisdom of my father, who would not allow his brothers to buy us even the simplest of things and how my mother would clean her doorstep and ask others to not cross it, if they had ill intent. How fortunate I was to have received such fine guidance but still I had considered the taking of a life. These thoughts brought a feeling of great sorrow for the Liverpool boys. What was it that formed them? What environment had shaped their behaviour? They were just naturally unattractive, there was no air about them that was remotely likeable, nobody it seemed felt drawn to them. Not even to say hello. It was as though they were wearing some sort of repellent. The type you would want to wear, if adrift at night in shark infested waters. They sat alone, they were not listened to when they spoke, I noticed. They were completely ignored and to think I had been considering how I could punch them both on the jaw at the same time. It would not be a fight I could win. I knew that, but it would have made a statement and brought things into the open. These lads needed some sort of help and certainly not further violence.

It was during that breakfast, with everyone present, that the lamp trimmer, the boatswain's mate, came to my table with a kit bag and said, "you might need these things son, a change of clothes, a watch and what have you." I hadn't said a word about my being robbed to anyone, not a soul, but somehow the crew knew of my situation and from that moment on, the lads looked after me. It was as though I had fourteen elder brothers. In some ways they cared too much and when we hit Mombasa, our first African port of call, they insisted, despite my protest, to drag me off to the nearest brothel. I will never forget that first sexual experience. How can you with a dozen blokes standing outside shouting their encouragement? Life was good and on top of the adventure of travel, I was being paid twenty-one pounds a month. It was when we reached the African coast that I discovered that I had very little money to spend on any trip ashore. The only money I had coming to me was from accumulated overtime, that amounted almost to zero. It was a lack of money, that got the Liverpudlians caught. They tried to sell my watch to Steve and told him to not let me see it. They had scratched my name from the back and though the words were no longer to be seen, the scrapings and scratches, spelt *stolen*. Steve put two and two together and told the boatswain. The boatswain told the Lamp trimmer and the lamp trimmer took back the property, this included an empty and unwashed lunch tin, that now showed signs of mould. When Dad signed me onto the ship, he had signed a bank order to have my wages sent home to Mum. So being on the four to eight watch, I spent my time hoping that the next port we arrived at would be during the times of eight to twelve or twelve to four, in order that they needed me on deck to help tie up and get the gangplank down. If that happened, then I'd get overtime and I'd have some money to spend.

Between leaving London and our arrival in Mombasa, we visited Gibraltar, followed by Port Said, and then we sailed through the Suez Canal, where I had my first encounter with sharks. The temperature was so hot, I decided to take a dip in the sea. We were at anchor, whilst awaiting our turn to enter the canal. Our gangplank was down to allow company representatives to come on board, they came to and fro from land, in small motor boats. I walked down the gangplank; the sea was so very inviting. Without hesitation, I launched myself from the bottom platform but before reaching the water, I heard a shout from the bridge *SHARKS'S*!!! I swear I was barely wet before I turned and climbed back onto the platform, only seconds went by before a fin passed by, and then another, and then a third. Wow! How fortunate was I? Being at sea is a very dangerous business. Twice since leaving London I had come close to losing my life. That's something else to not tell Mum about I thought.

Africa in those days was Africa, as we might imagine it before globalisation. It was primitive and raw. The native people, mostly the women, wore bright and vibrant clothes made from materials that were no doubt produced locally by tribal people, they were beautiful. I had not seen anything such as this in England. Generally, our materials were some-what dower in comparison. Some people wore no cloths at all, perhaps they preferred it that way. This all added to the wonder I felt of being in Africa. The women, young and old, transported their goods in an African way, in baskets or giant pots, held upon their head. Everything was just like the pictures in the library books. At the slightest excuse, natives would chant and dance.

They did not do the fox trot but they moved their bodies, like fluid poetry. They had rhythm that at times made them look like they were boneless. Watching them made me move too!

It truly was a different world to anything I had previously known. I was elated to be a witness to this world. I was having experiences, that to my mind, no other person I knew would ever believe. Within a very short time, a gang of black workers had gathered on shore, alongside us. It was obvious, that these men were to be working on our behalf. There was a different air about them to that of the women, there was a resentment about them, they were bare footed and raggedy in dress. This air I speak of was very strong, it was palpable to the point that I stood back, not wishing to be seen. I knew nothing of the situation but I did feel a sense of shame. We were taking on a cargo of copper but not by crane, as would be the case in London, but by sheer manpower alone. Long bars of heavy copper ingot, like elongated bars of soap, sat balanced on the shoulders of the native men as they staggered up one gangplank, like a line of orderly ants, round to the cargo hold, where they were relieved of their heavy burdens and back down a second gangplank to pick up their fresh load. These men kept up that circular formation for hours on end, that turned into days on end. Relentless work. These men to my mind were slaving. They were watched over by stern looking armed guards. There were no tea breaks! No rest! No refreshments, that I could see! All this and despite the relentless heat, that wrapped itself around us like a hot and heavy blanket. It was hot!

The sun blazed in a cloudless sky like the rounded end of a red-hot poker. The working men voiced a melodic chant, which I was told, set their pace for the day. I did not ask what they were paid for their intense labour, maybe I should have. I may have felt better, if I had known they were well rewarded for their effort but I doubted this, the whole scene made me believe that the abuse of human beings was still very much a part of life in this part of the world. I told this story some years later to a musician friend of mine, who told me that the daily pace was set by melodic chants in the tobacco and cotton-picking fields of Americas Deep South. It was working to this rhythm that would ensure they reached a daily quota. It was this quota that kept punishment at bay. It was these songs, mixed with the relentless toil that formed the foundations of Rhythm and Blues, a form of music we can now be a great fan of, but the origins certainly sprout from a very painful time. I thought of those notices, stuck to the boarding house windows back in London. *No Blacks. No Irish. No Gypsies* and felt very sad indeed. One thing was for certain. There was an international view that did not respect the sacred nature of all living beings.

No-one I knew from back home would believe what I was seeing, no-one ever listened to a seaman's tale. They were beyond the imagination of those who had not had the time or space to have heard even a bird song. Things today are of course different now that we have television and other film media but there was a time, when there was a wide belief that the world was flat, so who would ever believe that there were sea creatures, that exceeded the length of a London trolley bus? They would now, they are called whales and I've seen one, hammer head sharks, how on earth did they get to look like that? Nothing in this world was beyond possibility and I now knew from personal experience, that greed and lack of empathy for the vulnerable knew no bounds. It took me less than five minutes, to understand, that the world was raping Africa. How could I not know this? It was under my nose and I saw it with my own eyes.

What a wonderful thing nature is? I had cause to think about this indestructible wonder, of how it covers every corner, every nook and cranny upon earth and spreads its wings out into the universe. Where there is space, we will find that nature is present, even at night, I would look up at the countless stars and wonder of the nature of them. I was pleased to have the opportunity to read points made by Darwin. I had seen a copy of his work whilst in the captain's quarters while being disciplined over my swim with the sharks, back in the Red Sea. The captain fined me what he considered an appropriate sum of five pounds and asked me what I had to say about his decision. He smiled when I told him, that I thought it fare. Then I asked him, if I could borrow his book. Days were passing in a very happy fashion, just as they did from when I was a child, I was watching points, often silently and often from a distance. Opinions and views were formulating in my mind and I truly felt confident for my future, though I must say that many of my thoughts, for a lad of my age, were rather profound indeed.

It was a long time before I shared my views in open conversation, most likely because I did not wish to discuss my goal of spiritual understanding in the wrong company. By wrong company I mean; to discuss these matters in front of a majority, that would not be able to see my point. I thought about how things evolve from the simplest of actions and how important it is to look ahead with vision, to see what effects our actions were going to have in the long term, not just on our own lives, but on the lives of others and ultimately on the planet itself. This is not to say that I became hesitant in my actions, but it did slow me down to become more thoughtful, more contemplative, not so rash. Mr Wilson, when telling me of his refusal to fire bullets at other human beings, to be a conscientious objector, said he would have also refused to work in an arms factory, as the man who made the bullet was as responsible for death as the man who held the gun and fired the bullet. "When my time comes" said Mr Wilson, "I do not have to face the consequences, of being an active link, within a very negative chain." He prayed that there was great benefit, not only to his fellow man but to the planet also. Certainly, he believed there would be a reward for him in the future, not a reward he sought but a reward none the less. Mr Wilson had, with his humanitarian views, unwittingly encouraged me to think. "The world needs visionaries" he would say. "Leaders who are able to foresee the consequences of their actions." When making decisions today, still I think of long-term results and it's all due to listening to Mr Wilson. Everything we think, say or do, have inevitable ripples.

I think of those who argued against the industrial revolution. Had they foreseen, that the need and absolute necessity for oil would lead to so much Middle Eastern conflict and death? I had heard that Leonardo De Vinci had designed a helicopter. He is said, to have destroyed his drawings, believing that the air machine would be highjacked by the military. He wished to play no part in future misery and mayhem.

History is littered by stories of the altruistic visionary. Unfortunately, it is also littered with the blind, who all too often are the powerful. The later are in greater numbers. I wondered again about the statues in London. How many subjects of these monuments were visionaries and how many, in the ultimate sense, were short sighted? It became a habit to look at all things around me. I thought that the development of the type writer was solely the result of early man having once drawn pictures, using a finger in the dust. Early man had unwittingly set the ball rolling for the quill to appear and then for the fountain pen and so forth. I formed the opinion that all species evolved through necessity or a wanting. I had a theory, that a tiger might well lose it stripes if lost to the wild and kept only in captivity. It would take a long time for the stripes to grow out, but without the need for camouflage, then why would the stripe remain? If we do not use it, we lose it, surely that is the rule, as with the human appendix. I wondered if the very first butterflies had owls' eyes on their wings, or did they develop these very useful aids, from a very subtle wish for safety from a predator? I was not surprised to hear about a species of tree in Africa, that became poisonous when over fed from by the giraffe. The tree has a survival system. It has a role to play and nature will take care of all angles would it not? I formed the opinion that humans were the danger. That our intellect is under used. That the masses are easily led. May be, I thought, procrastination may often be a good trait. It gives us time to consider consequences.

How wonderful it was to hear the monkeys that screamed, the parrots that squawked. What a wonderful and extraordinary world. Every day I blessed my good fortune for being a witness to it all. I swore that when I saw Prince Honolulu, if he was still selling his horse racing tips in the East End markets, I'd tell him I met his mum. Before leaving Mombasa I, along with a ship mate, Peter the orphan, went to buy a pair of carved antelopes. They each stood three feet tall. I had seen them in the markets, hand carved and ready for sale, each one unique in its own way. I wanted them for Mum. She can stand one either side of her fireplace. I also bought her tea towels, pictures of Africa. She would like these too! The carvings would help the crystal vase look more at home in the front room and the tea towels would remind her of me when I was not at home.

Lourenco Marques was our next port of call, the story here was different to Mombasa. I got myself in deep trouble, the place in those days was governed by the Portuguese and the Portuguese police carried whips, they did not need a life or death reason, or any valid excuse, if ever there was one, to unfurl this barbaric aid from their belts and use it openly and without shame against the natives. Trouble for me arrived when I ran to step between a policeman, his whip and two black guys talking. There was one hell of a commotion. The black men fled as did everybody else whilst I was arrested and marched off to the police station with my arm held firmly up my back. That hurt let me tell you. It hurt very much indeed. When the policeman eventually let go of his hold of me, I could barely bring my arm to my side, let alone use it. It crossed my mind to swing my boot at his groin, then thankfully I thought better of it, some things are better not acted upon, but I definitely was not a happy chappie. I had interfered with justice the policeman reported! *"Justice"* I shouted! *"What justice!"*

The police station was an old colonial building with high ceilings. It was dim inside despite the bare bulbs that hung from long wires that swung at least five feet above my head. An old colonial building with high ceilings to allow the hot air to rise high. The walls were glossed with a dado line about waist height. The top half a forest green and the lower half a dark brown. There was a fan on the ceiling. If it spun loose it would take your head off your shoulders. It swished around with an incessant hum. Without being given a chance to speak, I was marched into a cell which stank to high heaven of human waste and stale urine and I'm sure many other things besides. There I waited for a long time, refusing to sit down and not wanting to sit or lean on anything hoping I was not breathing in a tropical decease. I used the time to think whilst spinning and ducking to keep the fly's away. I thought of those awful signs again, those dreadful notices in the boarding house windows back home. *No Blacks*! What is it about the black people? Why the aversion? Why the abusive approach? Dad did not like them being in England. He said they were Okay as long as they stayed at home where they belonged. Like many men I suppose. Work was sparse and they did not want any unwanted competition. It was a wide spread view that two world wars had been fought to preserve our way of life, to make life better and no working man wanted to struggle for their war time sacrifice. It was narrow minded, a view based on ignorance but education was thin on the ground for the ordinary working man so the survival instinct kicked in to over-ride humanity and good reason.

The policeman that held the key in readiness to lock me up was told by his superior that I had been arrested for assisting a savage. What exactly did that mean? The savagery was displayed by the policeman with the whip. It was not the other way around. I had no choice other than to await the arrival of my dear old boatswain. I had been polite and supplied the authorities with my details. Until help arrived, I shall keep my mouth shut and continue to encourage blood to re-enter my arm. That to me seemed to be the best tactic. The police let me go in the custody of my guardian, but before leaving custody they did their best to impress upon me that my behaviour and interference would not be treated so lightly next time, should I act in a similar way again. On our return to the Rhodesia Castle we went directly to the captain's quarters where he informed me, I would not be going ashore again until we reached Durban. That meant missing out on a going ashore in Darussalam and Byra. He asked me to promise him to behave myself and that I would make no attempt to embarrass him or the shipping line. I remember for a moment I didn't answer him and he repeated himself, asking me for my promise, and with a smile, because he wasn't angry, he just said he had a job to do and part of it was to take care of my welfare. I apologised to him. He was a good man and it was not my aim to stress him. The door was held open by the boatswain for me to step through. Before doing so I turned to face the captain and asked him what savage meant. He stared at me without answer, I could see he was struck momentarily dumb, so I asked him if it meant being black. Without invitation I sat myself down and in an enquiring boy like tone I asked him his opinion on why the blacks were treated so badly. Not just here in Africa but at home in England too. I knew I had hit a tender spot. His face changed colour and his skin became tight across his cheek bones. All of a sudden, his collar became too tight around his neck and his lips turned to an odd and worrying shade of mauve. I thought he was going to pop but he did not answer, instead he returned to his paperwork whilst with the brush of his hand he ordered me out of his cabin.

I asked the boatswain if he had an opinion on the ill treatment of the blacks. He did not answer my question though I knew he understood me, so I continued by asking if he could promise me overtime, that was with a smile on my face. I promised him I wouldn't get him into trouble and to keep me occupied, he gave me extra work, both of us were happy and the boatswain smiled too. The following day I was again summoned to the captain's quarters. We were getting to know each other. We did not always agree but I still liked him. I think we understood each other. I wondered if the Portuguese authorities wanted to see me again. This time he would no doubt come with me. That, I thought might spare me the smelly cell. I knocked on his door and heard the instruction to enter. The captain had been drinking, which was not that unusual, I had seen signs of it before. I could smell the rum in the air. The sweetness filled the entire space and made me feel sickly. The air felt sticky. He stood solemnly with his back to me staring out through his porthole. Hands clasped behind his back and his hat set accrue. Without any preamble, he turned to face me and without any hesitation he informed me that London had been on the radio. Your Mother wants you to know that your Grandfather has died. I stood for a moment and heard him say he was sorry to be the one to deliver such sad news. I nearly collapsed. My precious grandpop. I asked if it was alright for me to leave, the truth is I did not think I could stay, words and company were not what I wanted, it was necessary to escape this claustrophobic airless atmosphere. He nodded his head in a rather helpless way and I went out the door closing it behind me. I went straight to my cabin, shut the door and sat in that space between tears and no tears at all. I adored my cabin; it was my own special space. In a way it was the perfect place to feel my first experience of death and the associated feeling of heartbreak. Never have I felt so helpless. I thought that if we could go back in time, then I could nurse Grandpop to good health. Word soon spread. Nobody said anything but everybody knew. The Boatswain stayed close and gave me more work to do. It took me a couple of days to accept Grandpops passing. I reasoned that he would not have passed on unless it was his wish, or at least unless it was his time. I could feel his presence strongly as though he wanted to communicate something across to me so I saw him as a continuum rather than a loss. Whether I was right or not did not make any difference really because my logic, twisted or not, helped me to feel better. Grandpop was with me. And that was that! This feeling was more than imaginary as I saw him, as plain as day light standing directly in front of me. I could see him, his flat cap, loose German military belt and his shining shoes. I could even smell the wood smoke on his cloths from the fire he kept burning in the kitchen so mum would have hot water.

Grandpops moving on from his life here with me was a real landmark moment in my life. I was to become very grateful to him indeed, as beneath the emotion lay a great teaching. He taught me to cherish life and glean from it every precious moment but he also taught me to not be afraid of death either. Future dates, that we look forward to, like seeing a loved one at Christmas, are the same and no different from those dates that we dread, like going to the dentist or sitting through a job interview. They all come and then they go. All is dependent on the mind we face our future with. When we believe that all is going to be well, then generally it is. If we have a negative outlook on death, then I should think it would be a very stressful time, or at least a harrowing experience. Grandpop always faced the future with an optimistic outlook, so I had no doubt that he passed in same way as he lived.

With an absolute determination, I renewed my vow, that I would seek and find those spiritual answers I had thought as a boy to discover. My quest had been on a back burner for a while, not totally forgotten but barely simmering, and now things were going to change. Where ever Grandpop was, I was going to find him, then we would know joy again, as we always had. I wondered what Miss Harper or our local vicar would say, not that their view really mattered to me now. T.S Elliott wrote something on the lines of a hell being in man's mind. If that is the case then heaven is also a state of mind too, therefore I did not have any fear for Grandpop nor for his future. He was a good man and he had, by passing away, given me the inspiration to re- kindle my search for ultimate understanding. Okay! I had lost a mate but he left me with an enormous sense of direction. It was to prove a priceless gift.

It was at this time that views of Mr Wilson came back most vividly to mind. I started to make notes as I recalled his words. He had said that to travel the world would benefit me greatly, so I wrote this down. He said that I would find many truths and that my view on many things would change or develop. Goodness me! He was right! I only left home two months earlier and already I was wondering, if one day, I may write a book about the history of slavery, the general plight of the black race, and what I saw as being the truth of it all. This notion arose from experience and having an innate sense of social justice that was awoken due to exploring distant horizons.

I left my note book and pen on the cherished polished surface for several weeks, making notes daily, based on how my world was opening up, the thoughts I was having and on how I was changing as a result. My scribblings were a revelation to me. Imagine my wide-eyed wonder, my sheer delight when it dawned on me that I had not put my quest for spiritual answers on a back burner as I had previously believed, I had merely stopped paying attention to the pot itself. I checked through my notes and realised, without a single doubt in my mind, that I planted a seed when I made the sincere request for spiritual knowledge. That seed took root and it will not stop developing until I reach my goal. Several other realisations arose from my notes. I saw quite clearly that I would not find spiritual answers here in Africa, nor would I find them in many other parts of the world. I am traveling the globe so, as a person I may grow, so I can differentiate between what is right and what is ultimately wrong. At this rate and by the time I have travelled the rest of the world, then I will, no doubt, have enough work and investigating to do that would fill ten life times, let alone one. I had also sworn to find spiritual enlightenment and in doing so, both life and death would surely no longer be a mystery to me, I will continue to make written notes and keep my eyes and ears open so as to assess my thoughts and findings as events in my life were to unfold. I was inspired by the deeper knowledge that my life would be wasted if I merely used my time simply to survive.

Earning a living and being considerate toward my employer was of course important. To be idle in this area would display a nonchalance that in the end would cost me peace of mind, but I knew that this had little to do with the true and ultimate meaning of life. I had not read much on the subject of the slave trade, just bits and pieces that were written into other works that focused on the American civil war. I had no real knowledge of the history but my own trusted senses told me that the past had been ill reported. Whilst marooned on a desert island, Robinson Crusoe feared being captured and eaten by cannibals but he asked if he had just cause to call them savage when the rest of the world was awash with savage behaviour of all kinds through the decadence and misunderstandings of mankind. I did not think that white men for instance sailed to Africa, dropped anchor and simply went into the jungle pulling out young, fit and strong tribesman ready for sale. It would not be so complicated or thwart with so much danger and uncertainty, it would have been more organised, more of an industry. Bos told me, following my earlier arrest, that Liverpool docks was built as a result of the slave trade. There would have been big money in this business, big profits that kept fleets of ships afloat and bought their owners stately homes. Probably through a generation thing, there would have been a breeding programme of sorts and what would happen to those born weak, sick or deformed? And what happened to excess females?

It seemed to me that powerful Chieftains would round up and capture the strong from neighbouring tribes and sell them on to the Arabs who sold them on to others. This would reinforce the chieftain's position, as neighbouring tribes would always lack the man power to depose them. I also thought of the likelihood of rape and child abuse too. I wondered if any mixed-race children were commonly seen. Slavery I believed had a whole unwritten story behind it.

It was not the news of Grandpops death alone that allowed these thoughts to surface. We all die, I knew that and it had to be accepted. It was the business of the whipping I found most shocking. It shocked me then and I still find it shocking now, it's a feeling of disgust that's always been there and has never really gone away. Once again, I pictured in my mind, the signs from back home. *No blacks, No Irish, No gypsies.*

I took little if any notice of notes in windows as a child. I saw the message and knew on some dim level that it was wrong, but the depth of the wrong did not register, or fully dawn. I supposed I thought it was the landlords will, but I always knew it was wrong without really knowing why. But now I decided that I would always do what was right and stand up for justice. Grandpop would be proud of me! There was then, and still is today, a global idea that white is superior, the Brits are tops and in essence, the rest can serve our will. This did not take much working out; it was under my nose. Didn't need a debate, the evidence was there to see. I felt it was my duty to show foreign people the descent side to be found within an Englishman. A fellow human being. I kept this principle in China, Japan, Australia, New Zealand the Pitcain Islands, throughout the Caribbean, through the south China seas and across the globe. An attitude of equilibrium towards all beings. This brought out a happiness in me, and caused me to even think better of the Liverpudlians, who originally left me with the desire to never visit Liverpool or to have anything to do with their citizens. How small minded was I? Those two guys in the next cabin were no advertisement for their city but now they were slowly becoming a cause for me to practise compassion and understanding. I said many thanks to Grandpop and Mr Wilson. Mind you, my developing fresh view did not let my neighbours totally off the hook, if I ever saw them in future, I would continue to keep at least one eye open. This to me made good sense.

Being ship bound, due to my arrest in Laurenco Marques, turned out to be no punishment at all. In actual fact, when we tied up alongside in Cape Town, I had a funny feeling in my belly that this was a dangerous place. I had Robin Island pointed out to me as we slowly sailed in to port. I was told that it was a prison, that there was a terrorist held there, that his name was Nelson Mandela. He had been there on the island for many years. I was told he would probably die there. This information was enough for me, I decided the place was dangerous so chose not to go ashore. I was to go back to Cape town years later and chose again not to set foot off ship. I felt a certainty that it would have been at my cost. I suppose I must be among the very few, who ever visited the city of the table top mountain, who chose to not put his feet on the ground. No regrets. I was wary of the place. Though the air was clean and fresh and the sky as clear as any African sky might be, there was still something in the atmosphere that did not smell healthy to my mind. I likened this feeling to being in New York or any other major city I was to visit, there were certain areas that one would by instinct learn to avoid. I suppose that this awareness is something that it very ancient within us that is in reality the foundation of our survival instinct, we must ignore these instincts only at our peril. It made no sense to disobey myself, it did not add up to go against such strong feelings. I had the same feeling some years later too when visiting Accra, on the west coast of Africa, they still had the relics left from the slave auctions, stocks and pens. I felt in my belly that deep sense of shame again, that gut feeling that all is not right that always arose within my being given certain circumstances. Some of us listen to these inherent alarm systems and some do not. I thought of the moment Mum gave me the watch. The feeling was somehow the same, of not wanting the association with what others may well consider to be normal. I turned by back to Ghana, not wanting to be a party to such a horror that may in some silent and unseen way wash off on me and be the cause of my accepting it.

The captain on that occasion said "blimey mate, you're a strange young man of strong principles." To which I replied that I am not at all strange, "I'm just a descent individual who wants to stay clean. It's those who wish to gawk and take photographs that are strange to me, it's those who I find odd." That's how I've always been, just a person who has his own rules. I told him of my arrest years earlier in Laurenco Marques and he said he was aware of the circumstances. It was written in my sea going record. Wow! I wondered if it would be recorded if I had stolen another sailor's kit bag along with his watch. If that was the case, then I knew two guys who would have found it somewhat difficult to get another job.

On leaving Cape Town, which was of some relief to me. I went to the upper decks to see the captain, so I might put a case forward to go ashore in Laurenco Marques. We had begun our return voyage and all the ports we had called to we were to call to again. I mentioned earlier that the captain was a gentleman, though sometimes a rather drunken one. He listened to my plea, but he refused my request. He told me that he was not concerned over my future behaviour but he was concerned that I may be recognised should the same policeman with the whip be on duty. "If they arrest you out of spite" he said "then I do not know how I would be able to help you."

Being defeated by fear went completely against my grain, but maybe it was not fear. More like leadership and common sense. So instead of pushing I told the captain that I would not argue with him if he gave me work, therefore overtime, while the other crew members had the luxury of shore leave. He laughed and agreed. He was a good man. I suppose being a captain meant it was necessary to also be a bit of a politician. I spent those four days manning the gangplank for which I received double time. The only people not to go ashore during that period were the captain and two Liverpudlians. There is little point in my saying anything further about Africa. It was then a place that I had no desire to re visit. I had learnt much from my time there. I now knew from a personal experience that over trade and humanity, fair play would continue to count for very little. It was prudent for my own peace of mind to go visit elsewhere, as there was little, as an individual, that I could do to step in and prevent what I felt to be the rape of a nation by the rich, the blind and the powerful.

As we docked in London and tied our last rope to shore, the ship's crew had completed our articles and contracts of obligation. Our time on board the Rhodesia Castle was at an end and officially terminated by a single signature, so it was left to the crew to leave the ship and head for shore and the next chapter of our lives. Steve told me that his next voyage would be to Australia to see his wife. I told him that I did not know what the future held for me. I did not have a plan. We were no longer entitled to be on board, so we parted company wishing each other well and went our separate ways. He was the first person I saw on boarding the Rhodesia Castle and the last as I left. I felt somewhat mean of spirit when feeling thankful to have not seen the scoundrels who had lived next door. My only memory of them now is the smell of their cabin as I passed and the reminder of dirty socks.

I saw the boatswain on quay side, and immediately stepped forward to shake his hand. He asked me if I'd like to ship out with the Rhodesia Castle on her next voyage. He was a company man and stayed with the ship for the previous ten years. Same ship, same journey. I said no, I'm moving on, somewhere else next time. But I thanked him for his tolerance of me and we both laughed at the memories of my arrest. "Don't forget you owe the captain fifteen pounds" he said with a wink of his eye. "He had to pay the police captain to get you out of there jail." "Is that true Bos?" I asked. "Oh yes!" he said, "our captain is a very strong negotiator and as soon as they came to an agreement, I was sent off to collect you with the money in my pocket." He went off into a dream for a moment. "I do hope our paths will cross again" he said. He was as sound as a bell, and so it seemed was the captain. With those words I swung my rucksack up to rest comfortable on my shoulder and headed off toward the dock gate, the antelope's in a second bag held tight in my left hand. Mum will love these I thought with a cockney smile. We all love our mum's in this part of the world, I was feeling a little euphoric. But no further than one hundred yards along on my trek I was aware of a taxi that pulled alongside me. The driver told me to jump on board otherwise I would certainly not get through the gate, not even by Christmas he added. It will make life a whole lot easier said a voice from the back seat, it was Steve waving me over frantically. "I only live up the road" I said, "no need for the taxi." It will make life easier for you Steve repeated and have your five shillings ready for the gate police. I was to discover soon enough what he meant by that. As I climbed into the taxi, I caught the tip of one of the antelope's antlers on the door frame. The top inch snapped off and I cursed myself for not being more careful. I had guarded the wellbeing of these two treasures for months, making certain that even the return trip through the nightmare of Biscay brought to them no harm but I was able to recover the broken piece and put it in my pocket. It could easily be repaired later. I was now in a situation, along with other passengers, where if we did not give five shillings to the policeman at the dock exit gate, we would be searched and held and who knows even arrested if contraband was found or placed about our person. It was black mail. Given my mood with the breaking of the antler, it did cross my mind to prove difficult in my attitude but this did not come to pass. Like everybody else that ever returned to sign off from their vessel at this port, I paid to leave it. Behind us were a tail back of trucks, each heavily laden with cargo that had arrived to our shores from every part of the world. I wondered if any of the drivers had ever accepted a hand out from my uncles when times were hard? I hope not, I thought. "They may be asked to lose their lorry." This miserable thought made me think of what I had seen in Africa. There was corruption at every turn. Everybody was trying to make a living but always at the expense of somebody else, but in truth and given the circumstances, I did not mind and I understood why, in fact I smiled. This was a reminder of London from when I was a kid, everybody was out to earn a few quid, you scratch my back and I'll scratch yours. I knew enough to know that this payment to the policeman had nothing to do with private enterprise, it was an organised affair, corruption went from top to bottom. Payments would have gone up all through the ranks in the form of a wages system, like tips in a restaurant being shared amongst the staff. Not everyone would be able to bribe a policeman at will, it is something that would have been organised with proper agreements and understandings involved. How did my uncles have several unlicensed drinking clubs, several gambling rooms, if it wasn't for an understanding between the gangsters and law enforcement? When I was smaller, I overheard, then set myself up, to secretly listen, to the stories about the gangsters of the day. Billy Hill and Jack Spot ruled the roost. Then it was the twins turn. Times change but things remain the same. As far as I knew everybody seemed happy in a world of understanding where you give and take. Keep the wheels well-oiled and everything turns smooth and nicely.

There was an example of this, when two days later, I sat at Chippies market stall. We were having a natter, catching up and reminiscing. Along came a policeman who sat down too. Trade came to a halt with his presence, so Chippy gave him a tin of boot polish to get rid of him. "That's all he wanted" Chippy said. "I Give him a tin and he goes on his way" Everybody was happy. Everyone had their angle and I had mine. I wasn't going to doodle long; there was a world to see and no doubt, where-ever I went I would find corruption there too.

Whilst with Chippy, he mentioned that Vicky had moved over to the Angel Islington, but was not certain exactly where. He had heard that Vic had a few troubles, that he was not the same guy. He had changed. Unsure as to what this meant, I waited for Chippy to say more, but he didn't, he left it at that. I understood this to be a warning, that I should mind my own business and keep my nose out. "I will see him another time" I said. A sixth sense kicked in, just like the one I had in Cape Town, for now I will steer clear, but still I did not like Chippie discussing my mate having troubles and not knowing what they were, or maybe he did but did not wish to say. This told me that Chippie had changed too, but then I did not know the circumstances. May be Chippy was doing me a favour.

Mum had her antelopes and the broken antler tip was safely placed in a bowl on the mantel piece waiting to be mended and the vase looked more at home with the carvings as company.

Mum and I spoke for hours about my voyage and about Grandpop. She adored having me home and spoilt me rotten. Am I alright? Have you eaten enough? Do you want an extra blanket? Let me straighten your collar! It reminded me of when I was a small child, when she would spit into her handkerchief then scrub my face with it whilst chastising me for being grubby. But there was something in the air, something uncomfortable and edgy. Dad constantly walked in to the house and then back out again. He was more talkative and even showed signs of having missed me but he seemed nervous and told me that he thought it would be better for me to go off again. There was something he did not wish to talk about. That was obvious and I, like him, thought it was best to not drag my feet. I would go to the Minories tomorrow and get another ship.

There was a world to see and places to go. As I have mentioned earlier, there were days, when in my youth, when I would wander over to London's West End on my own. I was always a little self-conscious as the area made me think I was being watched, that I was somehow to not be there. I had not been dressed as well as others and I do not know quite why, but my left sock would not stay up, it never would. Our postman, who was always whistling, gave me an elastic band to keep it from sliding down my leg, but the band tended to cut off my blood flow and that made me itch, so thanking him for his kind thought I gave the idea up. I would continue to always pull it to my knee. I mentioned this to Grandpop once, telling him that I sometimes felt out of place, that when I grew up, I would never be scruffy. He told me he had just bought a few boxes of former military ware. He told me to go through the boxes before he sold the lot on. He often bought job lots cheap to sell in the pub. See if anything fits, he said. You can take what you need. He suggested I go visit my Uncle Tom as he had the boxes stored in his spare room. I had to laugh. Everybody was in on the joke. The boxes were full of cloths and they were all brand new, but there was no chance of me going anywhere, let alone the West End, dressed as a Japanese soldier. Who I wondered was going to buy that stuff? But Grandpop knew all sorts of people, maybe he knew a few nostalgic Japanese too? But it was not a wasted trip. Aunt Mary cut me a large piece of bread pudding. It was still warm from the oven. It was delicious and made me think of my overall good fortune.

I was up and out of the house before day break the following day. Mum was out of bed too. I told her I was off to find a ship and would be leaving home again very soon. "hopefully with the next tide" I added. The news seemed to shrink her like a balloon that was slowly losing its air. It hurt to see her physically deflating. There were times when she would change from young and vibrant to old and wrinkly in the blink of an eye. It was horrible to see. But showing her usual strength of character she said "it would be for the best." I knew there was a good reason for her comment but I did not ask. If Mum or

Dad wished to tell me something, then I knew they would do so. By having an early start to my day, I expected to complete my business early too, so I decided to spend the rest of my time alone with my thoughts, I would go to the national portrait gallery, the Victoria and Albert museum and perhaps, if there was ample time, I would visit also the National History Museum, just as I used to in my youth. That's what I wished to do with my time before joining my next ship which I was soon to discover would take me down under. It was to take me to Australia and New Zealand and to many places in between, but before leaving, I planned to visit Mr Wilson. It would have been wrong of me to not call in on him. I felt compelled, and I must say It was wonderful to see him. We spoke long and at length, I found our meeting to be a release to me. He thought that I had lost some of my spark and become a little cynical. He warned me of the dangers of this and reminded me that I was out in the world to learn about myself and in the process, I would learn something about the world too. Direction and purpose will come with time he told me and suggested that I should not miss the irony of life, as this would keep the smile on my face. He caused me to realise my discontentment's and I wanted to hug him for it, but teachers and pupils do not do that and we parted with a handshake. I saw Chippie as I made my way home and told him of my leaving again. He told me he had an Australian customer who owed him a tenner. "Will I remind him to pay his debt, if I should meet him" he asked? East End humour eh!

Sitting looking at the paintings in the national portrait gallery was always a wonder to me. I would look at the faces of the kings, the Queens, the Earls and the Squires and read them as though they were a book. The artist captured arrogance, aloofness and nonunderstanding of the poor. I would study there fine clothing. The lace, the buckles and the handkerchiefs. I now sat there wondering if the lace came from Holland or if the shoes were made in Northampton or may be Italy. The facial expressions arose from vast fortunes that were gleaned from overseas wars and now trade. Perhaps even from Africans who carried copper ingots on their shoulders all day for very little reward. I was taking note of all before me, so as to clarify in my mind, the ways of the world. Often, I looked at portraits and saw the lack of proportion between face and hands. I wondered whether it was the same artist that painted the expression and a different artist who painted the rest. Nothing it seemed to me was authentic in life, true and real, everything a deception. All my experiences of late showed me only deceit, nothing seems to be as it appears, but in the words of old Albie Banks who passed away two days after Grandpop. *"I would just have to get on with it... for now."*

Four days later I set out from Bethnal Green to join the Ceramic, it belonged to the Shaw Saville Line that owned many ships that regularly sailed to Australia via the Panama Canal. There were few jobs available at the time. The lady in the merchant navy office suggested strongly that I take the job offer, so I did, but would you believe it, I was to board the Ceramic in Liverpool. "Scouser land!" as I called it, was the last place on earth I ever wanted to visit. But life, I had noticed, had a habit of dishing out the exact opposite to your plan at times. It did not occur to me that there would be many decent people there, my whole view of Liverpool had been stained and completely tarnished by that awful pair of thieves I'd met on the Rhodesia Castle. I realise it is ridiculous to think as I did, but I was young and I had only my limited experiences to measure things by. It was years later that I was finally able to realise how wrong and damaging it is to our own inner comfort to have such wide sweeping and negative assumptions on places and people. It's so easily done. There must be good and not so good characters everywhere. In some respects, I was no different to Dad. I thought that everybody from Liverpool must be a scoundrel whilst Dad thought that every immigrant to England was after taking his job. People from the war spoke about the Germans as though they were all one warmongering person. Many of the adults I knew did not speak well of the French and some warned me to never trust an Arab, as indeed there were those with boarding houses that did not open their door to a black man. What did all this mean? Hearing this sort of nonsense is a subtle way to learn, to think the same prejudices as others. Mr Wilson had said, that there would be no end to national or international conflict until all people showed tolerance for the ways and cultures of others, but who on earth would ever listen to Mr Wilson? Even his marriage had collapsed due to his beliefs. His wife had been unable to withstand the disgrace and associated strains of him being sent to jail for his humanitarian ideals. Discussion must always come before conflict he had said. I had long ago made up my mind to follow Mr Wilsons example. Whilst in Africa I decided that I would treat every individual the same. With respect and decency! I tried to look forward to going to Liverpool. Whilst there, I would try and let my feeling of pending trouble go. With a cheerful heart I went to the Minories, the home of the Merchant Navy, to collect my ticket for Lime Street train station. Liverpool here I come. On arrival in Liverpool I decided not to drag my feet but to head for the ship and be there before dark. I had that same sort of feeling, what I came to call the Cape Town Belly. It was a feeling of real and pending danger that I had first felt some months back whilst in Cape Town, the difference being that I was now out in the open in Liverpool, feet on the floor and needing eyes in the back of my head. In Cape Town I was safe, I was able to be a witness from the ship and not a participant in life there. I know others have this feeling too, some in New York, others perhaps in a dark woodland. Some even feel the same discomfort within their own home, not wanting to go upstairs on their own or thinking there is someone, or something under their bed. With me the feeling arose when in Cape Town and Liverpool. The moment I walked out of Lime Street station I was struck by the monumental buildings that met me. Truly the architecture was magnificent. The city's history of centuries of international trade was directly reflected like a mirror from their facia. But before all else, my wish was to reach the Ceramic before night fall. If I was to see the city, then best to drop my bag off first and get myself settled. I asked a young lad for directions to the Victoria dock. He stood next to me. He replied by saying "give me half a crown and I'll take you there." No way I thought. I have fallen for a similar line in Port Said and it cost me dear. But I did catch a slight glance that the boy made to his left. I had read this fleeting moment and with great confidence I set off in that direction. "I think I remember now" I said. Half an hour walk from the station the lady from the Minories had told me. Not a bad guess I thought as I arrived at my destination less than an hour later. The wall that surrounded the docks was as impressive as the buildings I had seen behind me. It had no features or decoration as the town centre buildings had but it was certainly and without doubt a work of art, the mortar between the bricks running in perfect lines as far as the eye could see. I'd never in my life seen so many bricks and certainly not in such perfect formation. The wall was immense. Certainly, it was ten feet high and definitely mile upon mile in length. It sent me giddy just to look at it and to some degree it sent me into a mental turmoil. I thought of the irony and sense of humour that Mr Wilson had mentioned, as I do not know where it came from, nor do I remember why or how it started, but I had always, as long as I could remember, had one of those compulsory counting habits. I was always counting paving slabs and knew exactly how many there were from my front door in Vallance Road, down to the Blind Beggar pub that stood on the corner with the Whitechapel Road. This wall gave me a fine reason to break this habit. I would have driven myself bonkers and been counting until the cows came home. It was time to stop counting lamp post too.

As wary as I was at being in Scouse Land, I did feel a continued sense of good fortune for being in this forbidding place. If I was to practice my resolve of equaliculum towards all people, no matter their place of birth, then I needed to be tested and this was truly a fine opportunity to examine my resolve. Scousers eh! I walked with a steady step, the wall to my right. I kept one eye roving so as to see if I had become an item of interest to any lurking trouble. My other eye looked ahead for a sign to tell me that I had arrived at my destination. The cobbled streets and rows of terraced houses went off at regular intervals to my left. They reminded me of Victorian paintings I had seen in an art gallery in the London's Old Brompton Road. It was a gallery that I was asked to leave by a rather portly man wearing a giant-sized hat that matched his white linen jacket. It was a hat that Quintin Crisp might be proud of. His face was port wine red. Below it he wore a polka dot bow tie of equal flamboyance to his hat. I asked him if he would let me in, if I returned wearing a Japanese army uniform. He may have smiled if he knew the story.

The shoeless children seemed to come from another era. They appeared like Dickens fiction but even in London I think all kids had shoes, some with holes in the soles and lined with cardboard, but shoes none the less. I had a hole in one of my shoes once and used a corn flake box to cut an inner sole. This helped keep the cold weather out but I still had to avoid the puddles. I cut it with great care to make certain that the head of the cockerel could be seen should I lift my foot. I don't know if this was a glimpse of an early artistic tendency or whether it was my sense of humour. The care I took, trimming and re trimming did give me a certain amount of satisfaction and it made me smile too, it was almost something to be proud of. I thought my part of London was poor as even the lady at our library in Bethnal Green checked my hands for cleanliness before she let me anywhere near a reference book. But here, as much as I tried, I saw no child that was free from grime and I had a feeling of certainty that they were unlikely to ever visit a library. Thinking of Dickens, I wondered if he actually wrote that immense body of work he has been credited with. I had read much of his writing and learnt so much by it. I am very grateful for the solid advice given by Mr Micawber and dear old Mr Dicks but a Tale of two Cities I found impossible to read. Twice I had tried to read it and twice gave up on page 43. How did this renowned writer produce so much work? Apart from him being a journalist with only a quill and candle light to work by, he also had a family life, a wife and ten children. He was a well-known and highly respected sketch artist too. It was his work as a journalist that helped to establish the Battersea Dogs Home, that was much needed as the population of London grew and the amount of street dogs expanded with it. Within weeks of the Dog's home opening its doors, it had nine thousand abandoned dogs under its roof. I wondered how a man could achieve so much in one short lifetime. I thought that one day I may look into it and use the life and times of dear old Charles as an inspiration for my own future, but then I asked myself whether it mattered or not, I would let dear old Charles rest in peace whilst simply making up my mind to not get involved in trivia or any activity that would be a waste of my precious time on earth. If I was of a mind to waste even a single moment, then I would be leaving a door open for dissatisfaction to enter my being, and that could potentially lead to misery. I had seen this happen to Dad and others; it was not going to happen to me!

Liverpool, from where I stood, was a very sorry place. I hoped there was a life worth living for people here beyond what I could see. I mentioned this to a lad on the Ceramic, a Barnsley boy who I immediately took a liking to. I asked him what he thought of the local landscape. He had such a good-hearted way about him. I told him about the scenes I had seen during my walk from Lime Street Station and gave him my thoughts on Africa. Then I thought of the portraits in the National gallery and the buildings in major cities that did little else other than to display the immense wealth that had been generated from trade, but had contributed nothing to the comfort of the ordinary man, woman or child. Harry, my new-found ship mate spoke with many a "*thee* and a *thou*" as he told me of life in Barnsley. "It's poor there too" he said good naturedly. No doubt there was something amiss in this world of ours but for now I would think no more of it. I was off down under. Mr Wilson foretold that I would see the world, that not much would escape me. I wondered what I would discover whilst in the Pacific. Places better than Liverpool I hoped and better than Barnsley too, so I had just been informed.

Harry was great company, he sounded like a comic with his northern accent, just like Little Jimmy Clivero, who Mum and I often listened to on Sunday radio. Little Jimmy would be remembered by many from that era. He was a grown man but looked like a fourteen-year-old boy. He made Mum think about her brother, my uncle George, who stood on the hand of the tattooed man.

We had two days on board the Ceramic before we set off for Genoa, our first port of call. From there we were to sail to Naples before heading for the Panama Canal, the gateway to the Pacific. I used my off time to explore the city of Liverpool, or at least as far as I was able in the few hours available. Avoiding the pubs and bars that were plentiful, I went off alone to find out about the Scouser, the ones that lived here who had families. I wanted them to give me a clearer view about the city and help me to re assess my opinion on them. I wanted to be rid of my feelings of superiority that I knew to be distorted. I found the locals that I spoke to, to have a strong sense of humour and a helpful nature about them. But maybe they needed a sense of humour as a survival mechanism. I was uncertain as to whether their helpful nature was to relax me before setting a trap that would ensnare me for their dreaded gain, such was my distrust.

Shop keepers and stall holders were very kind and eager to tell me about the history of the city. I asked one man about the relationship between Liverpool and the slave trade. "Did you know that many slaves had limbs amputated as a punishment" he said. "They had wooden limbs made for them that were hollow and used to import contraband?" On hearing this I felt I had heard enough about the slave trade for now. I was emotionally exhausted by it all. Knowledge of this nature sucked the air from my lungs and created a sickness in the pit of my stomach that was difficult to bare. The Trojan horse was one thing but this was quite another. It did not matter where I was in the world. There was always a new horror story about the slave trade and general injustice. I knew it was a bigger trade than I had first imagined but how many limbs would have to be amputated for it to be worthwhile for the contraband trade? It was beyond my imagination.

The ships new crew were coming aboard in dribs and drabs, slowly all births were taken and I was able to assess what kind of voyage this was likely to be. By the time we arrived in Genoa I once again knew I was among good men. There were no problems and plenty of laughs. Everybody and everything were light hearted and even joyous. Everybody swopped names, we soon got to know each other and would you believe it. There was not a single scouser amongst them. I thought I was in heaven. Let off light this time! Harry and I got on like old mates, both the same age, both on twenty-one pounds a month, both willing to do a day's work and in many ways our friendship reminded me of Vicky. The only disappointment was that we were given a double birth cabin to share. I hoped he washed his socks!

We let go our heavy ropes and wires. I watched as the ship slowly distanced itself from the quay. Five and then ten. Then twenty feet and then the beginning of a slow turn that was to put us on course to catch the midnight tide. I had once more signed up for the 4 to 8 watch so I was immediately grateful for overtime. Money to spend! I had managed on my overtime pay before so again arranged for my set basic pay to be sent home to Mums post office account. I was earning some pennies. It had crossed my mind to stop my wages going home every month but then thought I would renew it as it also, in a way, acted like a letter. I did not post any mail home so whilst Mum was receiving the payment, she knew that all was well with me. I got by and Mum might need the extra cash. I only had two wishes. That Mum was okay and that I had enough money for my adventures of discovery. It did cross my mind to not refresh the monthly payment, it was only a fleeting thought as I thought of Dad, I had no wish to subsidise any gambling habits. But there you go! It was too late now to think about it. I had made the agreement. Aussie land! Here we come. It didn't take too long for the weather to become truly favourable. We were up on deck following instructions and doing general maintenance with the sun shining and the sea air heavily salted brushing our skin. These are experiences that never leave the memory. I had no thought whatsoever of home, literally no thoughts at all. I'd left East London; my grandpop had died and it was only his memory in my heart that I took with me. All was well. Chippy had even given me a small tube of glue, so dad could repair Mums antelope.

The crew was another fine bunch of guys, there was a few guitarists and in the warm evenings we had a choice of some private time in our cabins or going up on deck and listening to some music. I asked the captain, who was once again my legal guardian, if he had any travel books I may read. "I have" he said "but tell me do, why should I allow you to borrow them?" "If you don't lend them me" I said, "then I will tell my mum and then you will be in deep trouble." He laughed and gave me a slap on my shoulder, the kind that a jockey may lay across the rump of his favourite hurdler. It was affectionate but it still hurt. When I returned the first book I borrowed, an atlas of the world published by the Reader's Digest, I gave him a similar slap on the back. I know he felt the affection because he smiled like I imagined a loving father may do, so I knew he was not hurt by it, emotionally or physically. His personal steward was the first homosexual that I ever met. Well I may have met others and not known it, but Sissy, as I came to know him, was out front and open about his preferences. I was interested in what caused a man to wish to be a woman, so I asked many questions, just how Vicky and I asked dear old Abie Banks what it was like to live with one leg. But unlike Albie, Sissy didn't just get on with life, I think he enjoyed living with his particular mind set and lived with no sense of what might have been. I think he enjoyed the attention and most likely went to sea for the personal freedom it afforded. Maybe better than a life ashore in those days.

Since Vic fell off the roof and broke his pelvis, I'd become somewhat careful of heights. If fact I had developed a wariness of them. I knew that I would not fall if my feet were well placed and if I had a good grip but it was not the common-sense aspect that troubled me, it was the fact that I developed this insane wish to jump. It took a lot of resistance. Where did this come from? It was madness to be drawn to leap, but there it was. It had become a trait: so, I was none too pleased when the Boatswain told me, that if I wanted to move above a boy pay rate on my next voyage, then I would have to become skilled at the same jobs that the elder lads did. Tomorrow he said, "between us we will paint the top mast." This is something I'd not done before but I must say the idea of being winched by a pully eighty feet above deck seemed quite exciting in a way. I was becoming a sailor and I loved it. I had been taught all the knots and ties while on the Rhodesia Castle. The Lamp trimmer and the Boatswain taught me well. It was there way to give me a few hours overtime each week, so I was very grateful to them. They told me to never go up to any height on any ship unless I tied the knots myself. "That's all very well" I said, I'm happy to tie my own knots but I still would not leave deck unless he checks them three times over. The Boatswains chair is like a swing, from the swing a rope is attached using a boatswain knot, the rope goes up through a block and tackle and comes down to a winch, the winch turns at walking pace, which means the person sitting in the Boatswains chair walks up the mast until he is able to touch the top. This sounds straight forward enough but bear in mind, at the base of the mast it's the size of a reasonably sized oak tree and at the top it's no thicker than a boxer's bicep. Imagine on deck you might feel some movement from the ocean, a small swell maybe, but eighty feet in the air that small swell becomes a major sway. Imagine the state I was in, reaching one moment to paint the mast and hugging the mast the next, as the ship listed to either port or starboard. I was covered in paint and on top of this I was resisting the temptation to jump. The crew were a great bunch of lads, everyone stopped work to witness my initiation. All cheered and shouted their encouragement but I wanted to use this experience for a little more than a future pay rise or to entertain an audience. I wanted to overcome my temptation to leap from heights, I had no fear of the height in itself, it was the impulse to jump that was scary. I had a perfect opportunity to face my fear as I had no foot grip, my feet swung loose beneath me and the only thing I had to hold onto was a two-inch rope that I could only hold with one hand. The other had a paint brush in it, the paint pot hung from the side of the seat. Ten minutes into this exercise with back aching and bottom numb, the lads called up to me to say they were going for a cup of tea. Oh! How wonderful I thought. I was being teased. This was some kind of initiation ceremony. I thought I would use the time to make a perfect job of the painting. I tried my best to remove the brush marks and leave the finish smooth. I did not wish to be like the person who laid Mums bedroom lino. I wanted to care more than that, I wanted to leave a perfect signature. Like everything else in my life, I did not believe we should settle for anything other than our best effort. When the boatswain returned he told me not to be so fussy, slap it on son he called out, we will make it look better when we get down to eye level.

We had two days in Curasayo before being pulled by the *mules* through the canal itself where to spend a further day in Panama City. Curasayo and Panama were much the same as each other, dust roads with single story buildings made from stone blocks and sheets of corrugated iron. One roof was covered by an old but very large coco cola advertisement. Metal and strong. Probably better and longer lasting than any other materials available. Some places were lived in, forming dwellings, some were bars and others were stores or mechanic workshops. Everyone seemed to wear trilby hats and waistcoats. I noticed very few people held a cigarette in their hand, it always hung from their lips. There was a general air of resignation, though I didn't know of what, just an air that life wasn't going to happen. Like playing dominos in the street waiting for their house to fall down. A lazy, happy to do nothing atmosphere reigned. I did go to one of the bars, as I did not wish to wander the dust streets alone. My interest in seeing the world was one thing, but I could not see anything of likely interest that stood out above any roof tops. It was one big town of single stories that looked rather like a film set for a Mexican cowboy movie. Harry and I, along with a few of the crew went and drank beer, straight from the bottle, in a bar that had no chairs. I have a particular memory of an unusually high bar counter, in a very small space about the size of a single car garage with a man silently serving drinks from behind it. He looked at nobody, acknowledging nobody but had the customary cigarette dangling from his mouth. The smoke built up under the brim of his trilby, hiding his face. Odd is it not? Those small things we remember can become the overriding memory of an entire country.

The journey through the canal took us from the Atlantic through sixteen levels and set us free in the Pacific Ocean. There was a time when ships were actually pulled through the canal by mules. The mules were made redundant when they were replaced by small trains about the size of a low built transit van. All were made to last for decades and all were made in England. Following the death of Prince Albert, Queen Victoria ordered the building of the Royal Albert Hall as a memorial to her husband's memory. The steel structure of the roof weighed six hundred tonnes. It was made in Manchester in pieces and shipped to London by horse drawn cart. Certainly, we were a nation who knew how to manufacture in iron. I was happy to know that the actual live mules were no longer having to struggle through what would have been a hard day's work. It was a foreboding place. One man, for every yard had died while digging the Panama Canal. A large plaque to their memory was set deep in the cliff face half way through. Apart from this sad sight there was nothing to see. The whole place was industrial.

The older guys in the mess room suggested we settle down; we won't be seeing any land for a few weeks. They had sailed this route before and had their routine. We were heading across the largest ocean in the world and the next land we shall set sight upon would be Brisbane. But for me, there were many things to look forward too. I'd heard about the deep blue of the Pacific Ocean. I wanted to see this colour, I'd heard of its splendour and wondered if I'd ever seen it before. Perhaps I had seen it in fashion wear, or perhaps an artist had recreated it and I'd seen it in the art galleries of London. Maybe in the works of Monay. My first Boatswain, from the Rhodesia Castle, once mentioned to me, that at times the Pacific is so deep blue, that it appears to be black, like a woman's hair is sometimes so black, that it can appear to be blue. The lamp trimmer said, that on some nights, the sky is black and the sea is black too. There is no visible horizon. The only way you will know whether you are upside down or not, will be by the brilliance of the stars that bright the sky." I was fascinated by this description and looked forward to seeing it very much, but others told me that I had been spun a sailor's tale. Other than the blue, or black, ocean, I wished to witness the flow of water, as the force of gravity reversed when we travelled crossed the equator. I wanted to see the albatross, a giant sea bird with six feet wing span that never flaps its wings. It was said to ride on the air currents a thousand miles out to sea. I could not imagine this immense bird following our ship, when we were weeks from reaching land. Like a white kite, swooping down and catching flying fish in their beaks, as they swam at speed below the surface, then flew above it, in immense shoals, as wide and as long as Oxford Street. Thousands and thousands of flying fish rising from the waves as if in play, then disappearing again into the vast blue sea, like an illusion that left a person to wonder if it had appeared in the first place.

The fish followed each other, as though they had an agreed destination in mind. They were an exhibition of colour and wonder. They glistened in the sun light, each like a polished mirror, reflecting the sunlight in all its glory. They were chased by porpoise. Their hast being driven by the wish to not get caught and be eaten. Sometimes, they would leap so high, they would land on the ships deck, where I would busy myself to save their day. Using a coal shovel that stood to hand, I would lift, then flip them, back to the deep and vast ocean. This wonderous display of nature, would last for several minutes. When it was over, I realised I had not been breathing. The beauty of this spectacle, had taken my breath away. The porpoise and dolphins would play and leap. They would remove the barnacles from their skin, by rubbing themselves against the hull of the ship. The constant banging was enough to keep a man awake, but to me, they made music that was pleasant to my ears. I did not resent their presence, even for a moment. If they were happy then so was I. I wore a constant smile of complete contentment. I had never been so happy. We ran into a whale. I heard the loud thump as we struck against it. I remember Harry shouting, "look at the spray – a whale, a whale." It was just like I'd seen in Moby Dick, a spray leaving the whales enormous head. I couldn't believe my eyes. It rose through the six feet swell, in slow but deliberate motion. I stood and watched him continue to climb, as the crest of the swell past, I could see his full length. The sea water cascaded down his immense body. I swear he looked me in the eye as he reached his full height, before he momentarily stopped, then slowly slipped back into the water. He disappeared and was gone without leaving a single ripple. How fortunate was I to be a witness to such natural wonders? It was better than pushing horse dung on a barrow around the East End of London, that is for certain! The good fortune of being a direct witness to these events was not, I believed, limited to seeing the event in itself. I felt the good fortune was in being of a mind to recognise the greater message that had been conveyed. Think me crazy if you wish, but I can still see that whale looking at me. We met on a level where we had communicated. Words were not necessary. The whale reminded me to respect all life. *"No living being wishes to be harmed."* This is what he said to me.

I had read that the plains buffalo of America, were once so great in number, that it may take twelve hours for a herd to pass by in one single stampede. Imagine being on a high perch and watching buffalo rush past for half a day solid. The sound of dropping hooves would be like multiple thunder claps, one on top of the other. The sound must have been quite incredible. My goodness me! What had man done to the natural world? If the shoals of ocean life lived on land, then no doubt they too would be like the buffalo and be on the verge of extinction. I could picture Mr Wilsons face. I wanted him to know what I had seen, witnessed and realised about life beyond the limitations of home. If I were able to converse with him now, we would discuss the preservation of life. He would be able to point out those things that I had overlooked. He would be able to add his prospective to help me wake up further, to any deeper meaning. How far seeing he was, to encourage me towards a life beyond the confines of my birth place. I wanted to tell Mr Wilson that I was the world's wealthiest person. Not because I had money, I did not, but because I was privileged to be of a mind to respect him and listen to him. He had his whole life collapse around his ears due to his view for global peace but he had the decency, patience and courage to encourage me to embrace the world as my oyster. There is no doubt Mr Wilson very much assisted in changing the course of my life from something potentially narrow to something that was without limitation. I saw myself as being a global citizen who one day would hold a clear and understanding view. This planet I believed was for all life to flourish and not just the chosen few. Everybody, financially rich or money poor, all were locked into the life they knew and were born to. Few children would break free of restraints and see the wider picture. It was clear to see that money was a necessity, it feeds our family's but does little to satisfy the feeding of the soul, that vital element that makes us human.

Within the pages of my merchant navy registration book, I was described as being British. What did that mean I wondered? I had, if all went well, decades of freedom ahead of me to do with what I chose. This was a very important thing to be considered, to fully realise the privilege of my birth. This was something to be fully appreciated and therefore something to not be wasted. I decided that for me, being British would mean enormously fortunate. I actually came to the conclusion, that I was among the most fortunate human beings in the entire world. This, I thought was good reason to dedicate my freedom, to learning and understanding. Then Peter, my former ship mate, bright, illuminated and smiling, sprang into my mind. Why did my ears prick up when this lonely orphan friend of mine mentioned something about the hermit monks and nuns of the Himalayas? Why had I not asked more questions at the time? I know, I heard his words, and I know they deeply registered, but why do I recall them now, in this instant and why do I feel it of such vital importance to know more of their significance? Peter was a strange man. He carried an air of feeling inadequate that made me feel uncomfortable. He always apologised or made an excuse for any comment he made. Then one day, when we were talking about the bible, he asked me if I had ever heard of enlightenment. What is that I asked? It was then that he mentioned the mysticism of Tibet. Don't ask me how I knew, but I did, that the answers to all my questions to the meaning of life and the part we play in the overall scheme of things, would be found in the Himalayas. I thought of how my interest was drawn to the mountain range whilst in the library in Bethnal Green, not the Alps or the Andes but the twelve hundred miles of the mighty Himalayas.

I was on deck one late afternoon, ready to start my four o'clock watch, when I got into conversation with three of the stokers. I hadn't met any of these engine room workers before and in truth it did not occur to me that the ship needed to be fed with fuel in order to move. I suppose I thought it moved on its own. These guys were just about to release others from their four hours of coal shovelling. What struck me was, that they were already as black as the coal they relentlessly shovelled. They looked like miners, black faces too. There vests were dry, but would soon be wet again from body sweat, and their skin would be red from the heat of the fires. It was clear, that they had not showered or changed cloths following their last shift. Weary and exhausted they had eaten and then slept throughout their eight hours of break. I bet they stank down there in the heat of the engine room. It would be inevitable, and no doubt very uncomfortable for them. All three men were from Newcastle and I could barely understand a word they were saying, but it made me realise that within the world of a ship there were many needs and all departments are dependent on each other. Just like the greater world really. We all ultimately need each other. A ship is a small community, in a way it is like a village. I asked Harry to give me a hand with an old barrel that the lamp trimmer had offered me. We managed to drag and roll it to the door of the stoker's accommodation. We left it standing alongside a fire hydrant, from where we started our laundry service. Life was good and the stokers had fresh cloths every day. Not ironed but clean. All life counts and if we are able to help each other then we should, that was my thinking.

Later in life, I was to befriend a wild life vet, Dr Bill Jordan. Bill was a wonderful man who gave much of his life to the African elephant. He was tireless in his support of Daphne Sheldrick, who founded the orphan elephant sanctuary in Salvo National Park, in Tanzania. It was Bill who over saw the forty-monkey project that showed harmony among groups of forty monkeys or less. The trouble and in fighting began, when groups grew beyond that number. Splits and divisions grew my numbers, perhaps we humans can learn by this and choose to live in smaller communities. Bill was later to work with Peter Bloxham another dear friend of mine, together they were able to save the Madagascan pink Pidgeon from extinction. By throwing an immense net over a portion of forest, they were able to keep predators at buy until their numbers increased. Peter was also a vet. He had built his own boat and met Bill when sailing the world. I wondered how a small boat would manage in the Bay of Biscay.

The captain said, when he spotted our laundry barrel, that he had never throughout his career, sailed with a more harmonious crew. He had absolute respect for his lads and all was well. I was asked to take the wheel during a watch, when the sea was particularly rough, too rough to rely on automatic pilot. Whilst fighting the wild ocean to keep on course, I thought of the guys working in the bowels of the ship. Goodness me they worked hard. For four hours at a time, they would shovel coal, they would keep the engines fuelled. Not matter what the conditions, in the roughest oceans, with all the dips and the sways; with all the rocking and rolling, they would keep their shovels shovelling.

The Port of Brisbane is in an estuary. In the mouth of the estuary, there was a meat processing plant. From it flowed a continuous flow of waste, that came from a large pipe, about the size we would imagine a sewer pipe to be. The waste came out into the ocean, so you can imagine the sharks that gathered there. I wouldn't say hundreds of them but certainly there were dozens of them. I tried to count their fins, but this was impossible, as they circled, disappeared and reappeared again, they made me giddy. The species of shark was called the grey nurse. I have no idea as to why they were given this name. There was definitely nothing kind or loving about this highly developed killing machine. I was mesmerised by their grace, their power and deeply disturbed by their obvious lack of compassion. I wondered as to why there were no hammer heads here. Perhaps sharks were like land born sharks and kept to their own turf. They are the most unforgiving predator. I would stand and watch them for long periods of time and think about my childhood questions of life and justice. What made men and women human? Why is a shark a shark or a kangaroo a kangaroo? The human is the only species on earth capable of choice, to change our ways, to alter our outlook, to widen our view, so what it is that makes us so fortunate, to have the ability to develop a gentle nature? I had a burning desire to know the answers to my questions. I knew that one day, the wider world and worldly experience would show me the unequivocal truth of existence. I wondered again about Peter the orphan, and what he had said about the monks and nuns of the Himalayas, and how one sentence may hold the power to potentially change a person's life. I wondered if he had been real, or was he some kind of messenger? Watching the sharks made me shiver. They truly were awesome! I recalled that blistering hot day, when the Rhodesia Castle was at anchor in the Red Sea. I could still hear that cry from the bridge *SHARKS!* I shivered so violently with the closeness of this call. Wow! How near to certain death was that?

I went below to my cabin. The note book was still on the side where I had left it. Finding the pen that had rolled to the floor as the ship had rolled in recent swells, I took to writing down those things that humans, animals, birds, fish and insects all have in common. The differences were clear to see in terms of body shape but what did we share as sentient beings? We all have eyes in common, so it made sense that we would all wish to see danger coming. We all had ears and would wish to hear a threat arising. We all need to eat and we all fear for our lives. No living being would offer themselves up to be caught, hurt or eaten and definitely not to be butchered, fried or baked in an oven. The human being has the capacity to appreciate. We can for example delight in scenery, books, art and friendship. I wondered if other species were able to delight in the same. I became distracted. I was wanted on deck. I would look forward to making more noted later in the day.

In reality, my answers were under my nose and I knew it. I reasoned, that if life is all around us, then so are the answers to it. A spell of work gave me a break. I was only able to think about these things for short periods. The concentration I centred on these matters almost blew my mind. I had to shake my head at times to clear my brain. I knew that there was, and always would be, a natural justice. Given time, then all things would balance out. *What goes around, comes around!*

I wondered what the explanation was, as to why I was here in Australia revelling in every moment of my life, and yet my old pal Vicky, with whom I had so much in common, was struggling at home. The answer to justice must surely lay in the fact, that we had more than one lifetime. I reasoned this as one short life span would not be enough time for all to pan out evenly, but this needed further investigation. Assumptions and theories were one thing but facts were quite another. If all life is sacred, then one sentient being cannot possibly be more favoured, or superior than another. In the short term yes; but in the long term, no. Every living being must have their opportunity to find rest; even if you are a shark, who can never stop moving, who is always looking for the next meal! I thought that, somehow, we could overcome suffering, but only the human being had the mind to do so. This would not be through financial success, having money would certainly bring its own worries. The thought of not having enough cash and wanting more, would not be a remedy for a peaceful mind. The answer surely would lay in spiritual understanding. Under those circumstances, aiming solely for material success could well be our downfall. Money hunting held the potential to be a major distraction from reality.

My contemplations came to an end, as the old temptation to jump from height came to tempt me once more. If I allowed the desire to continue, then I might act on it, who knows? I would land amongst the sharks. How weird is this? The thought sends a tremor through my body, a shiver ran down my back and an icy chill runs across my shoulders. It was the same chill I felt, when I leapt from near disaster in the red sea. Very strange! I turned away from danger and reaffirmed my determination to live a life of learning. May be one day I might discover where this weird temptation to jump from heights had come from. I had managed my obsession to count bathroom tiles and floorboards, and all manner of other things, simply by not doing it anymore, so I will do the same with this. If I do not think of jumping, then I will not do it. My concern was that I may get caught unawares. I was no scholar, but there was no good reason to think this tendency could not change, even the weather does that! I wasn't going to waste a single moment of my life. Instead I would take an interest in everything meaningful! Right now, I had the opportunity to learn about the aboriginals, learn to throw boomerangs and to play a didgeridoo. I'd go inland and find koala bears and kangaroos, look at the architecture and visit the museums. I had heard word, from an Aussie docker, about two aboriginal brothers who lived between Ares Rock and Darwin. These brothers were very well known and had been on television. Their names were Henry and Cecil Goodfellow. Both were over one hundred years old. Word had it, that they looked like brittle twigs that at any given moment may snap, but they knew what to eat and where to find their food, they were very healthy. It would have been wonderful to meet with them but time did not allow it. I had responsibilities toward my ship and took these obligations seriously. Some years earlier, I told my mother not to worry about my safety because I would live to be one hundred and two. I have no idea where this statement had come from, but I do recall the certainty I felt when I said it.

This caused me to think, that meeting the brothers may hold some deeper significance, and maybe I would seek them out one day, though I had no reason to think, that I would ever return to this part of the world. I did not believe that my spiritual quest would find forward momentum whilst I was here. I enjoyed Australia and got on well with the Australians, they had great humour and knew how to relax. But if I was looking for a needle in a haystack. and I was certain that the haystack was not here, then nor was the needle. I was more than happy to move on. I believed that any country that was concentrating on material growth would be diminishing on spiritual awareness. I was becoming a more complete person in terms of being able to understand the wider picture of life. Though not all that I had witnessed in my travels to date were to be celebrated. I was still to discover what I would call a treasure, a land where all were content, and free from the relentless struggle to survive. I had learnt enough about life to know it could and should be lived and not merely tolerated whilst under the thumb of an oppressive force that made freedom, in its true sense, a remote and distant dream. Why as a youth, had I felt such revulsion at wearing a watch? Had I, on some deep and decisive level known that I would not live my life by a time table, laid out and decided upon by the agenda of a nation that was not going in my direction?

After following the coastline of Australia from port to port, we took the four day hop across the Cook Strait to Auckland in

New Zealand. The whole culture of New Zealand was quite different to what I had previously seen in the world. The wild life was different, as was the landscape and the climate. Whilst here on this beautiful land I wished to explore the Maori way of life. I had heard of the Maori villages of Rotorua and Rangiriri. These villages were two places that the Maori way of life was still intact. The cities and what they offered held no interest to me, apart from food outlets that is, it's always good to taste a nations cuisine. It was time to speak to the boatswain. I asked him to exclude me from any overtime schedule he had planned. The Ceramic was due to under-go some extensive maintenance work, she was starting to look tatty, with rust coming through the paint work where she had suffered most from inevitable effects of salt water damage, but I wanted shore time, rather than the double time that work would have left me with. "Money was not my priority" I told him; education came first. Bos was fine about things and was very happy to grant my request. He asked me to not be away for any longer than one week.

The first person I was to meet and commit to memory in New Zealand, was Ma Gleeson, who must have been the heaviest women in the whole entire world. It crossed my mind when meeting her, that it was highly unlikely I would ever see a larger female again, she was huge. Shaking hands with Ma was like shaking hands with a transit van, even her ears stuck out like a pair of large wing mirrors. Mrs Markavich and Aunt

Mary didn't come into it, they would be like seals in the lap of a whale. In comparison to Ma, they were true light weights. If being heavy had been an Olympic sport then no doubt Ma Gleeson would take the podium. She looked like forty stone of vast rolling landscape. I had heard of Ma Gleeson when I first went to sea, she was a legend among the sea going men and was spoken about often, not just for her size but for her agility and awesome speed of movement. It was said that she could fight like a man and often did, as she kept order in her bar that stood across the road from the dock gates in Auckland. It was a rough place with few stalls and no chairs, and come to that, like in Panama, there were no glasses either, everybody stood and drank from their bottles. I went to the bar, because I wanted to see one of New Zealand's land marks. To visit New Zealand and not see Ma Gleeson would be like visiting London and not going to Regent Street.

Some months later, I was to hear of a similar lady who had been a chieftain on the Pitcairn Island. I do not believe I ever knew her name, but she was the leader, or chief, of the tiny population. Pitcairn was the closest thing to the Robinson Crusoe island that so enthralled me as a child. Goodness me, it was so beautiful there. It was completely pressure-less. The whole air was one of worriless existence. There was no natural harbour and no port for us to enter, therefore there was no land for us to tie to. We dropped anchor and went ashore in the dugout canoes that came out to greet us. These canoes were not small by any means, they were carved to perfection by craftsmen who followed an age-old tradition of boat making. They were deep enough to hold the cases of medical supplies we had brought to them, and crafted to ride the high and crashing surfs that noisily formed around the island. The currents were very strong. The sea was Lapis blue and the white rolling surf was as pure in colour as fluffy summer clouds. A turtle, four feet across from side to side, arose from the depths and cruised alongside us. Its head the size of a rugby ball. Water ran off from its shell, that made it gleam beautifully in the sun light. A sword fish crossed our bow and both disappeared to not be seen again.

The Canoes were kept on the beech like a row of sleeping fish. They were of varying sizes, some big enough to carry twenty men, others would carry just a lone fisherman. The island population was made up from the descendants of those who survived the Mutiny of the bounty, along with a few church missionaries. The Bounty was a Royal navy ship, that in 1780 had been taken from the control of Captain Bligh, who was set adrift with several of his loyal shipmates in a rowing boat. Don't ask me how, but captain Bligh and his men managed to travel over four thousand nautical miles back to England from where they were able to resume their maritime career. The mutineers made a life for themselves, spread out across several islands where, bar the few, that were later captured, spent the rest of their lives, I suspect in peaceful bliss. There was no money on Pitcain. I exchanged a pair of shoe laces for a water melon. It was delicious. The chief owned the only horse on Pitcairn. Legend tells of how she fell from its back when out riding. Her tumble came to a jarring, and I would believe a very painful stop, as her leg jammed tight between two boulders. To free herself she took her knife from her belt and cut her own leg off.

In essence the Maoris were a warrior race, built to win battles and rugby world cups. In deed they had defeated the British forces at the battle of Rangiriri in 1840. The British had decided it a good idea to carve New Zealand into areas and hand large estates to English Noblemen, Earls and Dukes, but the Moari would have nothing to do with it and stood firm to battle. Unfortunately for them, they misunderstood the flying of the white flag of surrender to mean a wish to negotiate which led to their downfall. The Moari downed arms to chat and were soon overwhelmed.

They were great fishermen and built the most extraordinary living structures. Though their villages were close together, they lived in small groups and ate together in a central community building that we may call a hall that had no walls, it was open from all sides. They cooked their food on hot stones that were buried under soil. Everything including the Maori faces, torso's, legs and backs were covered in art. I had bought small gifts for Mum in several parts of the world. The antelopes in Africa, tea towels and a pair of boomerangs in

Australia and I wondered what I may take to her from New Zealand but strangely I struggled to decide on any one piece of carving. I was not certain as to what the motifs meant and did not wish to give my mother a gift that just maybe carried a message that meant nothing to her. I know the chances were small as all in Rotorua, where I stood among the tourist stools was all very happy and jolly, but I had once seen other art works that carried war chants, and I had no wish to take any chances, not with my mum and her wellbeing anyway. I once showed a picture to my Grandpop. It was of a swastika. I mentioned to him the detail. He said, "that not all things are for putting up on your wall, even though they may be well designed.

I often wondered in later years, if men and women knew the true meaning behind the tribal tattoos that became so very popular. I know some would say that it is merely a design but in truth it is something much more powerful than that, like eastern mantras, they bring with them something subtle but very powerful into the world. Like the East End signs in the boarding house window. No Blacks. These maybe a mere two words but the depth of meaning behind them is immense in ignorance and hatred. Such was my mistrust of motifs that in the end I did not purchase a wood carving for mum, but instead picked up a small but highly colourful rock from alongside a hot spring of which there were many. It was the perfect size, not to heavy as I had to carry it but not like a pebble either which would seem inadequate as a gift for the one person in the world that I loved and cherished more than all others. I decided to polish it and the boatswain oiled it, it was beautiful. It would look wonderful alongside Mum's Irish cut glass flower vase. A rock from New Zealand, covered with the most colourful veins, and a vase from Waterford that lit up like a rainbow when caught by the sun light, how about that for mum? I decided to buy Mum tea more towels too. They were depicting local scenes and I thought she would like that.

I left Rotorua knowing that, in regard to our place in the universe, I was getting closer to the answers that I had sought from my youth. Sherlock Holmes sometimes found his answers by eliminating those who were unlikely, until he was left with one who was most likely. This is how I was working my search. I had found many peaceful beings but this was only whilst peace was in the air. No doubt that even the Kray boys or my uncles for instance were able to rest in peace at given moments, but this did not make them peaceful people. Even my grandpop who could not always be peaceful in his environment. I think the one person I had found closest to peaceful was Mr Wilson but he was a one off, he was not peaceful due to a community and its way of life but despite the community and its values, expectations and teachings. I remembered back in England when in a church for a family wedding or christening. It was bearable for so long but then I became overwhelmed by a feeling of wanting out, like I needed air. The experience of claustrophobia, of the walls closing in was very strong. It was not my habitat. I had felt this way in many places in our world and therefore I concluded that I had not found my perfect surroundings, the one where I would feel the most comfortable without any sense of discomfort.

Following my few days inland, I arrived back at the Ceramic with the wish for this voyage to be over. I was now wasting my time and I knew it. The boatswain soon put me to work and I felt like most other people in the world must be feeling, filling my days with activities that were against my will but in the words of dear old Albie I had to just get on with it. There was no use fighting against the grain, the tide would change as and when I found a new adventure in a fresh part of the world, a place I was yet to discover. I was to realise later, when in the East, that a peaceful mind reigned despite outer conditions and not due to them. Peace is an inner thing. It is the fruit that appears from the virtuous practise of wisdom and compassion. If I had been awake to this indomitable knowledge at this time then I would not have faced the drudgery I now felt but I had signed a contract and I had a responsibility towards it. Being honourable and fulfilling my pledge would make me feel better.

With paint still not dry and with the windlass oiled and sparkling, we left Auckland to begin our tour of New Zealand. It was good to feel the salt air on our skin, the gentle roll of the ship and the sea breeze brought with it a sense of progress. It was good to be on the move again. The sea in the Cooke Strait was always quite choppy, but I had not been sea sick since my early days in the Bay of Biscay and that was something else to celebrate. There is always a positive to make us smile and our crew cook, after months at sea, had finally discovered how to make porridge that was consistent in texture from one day to the next, so that was good too.

I wanted to say thank you to the boatswain for allowing me time to visit the Maori villages so I told him I was at his disposal and that I was not bothered about further shore leave. I would be happy to work. This was not a big decision; I had no will to walk around the shops nor go to the bars. Why would I? We had them in London, they could be found throughout the world. They were all somewhat different but in essence they were the same and held no interest to me. I thought I would save my shoes before I found the need for another corn flake box.

I did go ashore in Littleton, on the South Island, where I nearly lost my life again. Not by shark attack this time, it was a mountain. Harry and I decided to go climbing, goodness me how high we climbed and what fools we were. It's not as though I wanted to absorb the magnificent views. I knew that if I was to pear over my shoulder then I would likely feel that dreadful urge to jump. We were a long way from the ground when a mist dropped. So dense was it that I lost the end of my nose. I laid as best I was able, against the rock that rose above me at an angle of two minutes to twelve. With my toes on a goat path, with my calves fit to explode due to the effort of clinging on by my toes. I don't know how long the mist lasted but I know I had a one footed confrontation with what I think was a rather large mountain goat. It nudged away at me with a stubborn wish to pass. It made me laugh as I quoted Albie Banks to him 'you just gotta get on with it mate' I told him. "You will have to find another route around tonight". My time in the mist transported me back to the East End and the smog. I spent my time in reminiscence. For a while I missed and even pined for Bethnal Green but things soon changed as the mist passed and the sun came through. Impermanence at work! Harry was nowhere in sight so I made my own way down, only to find him waiting for me at the bottom. I thought he would be safe as I had not heard a long drawn out scream of terror but then Vicky did not make a sound when he tumbled down from the roof of the three-story building in Bethnal Green. Maybe the movies had it wrong and people fell with a silent resignation. Harry took a real risk; rather than wait for the mist to clear, he found his way down and managed to survive despite the dangers. I asked him if he met up with a mountain goat. He said he did not and then ask "did thee?" I was to tell this story years later, to Chris Bonnington, the renowned mountain climber. Chris had survived many adventures and surmounted every one of the world's major peeks, including Everest. He did not say anything in response to my story but the look on his face said it all. I think he thought me an idiot.

That was the beginning and the end of any mountain climbing for me. From now on I was going to concentrate my time on my real interest and not be distracted by such fool hardy pursuits. Little did I know, that I was to spend many years in the Himalayas, where I would always be happy and content to look at Everest, K2 and Annapurna and any other peak from a distance. Never did I think about putting even a solitary foot upon them.

Years later, my son and I stayed in the Nepalese village of Tingla in the remote region of Solukumbu. We were the only white men to have visited the region since Edmund Hillary stayed there to acclimatise for his Everest expedition in the 1950's. Local nomads who still lived in the traditional way, offered with great generosity to guide us to base camp for the view but we were both very happy to remain at the monastery that clung precariously, it seemed, like a giant bees nest to the side of the mountain, though still in the foot hills the scenery was stunning. It was in Tingla that I met the most beautiful women I had ever laid my eyes upon. She was in her eighties and still did a full day's work. We would see her walking the vast slopes laden with grass and herbs that she carried on her back. In the evenings she would cook for us, a wonderful vegetarian meal that she cooked on a charcoal fire in her stone built ancient house. The interior of her dwelling was black from the charcoal. If we did not eat all that she so kindly served us, she would chase us with her broom. Her face was burnt and dry, the lines upon it were a map of her life and her broad and genuine open smile reminded me of the sun as it rose in the morning to illuminate all that was around it. She would sit on her porch, spinning her prayer wheel whilst muttering her mantra, her eyes alive with joy. She did not have a single tooth in her head and her chin folded to touch the tip of her nose. I had admired several women in my life but she took the biscuit. I thought her to be the most perfect woman on earth.

I was surprised to find so many Scots people on New Zealand's South Island. There is a port called Dunedin with a large population with half coming from Dundee and the other half having emigrated from Edinburgh. It was strange to be in New Zealand and thinking I was might be in Scotland, but all this information meant little to me. I was fed up and wanting to return to England, to see what might happen next.

It was a relief to set sail for England. We finally docked in a near birth to the Rhodesia Castle. It was good to see her being laden just a few births along. Off we went, same routine, to collect what pay we had coming, a few goodbyes and see you again to those crewmates we had sailed with. Then off to be one of the five in the back of a taxi with my five shillings ready to get me unhindered through the dock gates, leaving the policeman to count his coins and home to see Mum. She had no idea I was about to arrive; I had no communication at all with her. I was to be a surprise. It was not difficult to enter the house. The street door had twisted during the Blitz and had not closed properly since, so I was simply able to push the door open and call out for Mum. She screamed in delight at the sight of me but the air in the house remained dull, nothing had changed over years so why should it, just because I had been away for several months. It was wonderful to see Mum and receive a punch on the arm, along with a smiling grunt from dad. We drank much tea and spoke about grandpop, but I was already thinking about another ship. I stood by the fireplace and noticed that the tip of the antelope's antler was still in the box on the mantelpiece. No point in waiting I thought, I'll check for a ship tomorrow.

The evening came and went and the following day I was up early making my way to the Minories. Ships were scarce in those days, too many sailors and not enough jobs. The lady I spoke to said they only had one ship available, it would mean staying on her for two years, and I would have to fly and meet her in Singapore. I asked the kind lady to tell me no more about the ship, but to put my name down for her. I told her I would accept the job, another adventure, a new part of the world and more opportunity to learn and explore. Tell them I am on my way! As I said this, a vision for the future arose in my mind. I will tell Mum that I will not be sending my wages home any longer. I was going to save my money and use it for my trip to the Himalayas. It was difficult to understand how I could travel the world and be away for months on end, only to return and find people who I knew, still sitting on the same barstool in the same pub talking about the same things. It is not easy to describe the awful air, the staleness of my old life. Nothing budged and it was very sad. Everything was stagnant and I wondered, if I may have kicked off a new beginning, if I had fixed the street door or sang a string of sea shanties in the street, but people were in their own routine and my discomfort was, that I was no longer a part of it. Sometimes it only takes something small to set off an avalanche of thoughts but there was something at home that drained me. Perhaps that is why the house seemed like death, because everybody was drained but had got used to it.

I had become close to the lady at the Minories. I had known her from my first visit and always liked her. Her name was Gloria and though a decade older than me I thought we had something very much in common, I looked forward to seeing her and she did me too. I thought about taking her a little gift to say both thank you and goodbye but then thought this act might be a little cruel, if not foolhardy, but I often think that I wish I had done. I had a date and time to return to her office as there was paperwork to collect. Not just flight tickets but a visa, some travel allowance and most importantly a passport. Gloria took this opportunity to give me more information about the ship I was to join. In fact, she gave me quite a vivid picture, she described it as a "rust bucket," adding, "please be careful, I would like very much to see you again." Gloria had a wonderful smile that radiated her sincerity, though I could see she had her worries too. Taking Gloria, a small gift would have shown my appreciation and probably released me from that lingering feeling that I still feel today, like not completing a spoken sentence, that there was more to be said. Things were left unfinished, swinging in the air and incomplete.

Ten days later I was sitting on board a 747, listening to the rather worrying sound of the airplane propellers as they spun to a blur outside my porthole. But it was not so much the sound that made me smile, it was the side to side shudder caused by the power of the plane as it built up a forward thrust against the handbrake. Wow! How fortunate am I! But my joy was stained somewhat by an equal depth of sadness. I knew that once again I was leaving people behind that had little or no concept of their being in a cage of their own making. My new ship never left the south China seas or the North Pacific, it spent a great deal of time anchored off shore, ready to go anywhere at any time, like a taxi waiting at a rank on a cold night and hoping for a customer. In our case we were hoping and waiting for a cargo, that would be delivered somewhere in the region. Shanghai tomorrow and who knows where then, maybe Japan or the Philippines, maybe Korea or Hong Kong, maybe Taiwan. Who knows?

Landing in Singapore was truly a breath-taking experience. I know this statement sounds extreme, but truly the whole experience did just that, it took my breath away. Everything was picture book oriental. I felt that the books I had viewed and flicked through back in Bethnal Green had somehow come awake from some dream state and I was in among the pages. The beautiful colours of the dress materials were spellbinding in their quality and style. The incense in the air and the racket and razzmatazz from the market life was incessant. Having had past experience of joining with a new vessel and feeling quite sure of myself, I followed my old pattern and headed straight for the ship. I was fascinated by life around the docks and was taking in every aspect with an enormous grin, until I saw the Patterson, the ship I was to join. Gloria was right, it did appear somewhat on the rusty side and when last painted someone with a sense of humour had renamed her the Batterson. I climbed on board with some difficulty. The tide had risen and there was no one around to let out fore and aft ropes or to lower the gangway accordingly. I hoped there was not a ten-foot tide as the ship would tip against the strain of its holdings and then there would be trouble. It took me a good five minutes to find anybody of authority, most of the deck crew were Indonesian's, only two others were English, one of them was the boatswain who did and said little to make me feel welcome but no matter, I had a purpose being here and I was content with that.

No longer a deck boy, now a J.O.S. a junior ordinary seaman, I was relieved to see I had a single berth. It was not the best space in the world. I was situated high in the bow and that meant that there were only three straight walls. The forth wall followed the shape of the fore front of the ship and housed a round shape that the anchor chain would run through. That was going to be very noisy but I soon settled in. A week later we were dropping tractors tyres, of all things, on Ochoa, an island off Japan, that was particularly known as the home of Karate. My living conditions soon became of no importance. Japan was a wonderful experience. This was a highly significant time in my life. I was to spend much time in Japan and I was optimistic about the prospects of my being here. Things were very quiet there. The people spoke quietly and with a respectful bow. Nobody shouted or appeared to use poor language. Even when doing noisy work, they did it quietly.

It was the silence of the people rather than the environment that struck me

most. They had a quiet efficiency and obvious dignity. The silence somehow had

a tangible knowingness about it. There was a wisdom that hung in the air of this

ancient culture that was very attractive to me.

I could not help but recognise how different this part of the world was to other parts I had visited over the past years. There would be answers here spiritually. I could feel it in my bones. I had witnessed spirituality in several cultures and could not say that I saw any realistic sign of it being embedded within the different populations as a lifestyle. I know we cannot generalise, so I give my findings knowing that some might like to challenge me about them. It had been an education to have visited Africa with all that Africa had to offer but my time there was, in the main spent in recognition of everything that was unfair about life. From my perspective the place was a horror show and I could not visualise things changing much for the African, certainly not in the short term. Australia and New Zealand were much the same as England. They were very much part of the commonwealth and looked forward to economic stability through trade. The Caribbean and other places I have not mentioned, all had their points of interest, of course they did. Visually the Caribbean was stunning in its beauty. Where the pacific was blue, the Caribbean was emerald green. In those days the oceans were relatively clear and we were able to often see the sea bed. The colours of the coral and the sea life moving across it, was truly poetry to the senses. The South Pacific islands were the same but none had the air of Japan and its silent awareness.

We raised and dropped anchor often. When on watch, I was pleased to do my job and help, but when off watch I was not so pleased to be woken by a great chain rushing past my head like an underground railway train. The individual links were as much as one man could lift. It was a scary piece of equipment. Life was just as Gloria had described, we were a tramp ship that lumbered from one place to another, dropping off both large and small cargoes, but it was the second trip to Japan where we held anchor for several weeks with no indication that things would change soon. We were not in demand. No cargo to run. No work expected of us and plenty of time to fill. I took the opportunity to travel into the country's interior where I found the Zen, Buddhist and Shinto temples along with the Zen, Buddhist, and Shinto monks and nuns, that occupied them. I made many friends and in particular a Shinto master, Master Jun. Master Jun was to become a lifelong friend, a most fascinating man, and most dear to me. He was so quiet and still, that when he sat silently, a bird or two would often come land on his head, shoulder or knee. I spent much time with Master Jun, I stopped over at the sacred Yakuoin temple that sat at the peak of a small mountain, the central mountain of three. All were snow-capped and set against a pale blue sky that looked no different to a typical Japanese fine silk or charcoal drawing. The region was still, quiet, ancient and full of mystical mystery. Everything was spotless, no litter, no dust and no leaves that might gather and become trapped in hidden corners. I remembered crawling under East End market barrows looking for discarded apples. I would find them under cardboard boxes and among unwanted tissue paper and all kinds of unwanted debris, some dumped there and others brought by the wind. This was a different world in so very many ways. It was polished, clean and orderly. The monks wore garments of an ancient design, not cut and fitted like an East End suit but square and loose that hung with perfect pleats. The temple guardians were in blue and white, no starched collars and no starched cuffs but elegant, clean and crisp. There hats were black, shaped and tall, silk and shining in the sun, not like the one worn by Prince Honalulu whilst selling his betting tips in Bethnal Green and not like an undertaker and come to that, not like Jack the Ripper's either but like a samurai warrior. They displayed strength, discipline and honour. All would carry a long stick and all knew how to use it too. I would sit and watch them go through their exercise routine. It was beautiful to watch and difficult to put into words. Whether in a group, or exercising alone, there was a poetry of movement, an ancient art on display. There was a long history of tradition to be witnessed. In Taipai, in Chiang Kai Shek Tien square, at six o'clock each morning, five thousand people would gather and flow through there Tai Chi routine. This was much the same. It was poetry of movement and something to behold. The scenery, or backdrop to this, was as I mentioned earlier, it lay in layers. At the back was the perfectly clear pale blue sky, and on top of that, the snow topped mountains and then the ancient architecture and then the blossom, and finally, in the foreground, the honourable monks who lived with a solid discipline passing through perfect grounds and gardens. Japan is the country side was truly a picture.

I refused to stay with Master Jun in his hut, as he lived alongside bears. They stayed clear of him and he stayed clear of them, but I was not going to take the risk of them giving me the same respect as they did to Jun. I would follow the footsteps of Jun as we made our way across the slopes. On one occasion I stopped in my stride and froze, explaining to my companion that a bear was staring intently at me, and that I was concerned. Jun told me to relax. "A bear can tell when the hairs on your neck stand on end, this will trouble him as will a quickening of your heart beat." This made me feel no better. Jun had been in a bad motor accident in Tokyo and deliberately slowed his heart beat so as to not lose blood. He had control over such matters but I was yet to learn such skills. I told Jun of how sorry I was to hear of his accident. He had nearly lost a leg but he brushed it off. He told of how he was grateful, in a way, for the experience, as whilst in the hospital, the recovery rate soared due to his positive influence among the other patience. Jun said that much good had come from it.

The bears were not so very big, not as large as a Canadian brown bear but there were several of them and I was not about to ask any one of them to join me for lunch. Master Jun had a developed sense of distance. He explained how he knew by instinct the perfect distance to keep himself safe and free of any danger. Too close would disturb the bears and to far would cause them to be curious. There is he said "a perfect place between the two extremes that caused the wild life no distress and therefore no concern." I thought this to be rather odd and maybe a little too optimistic but then again, a bird would land on Jun's head if he was not moving, so why would a bear attack him if he did not invade its space? No wonder I lost all sense of time. If I had been wearing a watch, then no doubt I would have missed these life enhancing lessons, and all to catch a mere ship, that in essence meant nothing at all. I was in a wonder world, like a small child absorbed in the pages of a pop-up picture book. I heard and saw nothing outside of my experience and I wallowed in the experience. Living in the temple was an elderly lady, word had it that she was taken in by a previous abbot as a two-year-old orphan and there were those who believed her to be one hundred and eight. Older people in the community said that they had first heard about her from their own mothers. I did not ever meet her and in deed I never laid an eye upon her. I thought she may be real but then at times I thought that she may not be. This is just one example of eastern mystery. Was this fact or was it fiction? Master Jun informed me of how she resembled a tiny porcelain doll, a fine, slender figure, that seemed to be powdered with chalk. She had never eaten a poor meal, nor had she ever witnessed aggression, known anger, heard a swear word or been a witness to anything other than positive, gentle and pure intentions. I thought of my old friend Chippy. He was white but not from chalk. In fact, he was more off white, the colour of lard. A different world. Though she had never left the temple, it was said that her wisdom knew no bounds. Like a farmer who spent his life alone in his fields but had a wisdom that went much further than the hedgerows. Women from miles around would come to the temple to seek her council, nothing it seemed was beyond her understanding and foresight. Her influence within Japanese society was legendary. Foreign visitors were strictly fore- bidden from visiting her with their troubles. Master Jun told me of how foreign business men were starting to come to Japan, they would often bring their wives who would spend their time soaking up the wonderous culture of the Japanese. At first all were welcome and many wives through an interpreter would tell of their stressful complicated lives. These stories were to our lady so very harrowing that her compassion caused her to display deep and heart felt concerns and the ageing process began to kick in. The Abbot decided that enough was enough and to protect their living treasure he limited the visitors to locals only. Though a foreigner and unable to sit with her, I understood the decision of the Abbot. The creators of the museums I had so enjoyed throughout the world would not be challenged for keeping a century old master piece away for direct sunlight, so why should we think it strange or mean for the temple authorities to protect their own prized asset? It made good and sound sense to me.

You can imagine this was a different world, so different that I had no regrets when I realised, I'd missed my ship. Mind you, I nearly fainted on the day when I went to the docks and saw no ships anchored off. The horizon was clear of any sign of life. For some reason unknown to me, I did believe that the ship would be there waiting for me. It had taken on board a cargo and left for the Philippines. One day had drifted into another, I became, in a sense, a student to master Jun. I did not ask to be his pupil and he did not suggest he be my teacher but I was there to learn, so in essence he was my teacher. I remained at the sacred temple for nine months. The day came of course, when I realised that it was time to move on. Losing my ship had become a wakeup call and alarm bells within me had started to sound. Questions were starting to be asked about my permission to be there, so I headed for the British Embassy in Tokyo, where I informed the staff that I had missed my ship. "No cause for concern," the man with the wonderful BBC news reader voice said, "what time did it leave? We shall contact the port authority and try to get you onboard via the pilot's boat." His attitude changed when I told him I had no idea when it had left. When I told him, I had last been on board a month ago and that I had been in Japan for 9 months he was none too pleased. I was held at the embassy and interrogated as to my activities and though my ship was due back in Japanese waters the authorities decided I should be placed on the next British ship to leave the island, which meant, back to Australia. I was to be held within the Embassy walls before being transferred to The Ionic, a sister ship to the Ceramic that I had once sailed on.

It was whilst with master Jun, that mention of the Himalayas once again surfaced. Master Jun told me that I would not find the answers that I sought whist searching in the wrong place. This statement was not made to decry the Japanese approach to spirituality, far from it, but to point out the different dispositions of individuals. It was His belief that I was tailor made for Tibetan Buddhism. He believed that I would find my answers in the Mayahana teachings of the Buddha, the teaching of the middle way. I had no doubt that he was right, as earlier, whilst in Taiwan, I had the good fortune of spending time with a Tibetan meditation master from the Nyingma tradition of Tibetan Buddhism. His name was Yurmy Tinley. He was a Khempo, a title given to a great scholar, practitioner and teacher. He was in Taiwan to represent His Holiness the Dalai Lama at a world peace conference that was set to take place in a Taipai theatre. The Khempo could not speak or understand a single word of English, nor could I speak a solitary word of the Tibetan language, but in his silent, deep and still manner, he delivered, or transferred to me, the most profound teachings. His quiet stillness was of such a profound manner that I wished in that moment of meeting Him, to discover its source. Khempo Yurmy Tinley was a guest of Master Wu Chi, a Chinese Kung-fu master, who like master Jun from Japan was to become a lifelong friend. Wu Chi's father had been a guard to the last of the Chinese emperors. This was an extraordinary world of sworn and unlimited dedication. I can picture that world now. The clothing. The colour. The warriorship and the moment to moment discipline and unquestioned devotion. It would have been an ancient world lived by ancient traditions with scrolls and obedience. Guards were not permitted a weapon such as a sword or even a shield. It was purely kung-fu skills that were relied upon to protect a God King. Wu Chi carried on the family tradition by mastering the skills passed to him by his father. He grew up in this world and later became a teacher of the Praying Mantis tradition of Chinese Kung Fu. The family left mainland China following the cultural revolution when Buddhist became persecuted. They settled on Taiwan, an island set off the coast of China that to this day struggles to remain independent of main land politics and influences. While still in his youth, Wu Chi founded the praying mantis school of martial arts. It is to be found in the bamboo forest in the foot hills of the Quan Yin mountain, that stands over Taiwan's capital Taipei. I was to know Wu Chi for many years, my son was to attend his school during the 1990's. I was astonished to witness the athletic skills displayed by him and some of his advanced students. They would leap and spin in the air, turning and twisting like a leaf in the autumn winds but it was he who once told me that the defence skills of Kung Fu were limited, that they merely mastered the physical potential of the body. He went on to say, that the true and ultimate art was to master the mind, that the great meditators, who had realised boundless wisdom and compassion were the true conquerors. Wu Chi bowed at the feet of The Khempo, just as his father would have bowed at the feet of the emperor. To experience the cultures of the East was highly auspicious for me. Those questions I had asked the vicar, Miss Hobart and others as a child. The questions they had no answers for were clearly understood, it appeared to me, by the accomplished meditators. They were no push over. They were men and women of great strength and character with immense moral standard.

I first saw the Khempo sat upon a large flat, circular rock. It was a grey rock covered in part by a deep green moss. He was dressed in His maroon robes of the Tibetan Buddhist schools and bright yellow sleeveless top. These colours complimented each other to form the perfect picture of deep meditation. It was the perfect postcard. Everything was harmonious. He was in amongst the bamboo shoots that stood tall beyond Wu Chi's enclosed compound that lay quiet, though I could still hear the sounds of the students, even though there were no students there. I had as a boy, on several occasions, been inside Highbury stadium. The home of my beloved Arsenal, when it was empty apart from the groundsmen mowing the grass and renewing the white lines that defined the pitch. Though empty the roar of the crowd was in the structure of the stadium. I could dream and recall my treasured memories, my favourite moments, the goals I remembered. I employed the same recollections when the school dentist told me the needle would not hurt. I would take myself off into a dream and avoid any discomfort. The bamboo shoots were as thick and round at their base as my own waist line. When on occasion, when the high winds blew ferociously through the forest, the bamboo would sway and brush against each other whilst producing a hollow, clicking, whistling sound. It was a wonderous tune of nature to the senses, to sit and listen to the free movement of a dense forest that was in effect no less than one of nature's dancing orchestras. Khenpo was a large man, He was the shape of a pear, his hair gathered to a ball that sat on the crown of his head. He was as silent, like a night time sky. He sat on the raised stone, unmoving for much of the day and long into the evening. This I found to be astonishing but Wu Chi told me, that a master of the Khempo's accomplishment was able to sit like that, as solid as a mountain and as deep as an ocean, without food or ablution, for 10 days or more. I found this information to be extraordinary. The Khempo took my breath away and left me in a daze of open-mouthed amazement. He didn't seem to be here, but he didn't seem to be elsewhere either. There was a stillness around him that radiated, to my mind, throughout space. I witnessed His form but I had to look closely to assure myself that He was not transparent. I would not have been surprised if it had been a dream, that I had been asleep to wake and see Him missing. He had no need to arrive as such and had no need to go, whether here or there he seemed at home and ever present, so everywhere was the same. It is very difficult to explain such a profound experience but Khempo was no different to a view from a mountain top. His presence can only be described as limitless, boundless, all encompassing. Like an ocean that had no beaches or a sky that knew no end. I could have used this experience as a story to tell at any future dinner party. In - deed, I have done so. I could have returned to normal life and merely put my experience down to a tourism event but to my enormous good fortune, for which I am most grateful, my enquiring mind wanted to know more about this mystical phenomenon. These precious golden moments were not going to waste. They would become my spring board into a world filled with mysticism and magic. A world of miraculous events. A world where all fears are dispelled, where there is no old age, no sickness and no death. Without a word spoken I had received the message loud and clear. We could say it was my karma to see the message written so vividly in that moment. At the time I thought a miraculous message had been delivered me through miraculous means and I still believe it to this day.

My mind went back to the East End of London, the starched collars and cuffs of the gangsters, the well-cut suits and the shiny shoes, where everyone undoubtedly had an agenda. I thought of the corrupt policemen who demanded money from us seamen before we were allowed to pass through the dock gates and allowed to go home. I thought of the Africans carrying copper ingots, the sweat that oozed from every pore and the policeman that arrested me and in effect sold me back to my ship's captain. All at the same time, memories ran through my mind. I thought of the aboriginals and how in vain they tried to save their culture. I thought of the Maoris trying to keep theirs too and here I was sitting witness with a man, a simple monk without an agenda, with no wish or want, whose happiness was installed and abundant despite worldly affairs. There was no doubt in my mind that the world was heading toward its demise, due to a distinct ignorance of reality. A relentless search for material growth, greed and a wish for more riches could only be limited and never be the ultimate goal. I could not imagine that this fever would stop this side of man's ruination. But here I was, sitting before one man who was born, brought up and educated in a country, a culture that was awash with such men and women. I asked an endless amount of questions to Wu Chi. He showed great patience and always answered in a gentle tone. He told me of the atrocities perpetrated against the Tibetan people and their culture. I heard of how monks and nuns had been arrested, incarcerated and some tortured at the hand of the Chinese liberation army. I was told astounding stories of unimaginable hardships, of how those in robes were able to use their experience of horror to further their practice of equanimity towards all sentient beings by retaining their compassion for their captors whilst forgiving them for their brutality. It was while with Wu Chi that I made firm my aspiration to follow my feelings and head for the Himalayas as soon as the opportunity presented itself. This aspiration was further reinforced by the guidance given me by my dear and treasured friend Master Jun. I remained a seaman for some time following this experience but not for a day without the knowledge that my life at sea was to come to an end, certainly I felt that the energy and enthusiasm for such a life was very close to being exhausted. My single wish was to live and abide among the enlightened ones.

Once back in England, I attended the library where through maps and the written word I was to gather a great deal of essential information necessary to fulfil my intention. It was a highly energising experience as two realisations came clearly to the fore. The first thing being that I was definitely heading to the Himalayas but unlike Jun, I would need the semblance of a plan. I could just leave and head in the right direction, just as Jun would do. But I did not wish for my journey to take months or even a year or more. I wished to arrive at my destination so as to receive authentic information, rather than gain experience as I went from worldly hindrances. This was going to be the adventure of all adventures, very little money, no experience, but an absolute feeling of certainty, that if I couldn't pay the fare, then I would walk. It became a saying of mine, that if I wished to travel the world and haven't got the money or means to do so, then I would swim. I had no doubt I'd get to my destination, no doubt at all. This was the strength of my determination. Money was my dilemma. I had not signed off from my most recent voyage as I was not onboard to do so. The shipping company had deemed to not honour the contract we had between us, on the basis that I had not honoured my end of the agreement. I was most grateful to them for not leaving me completely high and dry. I was offered a settlement fee for the time I had worked, that without delay I accepted.

One option of travel came quickly to mind. I could join another ship that would take me to a place that gave me access to India with no water to cross. With this possibility in mind I once again headed for the Minories to investigate this potential. I headed that way hoping that I may see Gloria. I expected to get a cold shoulder from the shipping authorities due to the black mark that would surely be against me due to my having missed my ship when in Japan, but to my surprise nothing of that was mentioned and I was offered a ship that would take me back to Singapore. The question was, did I want to accept this offer or not? The potential was there for me to once again jump ship and make my way from there to India.

Gloria was no longer at the desk but was working from an office in the rear. I spotted her through the large glass window and with hand signals and silent lip movements I asked her to lunch. She looked up at the clock and mouthed back that she would be free in thirty minutes. I smiled and with my thumbs up told her I would wait. I negated any idea to dishonour my contract by telling Gloria my plan to head for the Himalayas. I knew as I was talking that I was throwing a spanner in the works, but no matter, whether it was subconsciously or consciously, I was pleased to do so. I knew as my words poured off my tongue that I was back to square one but I was confident that I had done the right thing and immediately felt the benefit of honesty. The good fortune that had followed me all my life was still with me and I wished to make wholesome decisions for the rest of my life, that would be the cause for this continuum to flow unhindered. I did not feel content to join a ship when I knew I had no intention to see my contract through. The disquiet I felt in my mind was in itself a message that it was not the right course of action. This was not my way and any pre-conceived intention to deceive my employer had to be dismissed. I thought of Paul. He had thought of digging a hole for those who had crossed him. If I cross others then I believed I would be surely digging a hole for myself. I understood the offer of this ship as a test of my character, my faith and intentions? The wrong decision would no doubt lead only to difficulties, barriers and hurdles and at worst to regret, misery and even failure in my quest. I remembered the ten commandments from school. Do not be led into temptation.

Perhaps the bible did have a message for me. Deceit would no doubt have its cost, as it always would, but I never ever stopped looking for my early questions of spirituality to be answered, particularly after the death of my precious grandpop, and here I was with the seemingly perfect opportunity to further investigate the meaning of life. My grandpop came often to mind, had this been to encourage me to cheat my way to my answers or was the it later, to warn me of the consequences of what would be after all, poor behaviour? The question was easy to answer. Grandpop was an honourable man and would always encourage me to be the same. What would grandpop have done? He stole a belt from the waist of a dead German soldier to hold his trousers up. Was this wisdom, opportunism or was it just plain theft? This thought was hardly an equal to my present situation but Grandpops actions from so many years ago came back to cause a quarrel between him and his beloved daughter. This very story was strong enough a lesson to know that if I wanted a future without, or free, of the potential of quarrels then I should not lay the ground for them now.

What I saw in the North Pacific and in the cultures of the South China Seas was a completely different way of looking at life and existence. We are not the same in the West, our mind set is different. We tend to push issues, to lack in patience, to manipulate outcomes. I could not imagine, not even for a single moment, that the Khempo would display impatience. I had wanted answers to spiritual matters for as long as I can remember. But seeking spiritual answers and cheating to get them would not work. The silent Khempo had taught me that this would not add up. I had to be patient, show fortitude and rely on good character. These three things, along with a sharp determination and focus would see me through. I'd spent time with a man in Japan who lived harmoniously alongside bears and a man in Taiwan whose father had been a guard to a god king, ready and able to defend the throne with his bare hands and kung Fu skills. I'd been presented with many examples of what seemingly appeared impossible, so who, or what, could prevent me from reaching my own goal? I would face what comes my way and I would look to enjoy every moment of it with always an ultimate goal in the fore front of my mind.

I was home again with Mum and Dad. Nothing had changed. The broken antler from the antelope was still on the mantlepiece and the street door still would not close. I said nothing at this time to Dad but chose the perfect moment to tell Mum that my life at sea was drawing to a close, that I had made up my mind to head for the Himalayas. I told her that I had been to the Minories and accepted one last voyage that would give me the money I would need, if I was careful, to make my journey. I also told her of the potential to jump ship to see what she may say. We recalled my early child hood interest. Mum was not surprised that my interest had grown in strength and not diminished. She was pleased that I had a plan for my life. Mum asked me to follow her up the stairs to her room. This took me back to the day that she presented me with the watch. It was as though very little time had passed since that day. Dad had decorated their bedroom and it looked fresh and very comfortable. A new carpet had been laid and I was happy to see the floorboard no longer visible. This made me smile. I was pleased for them. There are times in our life when we fully appreciate our mothers. Times when their love and devotion to their children are truly revealed. She reached to the same spot that she had produced the watch so many years ago and brought back an envelope that she clutched to her chest. "When you went off to sea" mum said, "your father had your wages sent home to me but I have not spent a single penny of it. Here it is, every penny, in this envelope, it is yours to do what you wish with it. Take it and use it wisely but promise me you will not sign a sailor's contract with the view to break it and your word. Promise me you will pay or earn your way to India and be therefore honourable from the outset."

Mums generosity of spirit and words of advice, caused me to break down. Her undiluted love for me was too much for me to contain. I could not control my tears at the perfect timing of this moment. Mum cried too, then asked me to "not tell Dad. It's no bodies business but our own" she said. I had no idea as to how much money I would need to pay my way to the

Himalayas but I was certain that I would have enough to cover cost, particularly following a further voyage. Why would I not?

I kept myself busy over the following days. I went back to the Minories to seal my interest in the job I had been offered. This brought a great deal of relief. I felt light, happy and content, even the knowledge that it was to be my last voyage brought with it a lightness of spirit. I had no wish to be at sea any longer but I knew this last voyage would allow me the time to prepare a realistic plan

With a spring in my step, I headed for Chippy's market stall, where I purchased a tube of glue. If I was going to purchase anything, then it may as well be from a friend. I also had another motive. I wanted my mate Vicky's address or at least some information that would help me track him down. His mother had moved home too and that is all I learnt.

With glue in hand, I returned to the house to fix the broken antler. It took only a few minutes to mend but during that short time, every single memory of Africa returned to my mind.

On my way back home, I had called into a carpenter's work shop to ask how much money they would charge to shave our front door into shape. The boss told me they had no time to do such a job, but offered me the use of a plain as he knew my uncles. "They are good men" he said. They have done much to help me. I asked no questions, though I wondered just how he would recognise me and how on earth my uncles had helped him. Did he not know that all favours had to be eventually paid for in this part of the world? I thought of China. To receive help in china one understood that this became an obligation to the helper. Content with the plane, I nodded and told him I would return it in a day or two. I used my time well. The following morning, I got started on the street door. Dad soon appeared to give me a hand. To my surprise he eagerly proceeded to take the lead over the task. It was I who was to help him. He took full charge telling me I would not do the job right if left to it, that I would cause more damage than the job was worth due to my inexperience. He wished to do the work. This suited me as I had little idea as to how to go about the job and the man at the carpenter's shop had warned me of the difficulty of re hanging the door once it had been off its hinged. Initially, the air between us remained thick, as it had always been, but things soon changed, I became grateful to spend a couple of hours with Dad. I thought at first, that it would be an awkward time of silence, but I was to be proved wrong. Dad took the opportunity to talk with me. We spoke about a life at sea, about my experiences and about Arsenal and all manner of other things. I told him I had fixed the antler and he said he had noticed, adding that it had been on his mind for a long time to get these jobs about the house done. I mentioned my intention to go to the Himalayas. Mum had told him and he was not slow in pointing out his concerns. "Monks do not work" he said "and if you do not work, then you will not pay your bills." I did not say much in reply, I just smiled. How wonderful it would have been, if he had been with me and met the peace of the Khenpo, if he had met Master Jun and dear Wu Chi.

That afternoon, I went to see Mr Wilson at my old school, only to be told that he had left and was now teaching else- where. Fortunately, the secretary informed me as to where I would find him. I was very grateful to her. She went to some length to help me. She was very generous and asked no questions as to my motives. Something that may not happen in the climate of today. She asked me to pass on her regards and best wishes. The day was moving on, so I decided to use what was left of it to track down my old mate Victor. I do not think it was a conscious decision but I was tidying up my old life before moving on to my new. I look back on this and see quite clearly that the future was set to be a new life and any distracting thoughts of the past required attention, so I would have no regrets and things to concern me. I suppose like dying. It would not be a good idea to lay on a death bed whilst wondering what happened here or there. I was tidying up my affairs so as to move on with a clear and happy mind. Mr Wilson was in fine form. A few years older but so were we all. He looked fit and healthy. He had become football coach to the under fifteens at his new school. This is where I caught up with him, on the touch line of a pitch on Hackney Marshes. He saw me approaching and I saw his smile. He did not take his eyes off the play and simply said They all want to play for the Arsenal. This was not the best time to talk as we were often interrupted by his calling out his instructions with great enthusiasm and sometimes frustration. At half time Mr Wilson invited me to visit him at his home. I accepted and he told me to call him Stanley. We had little time due to his commitment to the lads. He kept looking at his wrist but there was no watch. "Old habits die hard" he said, "I will get a new one, one of these days."

It was a pleasant surprise to visit Stanley Wilson at his home. His wife had returned and his two teenage sons were playing in his football team. It was a very happy home and I was delighted for them. The kids had good and caring parents.

The Wilson's lived in Cable Street, Stepney. This was not the best address in the world. It had a terrible reputation for villainy.

Served with a hot cup of tea and cheese sandwich, I told my old teacher my story and passed on the good wishes of the secretary for which he was most grateful. Stanley Wilson had such an open mind. He was a man of great intellect. A man of principle but never stuffy or aloof. The humour I witnessed between him, his wife and his children were heart-warming, and I must confess left me with a pang of feeling, that I can only recognise as jealousy. Dad and I could have been as joyous as the Wilsons but this was not to be. I told Stanley, that Mum had given me the money she had saved and that I was to take one more voyage before entering into an adventure to study Eastern philosophy. He was disappointed and told me so when I mentioned the possibility of jumping ship in Singapore had crossed my mind. He asked me "where on earth had that thought arisen from. For that thought to enter your mind is an indication that a side to you is fully prepared to cheat" he said. He went to great length to impress upon me "that I should think about his words, as cheating led to further cheating and constant cheating would lead to a life riddled with dishonesty, "and your mother," he added, "is of sound mind to tell you so." We shared a wonderful evening and all too soon the time for me to leave arrived. At the door I asked Stanley Wilson to accept a gift from me. It was wrapped and I asked him to not open it until I had left. With this we shook hands and I turned to walk along the street. I had given Stanley my watch, the one that Mum had gifted me so many tears earlier. I knew I may not have the opportunity to consult with my dear friend and mentor again. I prayed the watch would bring him good memories of our friendship and of my gratitude toward him.

On my return home, Mum asked me why I had not packed my kit bag. Not for the first time in my life, I had lost track of time. I was set to leave for Singapore on 'tomorrows mid-day tide. I was not going to see Victor. Perhaps this had been for the best. I had heard nothing of him. Not even a rumour.

PART THREE

India and the Himalayas

Singapore was a most fascinating place for me. It had its unique qualities. I felt it to hold a twin personality, an underlying sense of danger and an irresistible excitement that was tangible. There was an electricity buzzing away and sparking on two equal levels. My first thoughts on arrival were to keep alert for spies. I say this with tongue in cheek as the activity in the dock area, once again brought to mind, the works of John le Carré. Singapore appeared to me the perfect place for underground activities. I could imagine contraband of every description and espionage too. It was the perfect setting for the novelist to allow his or her imagination to run riot. All the elements were there for a good story of intrigue. Despite my thoughts that made me smile, I was very happy to be there. I could not help but to have a spring in my step. The dangers here were not the same perceived dangers I had felt whilst in Cape Town or what I felt in my stomach when in particular parts of South America. Anybody could come to harm in those places simply by wandering around in the wrong district but Singapore I believed to be different to this. Trouble would only come my way if I placed my nose where it was not welcome. I would tread carefully and avoid the wrong establishments, particularly the opium dens and gambling houses, then all would be fine. I had made the right decision to take this final voyage. I was happy also, because I knew I had made the right decision to see my contract through. There is peace in honour. Along with my decision, the sun on my back, the scent in the air and the mystery of this ancient city made for great contentment. I had never felt so fit, strong and ready for action in my life. Optimism was in the air. I wondered if Grandpop had felt like this when the war came to an end. It was a feeling of being almost home and that all things for the rest of my life would be perfect. It was a similar feeling to what I had as a child when at the Arsenal. We would be a goal up with only moments before the final whistle blew. The tension had subsided. We had won the match. I could relax with great joy in my heart. Happiness showed by the broad smile on my face. The world was my oyster. I was earning money and spending very little, whilst making enquiries about my future route that would likely take me through the spine of India and through to Northern India and on to Nepal. The Himalayas stretch across 1200 miles and I had every intention, in the search for spiritual answers, to trek the distance. I remembered with a shudder, my experience of mountain climbing in New Zealand. I had several memories that brought about what I term as holding the cringe factor. Those memories that we re-live, thinking there may still be a tragic outcome. Most of these memories were associated with shark encounters and others were whist gripping the top of a ships mast with a paint brush in one hand and nothing but thin air in the other, or those of being thrown around like a ping pong ball whilst trying to survive the Bay of Biscay. With these experiences in mind, I had no intention to attempt a climb of any mountain in the vast range of the Himalayas. Once burnt twice shy. The only mountain I wished to surmount was that of my own ignorance to the ultimate meaning of life. In the mean-time I would explore Singapore and look no further. The once officers club of the Royal Navy was now the Centenarian Club, an excellent meeting place for those who had reached the grand old age of one hundred years. My fascination with longevity continued. Master Jun and I, as I have mentioned earlier, talked at length of the causes for long life. He had told me the most interesting and inspiring story of the lady that had lived in the temple from her youth. I had the absolute pleasure to have heard of Henry and Cecil Goodfellow, two aboriginal brothers who had reached a fine old age in Darwin. Henry 105 and Cecil 108 and now I was to meet the Chinese people of Singapore who had surpassed the one hundred mark. I walked around the building on the day before I entered. I felt it prudent to be familiar with the land scape before I innocently wandered in. I did not know the reception I would receive. I may be poking my nose in to the business of others and need a quick exit. I had no idea what the elders thought of the British. I did not know the history. My presence may be a cause for resentments to rise. It was best to be safe than sorry.

I entered, the following day, the rather grand old colonial building that had been erected in all its architectural glory by the British whilst Britannia ruled the waves. The long and powerful history of the Royal Navy was displayed in every aspect. The steps were wide and deep. The double entrance doors were heavy, thick, dark wood and strong, with large and very heavy shining brass knockers. The Centenarian club, with its high ceilings and the most decorative cornice imaginable, housed a dining room fit for kings and queens. There were many tables, easy chairs and deep buttoned sofas. The floors were wooden, worn and polished to a high shine. Despite the tangible serenity of the building's new occupants, the power and the authority of the Royal Navy was still very much in the air. It was soaked into the walls and into the brick work. All but a few tables were occupied whilst all easy chairs and deep buttoned sofas were free and ready for use. There was a lonely forgotten air around them. I wondered if ever they were sat upon. It was not a Chinese habit to lounge.

How taken back I was. I could not quite believe my eyes. Being of an older generation, the club members wore more traditional garments though their younger guest were certainly more modern in their attire. The elders, all who appeared wise, had long and pointed beards, some with knots in them.

Their hair was long and tied in buns or pony tails. All eyes fell upon me whist my eyes went to a man who sat alone. I introduced myself, happy that he was willing to speak with me and that he was able to speak English too. I introduced myself, palms held together, a slight bow and a nod. I happily told him of my interest in longevity, to which he kept his straight face, showing no emotion, he simply returned my nod. I did not know at this time that a straight-faced nod was a sign of welcome and encouragement. I was rather hoping for a smile and maybe a hand gesture towards a chair. A silent invitation to sit down and join him. I was in two minds. What shall I do? I took the chance and sat. He advised me to not seek a long life for the sake of it. Then he stopped talking and an awkward silence filled the air. He was a man of few words and I soon realised that I would have to work at receiving answers. I felt I was conducting an interview with a man who wished to keep his secrets. What we chase we will not catch he then suggested and went silent again before adding. "It is a worthy life that is a main cause of longevity" he said. "If we do not have a full and honourable life worth living, we will suffer ailments, the aging process will kick in, we will become ill. If we are discontent then why would our body and its organs flourish? They would surely shrivel and die." He went on to say that poor life shortening habits were born from being unhappy. In seeking fulfilment through excess food or carnal pleasures, we in effect commit a slow suicide. What he said to me seemed more like personal opinion built on his own experience. His words did not designate a profound and ultimate truth. On my travels I had visited dozens of church yards and burial places of all and every faith. There were many examples of old age, long lives, as in deed there were many examples of short ones too. There are those who lived under great oppression and those who lived through great poverty and a multitude of other factors such as sustained ill health that lived a long life despite their circumstances. Others came to join in on our discussion. I was to discover that my new friend was a mere 98. He was awaiting the arrival of his father who was 118 years old. Sadly, I did not meet him. I was amazed by this news. I was told he had lived long because he played the flute in silent secluded places. Others told me their long life was due to their growing chrysanthemums or that they sat whilst listening to bird song or rested by running water. There were many causes given but it seemed to me that each individual was citing an interest, an interest that they wished to get up for in the morning. Lying in bed for long hours was definitely a no no. I could easily relate to this as I knew from personal experience that idleness caused laziness and laziness was the cause of no action, so the blood did not have the opportunity to flow, which meant that the blood rarely became oxygenated. The lack of enthusiasm was the beginning of a downward spiral that led to physical and mental illness and potentially early death. I did not have the answers to longevity and I am sure I have heard some valid reasons for a long life but I knew from common sense that there was more to it than that. Common sense told me that my own life would not be long simply because I had a train set. I did not dismiss the words of the assembly but I did have cause to think about how necessary it is to have a hobby or at least an interest to prevent the mind from sinking into misery and thoughts of old age. But there was certainly more to longevity than this. I have previously mentioned, that in many countries including my own, I had visited burial sites and seen the evidence that historically, long lives had been lived in all and every community. It did not add up that all of these people had a life free of negativity, even kings and queens had died in their youth. They did not all have a hobby. Some would have had worries beyond our comprehension. This thought brought Jimmy Watts to mind, and his father. I wondered if Jimmy was still digging graves and taken over from his father in the local churchyards. I was certain that they had buried a few that had lived long despite the blitz. I wondered if Jimmy may be a father himself now and had a son who stood on his feet as he squeezed in through the turnstiles at Highbury. I figured that long life had to be brought about by a cause, that it was not associated to anything we may term as good luck. The ground for a long life had to be laid in the past. It had to be the result of something spiritual. Perhaps a virtuous outlook, the caring for the wellbeing of others may well be major cause.

Our ship was fully laden with a cargo for Singapore and we were to take on board a cargo of rice that was to go directly back to London for distribution. This made my working day easy and hazard free. I was also able to accept overtime by sitting at the head of the gangplank with my clip board. I thought of Steve who greeted me the day I joined the Rhodesia Castle. I wondered where he was now. Perhaps he was in Australia with his wife. It was strange to think about all those guys I had sailed with over the years. We were like spilt milk, splashed all over the globe, perhaps never to meet again. On a whim, on a bright and sunny day, I went to the upper deck. I had seen the captain. He was in full uniform, one foot up on the bottom rail and his elbows on the top rail. He had his fingers inter laced as he looked out across the harbour. He looked like he had time on his hands. I asked him if there was any potential to re- sign with the ship on a one-way contract. I told him of my plan to visit India. If this was possible, I would be very grateful. I would disembark here in Singapore and make my way by public transport to my destination. He did not think this to be a good idea and told me why. "You will have to pass through some dangerous territory," he pointed out. "Why would you risk the Khyber Pass?" he asked. Afghanistan and Pakistan are not holiday destinations. "They are unsafe" he said "and no place for a lone wanderer." He suggested I travel out as a passenger aboard a passenger liner if I wished to chance the overland route, but he advised against it. "If you were my son, I would not allow it" he said.

Back in London I signed the papers that brought my contract and therefore my obligation to my employer to an end. I said thank you to the purser as he counted out my accumulated wage and wished me well as he passed me the wad. This I stuffed into my back pocket and zipped it in. The loose change went into my front left side pocket as I kept the miscellaneous in the right-side pocket. I was always one for balance. Five minutes and five shillings later, the corrupt duty policeman allowed me to leave the Victoria dock unhindered and breathing a long sigh of relief, I headed for home. My plan was clear in my mind. I would travel on the cheapest ticket available and leave as soon as I was able. Tomorrow would not be soon enough. I would not drag my feet. Every moment here I found testing. It was not my environment. It was a waste of my time. I was most eager to move on. I knew what I was going to do. With the help of the captain, I had finally formulated my plan. All was now clear to my mind. There was a lesson to be learnt from this episode. For months I had contemplated my route only to find my question answered once I had spoken to another about it.

I thought no further than booking my flight to Delhi. I had no idea as to what I would do from there. There was no point to making further plans as things happen and sometimes plans get destroyed by unforeseen events. I would wait and see how new friendships may be made and unseen opportunities appeared from out of space. I would take one step at a time. I would be spontaneous. I sat in my bedroom and added the money I had accumulated to the money Mum had so kindly saved for me. I stood and took a deep breath. I did not realise it, but I had stopped breathing whilst absorbed in my thoughts. This is it I thought. It's time now. Placing the money into my pocket I headed down stairs. Mum was in the kitchen. Opening the front door that now fitted its space perfectly, I called out. I'll be back Mum and was gone before she answered. I did not need to carry a key as Mum has tied one to a length of string and hung it through the letter box. I caught the tube to Oxford Street and walked with great purpose to the travel agent I had chosen. Without hesitation I requested a flight to Delhi. One way I added. Ten minutes later I emerged with my ticket. It was as simple as that. I was to fly out on the following Friday. I had five days to take a deep breath and prepare myself. It was a long five days. Dad did not understand my plan at all. I gave him too much detail. I could see the disappointment on Mum's face as Dad was accusing me of idiocy. Mum peered over her shoulder from her position at the sink. It was a large, square butlers sink with a crack that ran through it from fore to aft. I do not know what caused the crack but it had not always been there. Maybe the rattle and shake of the led pipes that brought only cold water finally became too much for it. Let him go Mum said. "He won't settle until he has been. Leave him alone. Let him have his way. What is there here for him? He can't go to sea for the rest of his life."

It was a great relief to knock on the bedroom door of my parents at 4 am on the Friday morning. I'm off I announced. I'm going now. Mum had not slept. She was still awake. I smiled at her and we both felt the message of love that reigned between us. Dad had been asleep. He was half way down the bed. Deep beneath the covers. It was a war time habit designed to keep the sound of shelling out. I snatched his pillow and pulled his blanket back. I playfully smothered him before giving him a light punch on his upper arm. This was a sign of my affection and I knew he would remember this moment fondly. It was the manner that he had said farewell to me the day I went to sea. No hugs, no tears, just him and Izzy Isaacs punching me on the arm. I turned to leave the room, pausing for a moment to blow a last kiss to Mum. Goodness me I was choked but I would follow instructions, get to the airport and have a nice cup of tea. I could have had a last cup with Mum but it was better, easier, to be on my way. I was not comfortable with long drawn out good-byes. The emotion drained me and caused my throat to burn. I can still hear Mum's final goodbye. I heard it as I went down the stairs. All went like clockwork. I had done my dummy run to familiarise myself with the journey as I had done with the travel agent seven or eight days earlier. I knew where I was going and I knew what I was doing. There was no need to think. It was better also to not think too much about Mum and better to not think too much of the future too. Breakfast at the airport was a special experience. I was nervous but I was free. Like a millionaire. I ate well and sat long and relaxed to drink my tea. Nobody disturbed me. My mind drifted across my years lived so far. I relived so many experiences, so many friendships, so many ups and downs. My shoulders tightened at memories of times of tension and relaxed as I thought of my times of joy. If any person at this time had asked me how I was, I would have answered by saying "I don't know."

At ten o'clock my flight was called. I did not look over my shoulder. I simply went through the boarding procedure until I climbed the steps that would lead to my future. My confidence was slipping away. For a moment I did not feel so certain that my decision had been sane. Perhaps Dad was right. I had never appreciated his advice and I had rarely taken notice of him, but perhaps he was right. Perhaps I am an idiot. Our eventual landing in Delhi made my intentions very real. This was no longer a distant dream. It was now happening. I stood alone. For a moment I wished I had a companion, someone I knew and could relate to. But in truth I had been pretty much alone for my entire life. I am not certain that I knew anybody. There were people in my life but this was not the question. The question was, 'do I actually know anybody?"

The humidity made it rather difficult to breath though it was the middle of the night. Rather than wander off at this hour I found a somewhat comfortable corner and settled down to await day light.

My only luggage was a hold-all. I put my forearm through the loop of the handles, checked the zips and that my money was in my back pocket and soon fell into a deep sleep.

Long before I woke up, I could hear the sounds of the traffic and feel the heat of the day. Slowly I surfaced. The sounds getting louder and more vivid. The heat getting hotter and more stifling. I had been in hot climates before but this was beyond what I had previously known and I was not out in the sun as yet.

For a while I sat crossed legged against the wall where I had slept. I looked around to get my bearings. My mouth tasted like wire wool. A drink! I needed a drink. There were several places where I could purchase a lovely cup of tea. My mouth was parched. Maybe I would get some sort of breakfast too but I could not as yet stand up. I was exhausted, without strength in any one of my muscles. I could see several Europeans. Once I had found my orientation, I would approach some English-speaking people. I would get a good idea as to my next move by introducing myself to others and asking for assistance. My mind once again went back to my childhood and my playing the spy from a John le Carre novel whilst watching Dad standing fearlessly on his Corona crate at Speakers' Corner. I had not read Kipling's story of Kim. Perhaps if I had, I may have related to him too.

Eventually I stood and painfully stretched. I was not only parched but I was also as stiff as a plank. I went and bought a cup of tea and headed with it to a rest room. I would soak my head under a cold tap and freshen up the best I could, and should there be no hot water, I shall drink half of my tea and shave in the remainder. Feeling much better and ready for my day, that I was certain would work out well, I headed back to the food stall. The water had been hot in the restroom so I had drunk all my tea, but another mug would not go amiss. A short queue had developed and I was three back from the counter. I turned and spotted two English girls towards the back of the line that had quickly formulated. I knew the girls were English. I could hear their public-school accents. They were exuberant and full of genuine joy and laughter. They danced, skipped and leapt, making body movements to every word they said. They reminded me of the girls who danced in Africa but not so rubber boned. Once served and uncertain how to check my change, I carried my food to a table. On route I stopped by the two girls and ask them not to wander off but to come and join me. I told them I was looking for directions, that I had no experience of India, that I was in need of guidance. I was delighted I had asked them. They were very happy to pass their knowledge and experiences to me.

For whatever reason, I believed that they were leaving India and were at the airport to board their flight home. I suppose it was their sun tans. They were deep in colour. Toasted by the sun. They were happy and rested. It was my good fortune that they were at the airport to meet a friend who was coming out from England to join them. All three girls came from West Sussex. It was not a part of the world that I knew. They were rather posh, well-spoken and very confident. I sensed they each had a horse back home. They looked fit and toned in their colourful, loose Indian fabrics that many Westerners wear. It crossed my mind that they were preparing for the Olympics games. They displayed what I perceived to be a charitable caring toward me when I told them I came from Bethnal Green. Not a spoken display but something that crossed their faces simultaneously as I voiced my roots. They may well have asked me if I had enough to eat as a child or whether I ever went to school. But they did not say this, instead they told me they were in a perfect accommodation. "It was not the most expensive but it was not the cheapest either" they said. "It was a great place to stay for a few days, to acclimatise and ready myself for my next move. I could rest, get by breath back, take my time and move on only when I felt ready to do so." I felt comfortable with short hops rather than one long hectic unthought through rush. They were lovely girls and I liked them instantly. It was like having three elder sisters. Each wanted to mother me. Once again, I had fallen on my feet.

I stayed in Delhi for a week. The girls left after two days. They were heading for Goa. I thanked them for their friendship but was pleased to see them leave. I was alone again and free of their exuberance. This gave me the space to think and to reline myself. I had decided to travel to Amritsar by train. It would be a long and crowded journey. The railway line had been opened by the Sind Punjab and Delhi Railways in the early 1800's. This I discovered when I went to Delhi station to familiarise myself with the conditions before my chosen date of travel. Crowded or not, it was to be an experience. The train was likely to be the same train that originally rolled this line. It came to Delhi from Islamabad. Its route to Amritsar would take me through the Punjab. I would visit the Golden Temple, cross the giant river of Ravi and live within a culture that at present was so very unfamiliar to me. The girls had told me, that where ever I travelled to, I would find western people who would help me. I was very grateful to them and wished them every happiness. My confidence was up and I felt I would be able to manage from here on in without teaming up with others. There were times when a companion would have been appreciated, as I witnessed sights, sounds and smells that no-person I knew would believe when I told my stories in the years that were to come. The world was a wonderful and diverse place and I had witnessed much as I had travelled around it but no other place was quite like India. The train was over crowded to the extreme. People squeezed on and brought their live stoke with them. Painted and colourful ascetics stood at every junction along our route. Some stood on one leg. Some with their arm above their head, held in the air, where it had remained for years. Some with finger nails that protruded and inter-laced like unruly antlers. We shared little space and the heat was sweltering. Men climbed out of the windows and found sanctuary from the stifling chaos on the roof of the train. I was tempted to join them. Anything to get away from the sound of chickens. On one stage of the journey we shared the limited space with a donkey and on another with a pig. Who would be able to imagine such a journey? I loved the colours. There were Muslims, Hindus, others and me. The train chunked away, sometimes it whistled and sometimes it rattled and rolled. The carriages were often filled with smoke that laced the length of the train, leaving a trail that hung in the still air behind us before thinning out and disappearing as though we had not passed through or been present at all. We passed farmers who ploughed with the oxen. Ancient activity that had not changed across centuries. The farmers wore their turbans but no shoes. There were children too who chased the train who waved, skipped and jumped with great innocence. I threw them sweets that I had bought in Delhi. Colourful fruit bon bons and a hand full of pear drops.

To disembark from the train at Amritsar was like taking off shoes that were far too small to fit my feet. The relief was immense. I was so quick out of the carriage that I could have defeated an Olympian sprinter from the blocks. I had been under the impression that several travellers had sat on the roof of the train but as I turned around to look at the scene behind me, I saw that the train was barely visible. There were people, not only on the roof but others who were hanging like a human curtain, by their finger-tips around the edges too. The scene was both comic whist at the same time it was insane. Amritsar was to offer no rest to a weary traveller. The traffic was a jig-saw puzzle that inter locked so tightly that it was a wonder of the world that it was able to move at all. I had developed a method, or rather an attitude toward crossing roads when in Delhi. I would step out into the hooting and tooting mayhem with great faith that the highly skilful drivers would avoid me. This proved to be a skilful method. It was either that or follow a street dog, as they knew what to do and how to tread a course through the dense nature of it all. If I was to stand and wait for a gap in traffic then I would wait for eternity. Day and night the flow of vehicles was relentless. This method did not work in Amritsar. I took to climbing across fenders, or passing through the tut tuts, the three wheeled vehicles without doors. Among this traffic there were horse drawn carts, bicycles pulling loads the size of a small hay stack and giant-sized sacred cows who chose to sit down right in the middle of the whole affair. The whole scene was incomprehensible but somehow it worked. Deliveries were made and passengers reached their destination. There was great order to the chaos.

While I stood to scratch my head, I heard the hiss and whistle of the train behind my back as it built the steam to continue on its way. Life in India never stops. I made my way slowly towards the centre of town. I thought of my aunt Mary as I ducked and weaved my way through the garments that hung from every available space above the trading stores. Vic and I would run under the drying washing that hung between the flats as we went to get our bread pudding back at Dalston Lane. But these garments were not bland colours typical to western choice. These items were of wonderous colour and life reflecting India as I saw it. I passed a hotel that did not look like a hotel at all. If it had not been for a sign over the door I would have passed on by. Under the sign was a narrow passage that led to a narrow door. Certainly not a door that you would squeeze large furniture through. It was barely wide enough for a chair. I turned into the passage and pushed at the entrance door. I will take a look I thought. If I am comfortable with what I see, then I will leave my bag and go out again. I needed to eat and as importantly, I needed to stretch my body and if it was possible in this polluted atmosphere, to get some air in my lungs. I could still taste the smoke that had puffed relentlessly throughout the train. Inside the door was a small lobby, narrow and featureless. In front of me were a flight of stairs, steep, narrow and long. There was a carpet and it was clean. I could however smell the subtle all-pervading aroma of spices. Curry is the smell of India. At the top of the stairs was a young girl, perhaps eighteen with a hand-made reed brush in one hand and a hand-made dust pan in the other. She wore traditional dress and had a stud in her nose and more bracelets on her wrist than I could count. They went from wrist to elbow. I smiled at her and she smiled back. Her teeth were a brilliant white, shining against the brown colour of her skin. The stairwell had no need for a higher watt bulb, her face would light up the night time sky. I wondered if the hotel was indeed a hotel at all. No proper reception, no key or letter racks. Just a desk and an elderly man behind it. He looked up at my approach, then stood up with a welcoming bow. His turban was white and as bright as the young girls' teeth. He was bare foot. "Have you a single room" I asked? "Only one double is available" was his reply as he shook his head from left to right with an apologetic tilt. "Let me have a look at it" I suggested, "if I like it, double or not, I will stay for a day or two." "Yes! Yes!" he repeated. "I will show you now" whilst still moving his head from left to right. He led me through another corridor. Still narrow and still clean but still the aroma of curry. It was making me hungry. We went up one more flight of steep stairs to a lone room. We were in the roof. A double room and I was happy with it. I was able to see Amritsar through the window whilst laying on the bed. The bed was on a stage. Perfect! Though I did wonder what was beneath it. It seemed to be a lot of trouble to go to for no reason at all. The shower worked and as I did not plan to unpack my bag, it did not matter so much that the wardrobe had a slight odour about it. Not curry but something old and dusty.

An hour later I locked my door and headed towards the reception desk. I was going to pay in advance, before going out. I passed through the first-floor corridor as the young girl with the brush in one hand and the dust pan in the other came out from a room. Behind her I saw a single bed. "Is that room occupied" I asked? She did not speak English and I decided to not press it. I knew I had embarrassed her. She did not answer but I saw her slowly turn red from her throat up. I now knew that the hotel owner was a slippery individual. I had met a few in India as I had met many worldwide, London included. Scallywags were all over the world. I doubt whether there was more than a hundred yards between each one of them. With a broad smile on my face I told my new acquaintance, who was back behind his desk, that I would settle the bill on the day I leave. I gave him no opportunity to answer. I skipped out through the door, down the narrow staircase and out through the narrow street door. I looked around myself. Looking for land marks so I would find my way back here later in the day. The hotel windows were odd. They were office windows and not room windows. But no worries. I was happy and had my valuables with me. My wad in my back pocket and loose change in the left-hand pocket. I will sort the money thing with the hotel owner in a day or two. Until then I will say nothing. He will find out soon enough that I can barter too. I was in Jalmal Singh Road. Imagine my surprise when I discovered that the main square was only around the corner and the Golden Temple was merely a stone's throw from there. Here I was standing alone at the Sikh capital of the world. The golden temple at its core. In all honesty, once over the initial wow factor, I was not particularly impressed. It was in deed a golden temple. The walls were white but the roof glistened in all its golden finery. I had been in buildings all over the world from an East African jail cell to a former naval officer's club and many in between. The buildings I found most inviting. The ones I felt most comfortable with were the homes of the humble people. The bender of the Aborigine, the humble home of Stanley Wilson. Cathedrals and other major structures did little to inspire me. I suppose I believed in that age-old statement, that our church is in our heart and we do not need a building to attend for a display of faith or spiritual intention. There were thousands of people in the grounds of the Golden Temple. Heads covered and feet bare. Maybe my present hotel owner was here too but his faith and religious devotion did not prevent him from denying me a single room for the greater price of a double. It's a shame but I knew that my attitude had been stained by a cheat. It left a bad taste in my mouth and I had lost interest. Once again. I decided to not drag my feet. I would eat well, sleep well, settle my account with the hotel and head for Jammu. This leg of my journey would leave me 195 k short of McLeod Ganj. How exciting this was. I had no experience of McLeod Ganj but something told me that I was heading for my own personal paradise. I could sense it, taste it and feel it. I knew that I would not be disappointed. Jammu was my next stop. It was a city with a population of between half a million and one million people. The average being around the seven hundred thousand mark but much was dependent on the time of year. Kashmir and Ladakh received very harsh winters and many who populated these areas took refuge in Jammu during these periods. Built on the banks of the Tawi River, it was known as the winter capital of the region. I wondered how many people would be there when I arrived.

The journey by train was a repeat of my experience from Delhi. Overcrowding, livestock and smoke-filled carriages but I was happy. I was content. Within hours I would leave the railway behind. I would be up high and among the mountains that I had longed for, for so many years. I thought of Peter, my friend the orphan from Southampton. How wonderful it would be to meet with him here. How did he know about the Himalayas and about the monks and the nuns? I thought also of the hotel owner I had just left behind. I had left my room and dropped my bag at his desk. We need to go see your priest I said. We need a referee but as we are in India, we can call him an umpire. If he thinks that your guru would justify your cheating me then I will happily pay you. If he believes you set out to deceive me then I shall only pay you for a single room.

He was not happy at my suggestion. He became very animated. His arms flew wildly above his head. I said nothing, then he stormed off, telling me he wanted no payment at all. I turned and saw the young girl with the brush in one hand and the dust pan in the other. She looked worried. I gave her the price of a single room that I had earlier placed in my right-hand side pocket. I winked and she smiled, then I left.

I found a space in the carriage. Using my bag as a head rest, I thought I would get some sleep, but before I settled, I was disturbed by a French man. He was with a French woman. They asked me in English if I was headed for Dharamsala. They told me they intended to hire a guide in Jammu. They asked me if I wished to share their guide to bring down their cost of travel. They were getting short on money and planned to not spend a night in Jammu but to move on as soon as possible. They would rest when they reached their arranged accommodation in McLeod Ganj. I was uncertain about making such a rash plan and suggested we talk again once the train arrived in Jammu. I was interested to know that guides were available. It had crossed my mind in a dream, that I may get bogged down in Jammu. I had left Amritsar too early, too fast and too hurried. I should have stayed one more day, or perhaps two. This would have allowed me the time to contemplate my circumstances. I had broken my rule of one step at a time. In the dream I saw myself as a familiar stranger, wandering around for direction in back streets where there were no signs. That will teach me to not fall asleep on the floor of a smoke-filled train. I did not see the French couple when we reached Jammu. I found this rather unsettling. I am certain I met them but maybe they were part of my dream. I had heard stories about Doolally and wondered if the sun had started to get to me. Doolally was a British army camp and sanitorium. It was used to house returning soldiers in the late 1800's. It was their final stop before home. Many held there went mad through exposure to the sun.

Jammu was different too Amritsar. Less people. Less traffic and the temperature had dropped. Not a lot but a little bit. There were signs that we were approaching the mountainous regions. Again. As had become my tried and tested habit. I found a hotel to suit my means. I had no intention to rush from here as I had when I left Amritsar. I was not acclimatising well and I knew it. I decided to revitalise my sense of great anticipation. I had allowed my dream to take on a degree of drudge and this had to change. I knew that good feelings could be all encompassing, just as hatred could overwhelm us. I would stay her until I was full of joy. Not too long but long enough. When I moved on it would be because I felt fit and ready to take that next step. I slept well that night. I did not leave the ceiling fan running as I had in other hotels. I was free of its relentless whooshing and free of the thoughts of the African police station that it reminded me of. There was less traffic and the silence was golden. I woke the following day. There had been no disturbing dreams about single or double rooms or of a French couple wishing to share a jeep. I was hungry and ready to eat. There was no breakfast offered in house so I stepped out and went for a wander. The scenery was stunning and full of promise for what was to come. The Shivalik mountains were to the North. Locally they were known as the Trestles of Shiva, which struck me as a little strange as the local population was mostly Muslim and not Hindu. There were several Westerners. Some heading south and others heading north. I learnt from their experiences, that there were many drivers for hire who for a price would take me by jeep to McLeod Ganj, the home of His Holiness the 14th Dalai Lama.

Two days later I left with my chosen guide. We left on our own. Just him and just me. I saw no more of my French friends. I wished to travel alone. I did not want conversation. The jeep was decorated with many religious hangings. Prayers and images hung across the windscreen, from the rear-view mirror, or stood on the dash board. We bumped and lurched violently and the images did not move. They were no doubt glued into place whilst the hangings flew and whipped as though they were caught in a gale force wind. The scenery was spell binding. The name of my laughing guide was Jawahar. He saw the humour as we bumped up and down and slid sideways as we followed a challenging terrain. At times we went uphill and saw nothing but the sky. Other times we went down-hill and saw nothing but a precipice that spelt nothing other than certain death. There were vast open spaces and forest of Shai trees. Jawahar told me they were unique to this part of the world. I did not tell him that I thought they were pine trees

We stopped at roadway cafes for a welcome cup of chai and eventually, eight hours after leaving Jammu, arrived at our destination. Two hundred miles of avoiding loose and venomous seat springs had taken its toll. I was tired but strangely, not tired at all. I felt a surge of exhilaration. I stood and stretched and invited Jawahar to eat with me. He had been a good and honourable man and I wished to thank him for his kindness. He said no as he wished to return to Jammu, so I ate alone. Two hours later I saw Jawahar pass me with three Western travellers in his jeep. I smiled and thought how their must be some sort of communication between the drivers and the hotels. Why not? It would be the same all over the world. Business was business. I stood and watched them as they bounced and leapt from view. McLeod Ganj was very quiet. His Holiness was overseas and the tourist season was yet to kick in. The market was open and the cafes were serving. There were many monks and nuns. My old habit of counting objects kicked in and I soon became giddy due to every one of the monks and nuns being on the move. It was like trying to count every changing ripple of water as it shifted across the surface of an ever-changing ocean in moon light. The roads and pathways were a kaleidoscope of bright and vibrant colour. I booked, for one night into a hotel that was named quite simply, The Tibetan Hotel. It was inexpensive, safe and heart-warming. The welcome I received was genuine. The décor was typically Tibetan with pictures of the Dalia Lama hanging over the reception desk and another in the dining room. Tibetan art was everywhere. I felt at home. Tanka paintings lined the walls and Buddha statues sat serenely in all and every appropriate space. It was natural for my mind to drift back to my time in London, when as a child I would sit alone in the art galleries. I had not seen a Tanka before and new nothing about them. They told the stories of Buddhas teachings. The scenery was again spell binding. I stood on the balcony of my room and just did my very best to absorb the beauty. We were so high that we looked down on the clouds. It was a great cause of fascination to be above the buzzards that hung in the air like kites beneath me. I watched the monkeys as they crossed from one balcony to another. The hotel to them was like a tree. It was there and so they climbed it.

I stayed for a week and gathered much information. It was wonderful to sit quietly in the temple of the Dalai Lama. It was still under construction. Work was in process. Men and women with great care and devotion did their work. Some sanding floor boards and others plastering walls but the main hall, in which on several occasions, I was to later sit and listen to His Holiness speak, was pretty well finished. Though brand new, the place held an air of peace and serenity. Every day, I would go there and just sit with the monks and nuns who chose to do the same. There was an atmosphere of equanimity. There was no sense of male and female. No sense of them and us. It was a wonderful place that rested the mind.

Slowly and at great leisure my plan formed. I could see it rise like a misty but clear dream. I would hire a further jeep, and head for Nepal. I would put no date or time to it. I would allow the conditions and circumstances to happen as events would unfold. I knew from my experience with Jawarah that everybody knew each other and the introduction to my guide would come in the moment I was to mention my wish. Among the Tibetan community I saw no sign of the scallywag. I found no scoundrels. There was no need for a room key. These people could be regarded as friends. There was no need to ask anyone to confirm their word. Their word was their bond.

The walks and paths around McLeod Ganj were not dissimilar to walks and paths that are to be found in many countries around the world. They were in themselves no different to those we may find in the English countryside or from around an Ethiopian village. They were well trodden, somewhat potholed and lined with bushes or trees. But this is where any similarity ended. The views were dramatic rather than scenic or picturesque. The monkeys were friendly and followed as if they were my guardians. The birds flew high and swooped low with their beautiful song that was sung for the happiness and well-being of all sentient beings. They resonated with me a friendly communication like a human companion may do. There was a message of peace that pervaded the globe. I feel no sense of embarrassment when I tell you that I sat and spoke with them all. The wild life accepted me. They understood that, though in human form, I was one of their own. May all living beings know the causes of happiness. I had no further thoughts of home or having a companion. I looked at the sky and at the light and shade as shadows were cast across the land-scape. The colours were sometimes vivid and sometimes not. Sometimes the day was bright with a warmth from the sun and sometimes it was dark with the chill of a winter evening. All constantly changed. Nothing, not even for a single moment remained the same. The clouds moved across the sky at a fast pace of knots. They raced at great speed. I thought maybe fifty miles an hour. As they shifted, then so did the shadows. It was a vast kaleidoscope of natural movement. Paths that lead from the north, the south, east or west were strolled upon by me. I went down to Dharamsala to visit the market Place where I ate Indian curry or Tibetan mo mo's. It was a few miles to walk, but immersed in the beauty there was no sense of time or distance. The return to McLeod Ganj was a different story. It was all up hill and I waved down the first tuk tuk that approached from my rear. The driver took me to The Tibetan Hotel and came in for Chai. His name was Lhamo. He was a friend of Dolma, a young lady who worked in the hotel.

She joined us for refreshment and refused payment for our drink, By the look on her face, when I offered payment, I thought maybe I had insulted her. I asked for her forgiveness and she smiled and brushed it away. Lhamo asked me if I was had eaten a breakfast and ordered food. Dolma nodded and gave him the bill. This time I insisted that the cost was mine. The following day Dolma suggested I stay at the Tibetan Hotel if I planned to stay in McLeod Ganj. She told me that the hotel had a policy and would charge me less for my accommodation if I stayed. I wondered how on earth the price could ever be reduced. The fee was already next to nothing. My conversation with dear Dolma led me to mention my intention to leave at some point for Nepal. Ask Lhamo she suggested. He will take you. I smiled and asked how a tuk tuk would manage the journey. You be surprise she said. Toot toot go anywhere. This is what I fell in love with. The Tibetan people were full of mischief and never slow to make fun. Dolma told me that Lhamo was her cousin but later, on our journey, Lhamo told me that Dolma was his sister. Their relationship was based on how they saw it, by feelings and not by blood. I was touched by their closeness and respect for each other. Dolma stood at the door of the hotel as Lhamo and I prepared to leave for Nepal. She stood with her feet together and held a slight bow. Her legs and back were straight, she leaned forward at a 45-degree angle, mindful and in prayer. I placed my one small bag in the rear of the jeep and heard Dolma reciting her mantra of safe travel. She mumbled in Tibetan. Lhamo told me she had asked Tara to look after all sentient beings that were in movement. She asked for all beings to reach their destination without hindrance. Lhamo and i travelled only for an hour before we got a puncture in our rear off side tyre. I grunted and Lhamo smiled. He thought it was an opportunity to deepen our friendship. The positive mind. How wonderful it was to be in the company of a man who felt no wish to rush. He took all things in his stride. He was relaxed, laid back and happy. His well-being had no association to what happened outside of himself. His contentment came from within. Whilst in McLeod Ganj, I had no feelings of walking on egg shells that I had often felt elsewhere. Everything and everyone were relaxed, but none the less they were certainly stoic. These people had an indomitable inner strength that could not be disturbed by what I, as a westerner, may perceive as a negativity. I thought of a quote attributed to T S Elliot. "I had an experience but missed the point." I would be vigilant and be certain that this did not apply to me.

My arrival in Nepal was among the most emotional moment of my life. I wanted to shout out my joy so Mum would hear me. Truly I was fit to burst. The joy that filled me was almost overwhelming. I had enough sense about me to control myself before I leapt from a mountain top, but I felt a distinct sense of invincibility, that I was finally home and felt indomitable. I stayed my first night at a boarding house. It was a rickety three-story building that appeared to be held upright by the other buildings along the narrow passage in which it sat. There were no straight lines to be seen. The buildings looked like a group of drunken sailors, holding each other upright as they stumbled there way towards their bunk and sleep. The whole scene, the street traders and the antiquity of it all brought to mind the story of Oliver Twist. Though of bright exterior colours, the interior of my chosen resting place was bare. Steep stairs that were so uneven, dipped and worn. I felt the presence of several thousand people that must have trodden them over a hundred years or more. I felt impolite for filling the width of the stairway. I thought I should make room for the endless stream of ghost who made their way up as others made their way down. I was immersed in a history that brought comfort to me. It was my environment. In the hours I had been in Nepal I had felt no apprehension. I had asked for a single room and was led to a single room. Though in my western attire I stood out, no person appeared to take a second glance at me. I was not their business and I felt safe. The following day I paid for my night's sleep and set out to explore. I would taste the local food and seek directions to the monasteries. It was time to seek the enlightened ones. I had no idea as to where my direction lay, but I felt confident I would find it. Should I encounter any delays then I was happy with the thought of returning to my lodgings of the night before. It was cheap and cost next to no money at all. Should it be necessary I knew I had found a safe place from where I could familiarise myself with the city. Hungry and ready to eat, I entered a café where locals ate. This was a sure sign that the food was good and as important, it would be affordable. The waitress was a delightful young girl. She wore traditional Nepalese dress, with long earrings set with heavy blue stones. Her neckless was heavy too. She had white teeth but no stud in her nose. I thought she was not yet left school. She was so respectful toward me that I felt uncomfortable about her humbleness. She asked me in her way, if I was a Buddhist. I told her the best I was able that I was on a journey of discovery to which she bowed and smiled. I asked her 'where do I start?' To this she did not answer but bowing politely she shuffled backwards before turning and passing through a blanket that, serving as a curtain, was the divide between the seating area and the kitchen. The smell of the food was most inviting. I could barely sit still in anticipation. I had placed an order for, I do not know what, but I was looking forward to it. Fifteen minutes later, I was served with my food. It was brought to me by a man in a dark waistcoat and apron. He was wearing a battered trilby hat and wore earrings too. He lingered a moment to study me as I looked at him through the steam that arose from the noodle bowl that sat between us. "English," I said. "I have come to meet the Buddha." London humour eh? The meal was wonderful. Full and satisfied I pushed the bowl from under my nose as the man approached once more. This time without the apron and his hair freshly combed. He was carrying a mug of tea that he placed on the table with a hand movement that told me it was for me. When a child, I wondered how tea would taste in different parts of the world. Taiwanese buddle tea was my favourite but Nepalese chai took some beating too. I shrugged my shoulders to say that I did not order it but thank you, I will accept it. With this my new friend pulled out the chair across from me and again with the use of his hand asked if he may sit down. I had travelled the entire world. There was barely a country I had not called in upon but never had I felt so secure as I did in the Himalayas. I had no concern in regard for this man's motivation to join me. He was welcome. He pointed at his chest and told me his name was Sangmo and that he had both a son and a daughter. Both, he told me were going to Kopan monastery in the morning. Would I like a guide? They would happily take me. I was delighted at his suggestion and immediately thought of my immense good fortune. I had been in Kathmandu for less than twenty-four hours and if this played out, then I knew that good fortune was still with me. It followed me like a stream. Perfect serendipity. I stayed again in the place of the night before with the arrangement that I would be at the café for breakfast. Imagine my surprise when the following morning I looked from my first-floor window to see the young girl waitress who I immediately recognised from the day before, with a young lad who held her hand. She looked bright and smart, still in traditional dress and he wore a chuba, a traditional male garment loose and long sleeved that came to his knees. I thought I may buy myself one. It looked very comfortable. Like wearing an outdoor dressing gown. They were waiting on me. How on earth did they know where I was to be found? But no matter. "Everybody knows each other" I said to myself. I would buy them breakfast and treat them well all day. It felt good to have the potential of a friendship with their father developing.

It took twenty minutes to reach Kopan monastery in a tuk tuk. It was a fun time. We laughed at every twist and turn. The traffic was manic and the children giggled at my every flinch. Truly they were the most delightful children. Kopan was to be my first experience of a Himalayan monastery. Pictured in my mind were the beautiful temples of Japan with their beautifully designed dragon roofs. The stunning architecture, the beautiful gardens and the silence that said so very much. Little was I prepared for the din of Kopan. I smiled with delight to see young monks, some not yet in their teenage years running from one end of the courtyard to the other. I could see no reason for their back and forth stampede. I soon saw, that they ran for no reason at all, except they were full of the joy and unrestrained happiness of children. They ran and chased from one end to the other, simply for the sheer enjoyment of it. How wonderful it was to stand and watch one hundred youngsters or more, dressed in the maroon and yellow of the Buddhist schools so freely amuse themselves. My young and most delightful guides led me through the chaos without a word spoken. I asked several questions. The only answers I received were in the form of smiles and eager hand movements that said follow me. The young ones were very excited and obviously following the instructions of their father. They ran ahead occasionally coming back to pull at my coat to hurry me along. We entered the main hall where there sat a great image of the Buddha. Gold in colour, serene in nature. I saw that the youngsters had kicked off their shoes at the door, thinking of Japan, and respect, I did the same. There were other statues too and many musical instruments lay ready for use. There were drums, trumpets and conk shells, cymbals and others I was unable to name. There were monks who sat in meditation and others who were sweeping and cleaning. The children prostrated full length before the Buddha and feeling somewhat awkward, I did the same. From here I was led to a side room where the children stopped and stood before two monks. They brought their hands together and respectfully bowed their heads towards them. I saw Dolma do the same when she requested our safe passage from McLeod Ganj to Kathmandu. With this, and without a further word, they spun on their bare heels and skipped and leaped from the room. They left me standing there. They had delivered me as they had been instructed. It was very quiet if not silent. The only sound I could hear was that of the children as they joined the others in the running and play of those in the courtyard. This was my introduction to Lama Yeshe and Zopa Rinpoche. Kopan was their base. These two great Lama's were the inspiration behind the Mahayana Preservation Society that was taking root among Buddhist across the globe. They were at the time resident at Kopan so this was a perfect time to visit. The Mahayana teachings of the Buddha were put in danger of being wiped out in Tibet as the Chinese set out on a re-education programme that out-lawed all religious practice and philosophical study. To this end the Chinese ransacked the religious institutions, burning all books and text, with no regard for the ultimate value of these ancient and precious works, historical or otherwise.

Yeshe and Zopa Rinpoche certainly had their work cut out but from what I had heard they were great and learned Lama's and they had the support of many learned academics and scholars from all nationalities. Their collective task was to translate the teachings of the Buddha into every language. This would safe guard them for the future. It would be very difficult for future governments to destroy them. They would no longer be vulnerable as they were following the Chinese occupation of Tibet, the land of the snows. I was privileged to meet with these two Lamas. They supplied a perfect starting point for me. I would ask questions. Lama Yeshe was most interested in my back ground and had been to London. He and Zopa Rinpoche had founded a Buddhist meeting place in Stoke

Newington, a district of North London that was not too far away from the Arsenal stadium that had been such a large part of my youth. "Why would you suggest I study and practice the philosophy of the Buddha" I asked? His answer at this point was difficult to absorb. His reply was, that to find enlightenment would result in my escaping old age, sickness and death. My dedication would eventually steer many sentient beings from suffering due to their poor perceptions of reality. These two short sentences gave me much to think about and invited much investigation. I trusted Lama Yeshe. I did not believe he would knowingly mislead, not only me, but any sentient being. By reputation, he was a living example of wisdom and compassion. He displayed at all times these fine qualities and without doubt he was a great source of inspiration to so many. As I have previously mentioned, many learned translators from across the world were working under his umbrella. Books in every language were being produced to preserve the Dharma teachings. Who was I to brush off his comments simply because they sounded outrageous to my inexperienced ears?

It was at this time that I first thought that I would become a spiritual Sherlock Holmes. A detective who would study and ponder over the evidence before me. I would weigh the information. Sieve it and put it through a litmus test prior to any thought to disregard it. Conan Doyle gave Sherlock a Bunsen burner and a knowledge of chemicals to assist him with his enquiries. I would have similar. My ability to define and to employ my sense of right and wrong would be my Bunsen burner.

The time I spent with the community in and around Kopan monastery was highly valuable. If these early days were to lead me to the ultimate joy of knowing, then the value would be immeasurable. It would be worth more than an ocean of gold and more than a mountain of precious jewels. What on earth could possibly be more valuable than to be ultimately aware? I often ate with Sangmo when taking my regular trips into Kathmandu. If the café was busy and crowded then I would eat elsewhere for the experience. I bought Nepalese clothing and discarded my western ware. I came to know many locals. I was saying tashi delek, the local greeting, at every twist and turn. I was very grateful to the many people I met during this time but I was never totally at ease with my spiritual progress. In essence I was remaining the same. The gathering of knowledge was one thing, but to practise it was something different. I felt that I was acting when I made an attempt to display a similar generosity that was shown towards me. I could not help but think that a good-turn towards others was an investment rather than a genuine act of humanity. I did not want it to be, but at the same time, I hoped it was, just in case I ever needed help. I felt I was missing a one with one relationship, similar to the one I had with Master Jun in Japan. I meditated on these points at length. I would visualise the Khempo and try to rest openly just as He would do. My mind would always drift back to my experience with the Khempo. I have previously mentioned that no words were exchanged between He and I but none the less, His silent message was no different to the spoken words of the Kopan lamas. Having listened to the advice of several monks I knew that the Khempo was free of the three things mentioned. I knew that He was beyond old age, beyond sickness and beyond death. These were the essence of the spaciousness I earlier tried so feebly to describe. He was victorious, a true conqueror, not of external matters but of His own mind, His own ill based emotions. He had defeated ignorance and expelled all internal conflict. He was my spiritual hero, my silent guide and my inspiration for the future. His presence on earth was a visual example of our human potential. He would pass seamlessly from one life to another, unhindered, without doubt, with no fear and free of confusion. To further my investigation and eventual transformation, I would need both the spoken and written word but I would always have Khempo to measure them by. If I could recognise personal progress by recalling His all-encompassing silence then I knew I was on the right path. In effect the wonderful Khempo Yurmy Tinly had become my precious teacher. The guidance from other lamas would lead me to his condition. I was drawn toward the Nyingma school with a certainty and familiarity that spoke of previous experience. My trust was such that I truly believed that I was picking up the thread of the path from where I had once left off. The familiarity I felt with Nyingma brought with it a peace that was womb like, safe and cosy. I left Kopan for Ladahk. Then I left Ladakh for Mongolia and then I left for Mustang. I travelled many miles across the top of the world. I met many lamas and accumulated a great deal of information and had many of my questions answered but I did not feel that I had found my resting place so to speak. I was in the right region but not in exactly the right spot.

There had been times in my life when I had heard something and known it was said especially for me to hear. Like a holy message for my ears only. The time that Peter mentioned the Himalayas was one of these times. When my old school teacher, Mr Wilson, had told me the world was my oyster was another. I had the same feeling when back in Kathmandu and eating with my friend Sangmo. I told him of my feelings. I told him of my being drawn to Nyingma and would love to meet a Nyingma master. I told him of the Khempo. I hoped he understood me as much of the conversation was based on hand movements and facial expression. I sometimes used me shoulders and he did the same. He told me of his brother who was going to Bhutan. He went there once a year to spend time with his Nyingma teacher. Sangmo asked me if I would like to go with him. He will go next month Sangmo told me.

One week later the children came to Kopan to tell me that their uncle would be at the café the following week. They told me to come visit. This I did and whilst eating, Sangmo introduced me to his brother, whose name was also Sangmo, which told me that perhaps they were not brothers in the sense I understood but none the less brothers due to the depth of their relationship. I thought of Dolma and Lhamo. Not brothers and sisters but brother and sister just the same. Sangmo 2 was an impressive man. He had the appearance of an ancient warrior. He had a flat face with cheeks the colour of cox apples. He looked like a throwback to Gengus Khan. Born in Kham, in Eastern Tibet, he had been raised by an extended nomad family. The people of Kham were known for their hardiness, their ruggedness and their bravery in the face of adversity. His strength of character was obvious and immense. They knew the mountains on the Chinese border where they lived during the snows and they knew the valleys where they lived during the spring and summer months.

He agreed to take me to Bhutan. His teacher was Dilgo Khyentse Rinpoche. Sangmo told me many stories about this monk. He told me of Rinpoches Nyingma lineage, of who His teacher was and who His teachers' teacher was. He came in a remarkable line of great and renowned lamas that were traced back to the time of Buddha himself. The teachings had been passed orally from Master to student, unbroken and undiluted across centuries of tradition. I listened with great interest. I felt like a dear may feel, grazing whilst alert in a distant and remote meadow. Enjoying the lush grass but always with ears like radar scanners listening for all and any sound. I was listening to every word but still I was absorbing the scenery. We travelled on the back of lorries. I shudder now when I think of the dangers we faced. We rocked and rolled, held onto sacks and prayed. Our journey was long. It took us towards Anapurna. We stayed with Sangmo's friends in Pokera who were to travel with us to our destination. This was an annual event. All were celebrating. Food was set out on long wooden tables. Above us were long lines of prayer flags that snapped in the wind. Through the prayer flags we were able to see a clear and powder blue sky. In an instant, the wind would drop, there was no rhyme or reason to it. The sky was still and the flags hung in barely perceivable movement. There were so many flags. I started to count them but soon gave this up as the wind rose again. From Pokera we travelled by jeep, towards Anapurna and the Bhutanese boarder. The road was arduous, it clung to the mountain side and often it was a pass, more than it was a road. It twisted and turned following the landscape. We were sometimes held up by earlier landslides and sometimes I wish we were as our driver met speeds that seemed above safe to me. I held on tight and prayed. Nobody spoke to each other but everybody muttered their mantras and spun their prayer wheels.

It was with great relief that we eventually stopped. I was invited to stay with my new friends and I was determined to do my bit in setting up our tents. These were called Yurts and were usually carried from place to place by Yak. The poor old yaks must be very strong to carry such weight across such rugged country-side. I found it difficult to merely lift my corner as to moved it from our roof rack. We were here for a festival. It was to start the following day. There were to be great festivities. Families and friends were meeting here, having arrived from places far and wide. Old acquaintances were being made. There were nomad musicians and nomad dance troops. Plays were acted out by travelling theatre. The costumes, the mask and the music were unchanged from ancient times. The ground shook as the Horses galloped, ridden by great and expert horsemen who sat on top their mount as they thundered through the lush green meadow. Some hung under their ride, clinging to their most colourful saddles with ribbons of every colour of the rainbow, stretching and whipping in the wind as they fired off their arrows from their bows. The laughter and the joy of the celebration did not stop for three days. I had seen Dilgo Kyhentse Rinpoche sitting under His canopy, accompanied by other monks, all enjoying the proceedings. All sat on large and comfortable throne like chairs with large and comfortable throne like cushions upon them. They were relaxed and serene. I thought of the Khempo.

I had been in the long line of devotees who had moved slowly across the front of the canopy. All happy and eager to receive the blessings of Rinpoche. The moment I placed my eyes upon Khyentse Rinpoche, I knew that I had found my guide, my beloved teacher. I had travelled the world, from one place to another. I was always disappointed to find that my answers were not to be found in any of the countries I had laid my feet upon. How many times have we searched for a lost item to eventually find it in the last place we look? Perhaps this is a universal law but maybe it is my good fortune. I was at rest in finding my destination here in Bhutan. I would never have to doubt or question. I had been everywhere else in my search and with great confidence I can now rest in peace, I had found my source for knowledge.

Having trekked the Himalayan range. I found, at what might be my last port of call, a man before me that was a direct reflection of everything I wished to be.

I awaited my opportunity, until my moment arose. were no words spoken. Rinpoche was standing twenty metres ahead and side on to me. I could see His back and His right arm. His left arm was completely out of my view but He radiated a loving essence that I had not seen or felt since my time with the Khempo. So deep ran my feelings of certainty that I approached Rinpoche, holding my palms together, finger tips to my chin and head bowed. I was overcome by my emotions. It is somewhat difficult to explain my tears, except to say that this was not merely a memorable occasion but it was a Holy, truly remarkable event. I later contemplated the words of Buddha in regard to many lives, no end to the cycle of birth and death. If Buddhism was to be the means of the cycle of suffering to end, then for how many life times had I waited for this moment? I remember this time with great clarity. I had begun to practise Buddhism as a life style. The distance I had travelled had changed my outer appearance. I now resembled a vagabond. I was in Tibetan clothing. My hair was long and knotted. My face was brown from the sun and red from the wind. The dust was ground into my skin.

I waited for Rinpoche to finish His conversation. His kind face was extraordinary. The sky was clear behind Him, His face was like the sun. The wisdom and compassion glowed like a guiding lamp. I stepped up and asked in a quiet and I think pleading voice. May I request you to be my teacher?

Throughout my journey of the Himalayas I had visited many Buddhist monasteries and met with many Buddhist teachers and communities but had not until this day met with an individual of whom I immediately recognised as my teacher. My feelings cannot easily be explained in words. The knowledge came from inside. I had been told my friends, the stories of men and women who had several girl friends or boyfriends throughout their youth, but when they met the one, they knew they had met their future wife or husband. This was my experience with Rinpoche. I just knew He was my guide. There was no argument or conflict. The realisation I had held within it no doubt. I only felt an unquestioned certainty. I knew that the goal of a student was to blend one-self with the mind of their teacher. The aim being to, in essence, become the same. Inseparable from the pure intentions of a living Buddha. Rinpoche was a teacher from the Nyingma school but such was His knowledge and reputation that He spoke on all approaches from the prospective of all four Tibetan schools. Rinpoche was a scholar, a poet and author. The festival had come to its end. All was quiet. My friends had packed their yurts and left. They had shown me such kindness and went to great lengths to wish me well. I was here alone with the one goal. I will request ordination and possible remain here for the rest of my life. I really had no idea as to what to expect. I was blind to any possibility other than my own wish. It had not crossed my mind to be a lay Buddhist. This meant to me that I would be Buddhish and I wanted to do things properly. I understood the value of devotion. I had seen it in the Khempo. The skills of Wu Chi were the result of devotion. In the Western world devotion held no guarantees for success and prosperity but spiritually, devotion meant something different. It meant progress and eventual realisation.

It was a joyful moment when I was approached by a young monk. Rinpoche would like to see you he said. He is preparing to leave for France. He will be gone in three days. I had been the centre of attention following the end of the festival. I recognised the attention that others were paying towards me. I could see the questions they were not asking; they were hanging in the air. I was a source of great curiosity.

Rinpoche's room was very simple. We spoke for an hour every day prior to His leaving. I told Him of my experiences. I told Him of the Khempo. He told me I was blessed. He agreed to be my teacher and agreed that one day it will be likely that I will become a monk. He completely understood my reasoning. He said I should have a son before I took my vows. He suggested I return to England with the thought to one day return.

An hour after Rinpoche left, I left too. I made my way to the lorry park that sat in Thimpu. I asked the first driver I saw if he was headed for Nepal. He shook his head meaning no, but took my arm and led me across the park and pointed at a man leaning against the bumper of his most colourful truck. It was blue and orange, black and green, yellow red and white. All hand painted by brush and nothing painted with any particular sign of care.

The lorry was highly decorated with prayer flags fluttering in every direction. The wind blew in gust that were strong enough to cause me to readjust my footing. The wind was such that it stopped me in my tracks. I looked at the bald tyres on the truck. There was not a sign of tread upon them, then I thought of the mountain passes and the erratic driving in these regions and then I asked for a lift to Kathmandu. It was important to return to Nepal. It was familiar ground. It was a perfect place for me to sit and sort out my head. I had not been invited to stay in Bhutan and took this as a signal to leave. Things had to be thought about. I had realised my goal; I had found my teacher but the timing it appeared was all wrong. I felt much like I imagined a deep-sea diver may feel, who finds treasure upon a sunken wreck but due to conditions it takes months to bring the jewels to the surface. Maybe it was my own interpretation of timing that was askew. I had rejected a watch in my youth because I did not wish to be governed by time. Now here I was upset because I believed the time to be right. Rinpoche had mentioned returning one day in the future. Why could I not forget about my own sense of disappointment and simply be patient? I had been spoilt by the serendipity of my long and arduous journey. Goodness me! I had covered so many miles. Finally, with my last wind, I had found Rinpoche. With enormous expectations I had asked Him to be my teacher and now I am exhausted. I was so very, very tired. perhaps He had already begun to teach me a lesson. Perhaps He was teaching me something right now. There were events and happenings that I had to wake up to.

I booked into my old hotel, into the same room with the same view. The one that was held upright by the drunken sailors. It was good to rest. With no energy I was physically running on an empty tank. It was time to stop, to sleep, to consider. Such was my weariness that I had begun to stumble, not just in my movements but mentally. I was like a scalded cat. I was seeking familiar ground so I could lay down and die. I called in to see Sangmo and ate at the café. Delicious Nepalese food, good company and wonderful friendship. I went there full of questions. What should I do? Miraculously in his presence there were no questions to be answered. Instead I watched him. I studied the way in which he conducted himself. Nothing upset him. All was taken in his stride. I went to Kopan with the children. Lama Yeshe was not resident. I took this as a sign that nothing was wrong, that all was fine. If I had a dilemma then it was mine and relevant in my own head and not externally. I sat alone for long periods and studied the local people. All were at ease. All were loose and agile. None generated a situation that would cause them stress. Months ago, Lama Yeshe had told a young Australian visitor, that she should not be bitter at failing in her dream to become a nurse following a life changing injury. "Whatever you do in life you can be a nurse" he told her. We can nurse the environment for the benefit of all sentient beings, we can do this through our choices and life style he told her. Some who wear a nurse's uniform he said are not necessarily a nurse by nature at all. They may have the aspiration but not necessarily the aptitude for the realities of the profession. I thought about this. Of how I could be a student to Buddhism. That it was not dependent on my being in robes. The robes would come all in good time. I should relax, keep my focus in mind and await the moment. Should the moment not arise in this life time Sangmo suggested, then so be it.

Feeling my strength return, I decided to not employ my intellect to make any decisions in regard to my immediate future. It was far better to follow the ways of the relaxed and happy friends I had made in this remarkable region. I would move forward by following my senses. We all know for instance, that feeling, when it is time to go home. The air changes and our mind move's elsewhere, to other things and other places. We have this feeling of certainty arise within us when we visit family, or the homes of our friends. There always comes a moment when we realise it is time to leave. I was in no rush. I had no pressing appointments and nowhere to go. I had no intention of staying too long or for that matter, I had no intention to leave too soon. I was at Kopan when that irresistible feeling arose in my mind. I would return to London.

During the coming week I made my arrangements to return to McLeod Ganj in India. I said my farewells to Sangmo, his wife and children. It was Sangmo who organised the driver and jeep to deliver me over the mighty Himalayas. He told me his brother would drive me. I wondered if his name would be Sangmo too. They were the most wonderful people. It was not difficult to say farewell. I knew we would meet again. In Sangmo I had found a brother.

Back in McLeod Ganj and back with Dolma. She contacted Lhamo and asked him to take me to Delhi at some point during the following week. I was acting without thought. I had a guiding hand in the centre of my back that gently urged me forward. I did not even think about purchasing my flight ticket back to England. I would buy it when I bought it, whenever that may be. I was becoming familiar with space and time. I would fit into it rather than try and organise it to fit in with me. Life is easier when we avoid the self-imposed causes of stress

Part Four

London and new friends. Good food, film stars and a Princess

Not for the first time in my life, I felt a true sense of wonder and optimism. My burning desire to become a Buddhist monk and to continue my interest of spiritual awareness had for now been thwarted. It was good to look at this turn of events from a positive perspective and believe I had been thwarted by wisdom, though at that time I could not see it too clearly.

I believe now that much of the hurt I felt whilst in Bhutan was generated by the fact that I had not been previously thwarted in my young life and I think I took events personally, thinking that I knew best, that others were wrong. Being thwarted did not come easily to me, it made me grit my teeth, it made me angry and this in turn meant that I was not ready to take the vow's that would cause the renunciation of life as I knew it.

Dilgo Khyentse Rinpoche was teaching me well. I was able to keep a clear image of Him in my mind, His wisdom radiated. I could not believe that He would make a decision based on anything other than His ability to see through me and to act for the best. If Rinpoche was to be my guide then I needed to not only believe in Him but to trust Him. By trust Him I mean, from the very marrow of my bones.

If I learn to trust in Him then no doubt my good fortune would always continue to shine through. In this I developed great faith and good fortune continued in every respect.

I had no pull or desire to return to the East End, I did not even think about it. I fore saw pitfalls of the kind that Mum once warned me of, the kind that creep up on you, that alter your life before you are awake to it.

I had changed as a person and I knew there was nothing in Bethnal Green for me, other than potential mine fields. The East End is no place for a young man with idle hands. Jennifer may still be single. I may get into a relationship. To earn a living, I may take on a market stall. Mum may beg me to stay and not go away again. There was a strong potential that my dreams and aspirations may get bogged down and my ultimate goal may well go up in smoke. I was of a mind to not put what I saw as my future at risk.

I had no idea what I was going to do as an alternative but I did not think about that either. I decided that I would tread water for a while and allow fresh direction to appear in good time. It was time that would bring answers. Of that, from my experiences, I was certain.

It was on a Saturday, I went to the Kings Road in Chelsea to witness the fashion I'd heard so much about. The kings Road in those days was known throughout the world, it was where celebrities lived and was the playground of many. It was where I was later to enjoy a morning coffee with Dustin Hoffmann or afternoon tea with Sly Stallone.

Whilst having lunch in a café near the Habitat store that stood on the corner of Sydney Street. I noticed through the large floor to ceiling window, a lady holding tight to a lamppost, she was tearful and obviously in some depth of distress. She was a sorrowful sight and one I felt great pity for.

I quickly rose from my seat and stepped through the door to the street. She was smartly dressed in a beautifully styled winter coat that looked so snug and warm. The lady, whoever she was had style.

Years later when I took to painting, I often tried to reproduce its colour but never with any great success. I could not make up my mind as to whether it was predominately a shade of brown or whether it was orange.

On taking the lady's arm I led her gently into the café and sat her at my table. Whilst doing so I reassured her that all will be well. I called to the waiter to bring a cup of tea. The lady chose to not tell me the cause of her distress, but she did stay for tea and after ten minutes she ordered a toasted tea cake. This told me that she would recover and that I should not be too concerned for her well- being.

Before leaving, my new-found friend, in her beautifully cut and tailored coat, she informed me that her name was Mara, that she had a restaurant in Beauchamp Place in Knightsbridge and insisted I should go there for dinner, she wished to say thank you for what she called my caring nature.

We parted company, we had shared a nice chat and she seemed to be coping though certainly she still was not happy. I could not remember the name of her restaurant but no matter I had no real intention to go there.

However. One week later I bumped into Mara again. This time it was me who felt truly distressed as she chastised me for not visiting her restaurant and again with great force, insisted I should eat at the San Lorenzo. She was very firm about it. She was Italian and had a very strong Italian way of insistence about her. She threw her arms about her head and her overall body language left me with no doubt that it would be wise and even safer for me to obey her demand rather than risk her wroth should I meet with her again.

The following evening, as arranged, freshly bathed, dressed and combed I approached the San Lorenzo at eight pm. I was tired from a day's work. Earlier in the week, I had approached a builder and ask him if he had a few days labour for me. He did not, but told me, that if I had money, then he had a room for me. He would ring a friend and sooner or later I would find casual employment. This I accepted and two days later I was working mornings only. We had an early start and an early finish. This suited me. I had money to pay my rent and time to use as I pleased.

I had spent this particular afternoon at the Tate gallery when all I really wanted was to rest. The morning hours had been hard-work, mixing cement for a plasterer who was very fast with his rendering. The afternoon had been relaxing as I eased my aching limbs whist viewing the creative work of modern artist.

But like any time spent alone and in silence, my speech, or at least my ability to converse had the tendency to dry up. I always knew what I would like to say but the words would not transfer from mind to tongue. I hoped my evening with Mara would not be too full of um's and ah's, she deserved better than that.

The paparazzi helped wake me up. I was soon to become alert. I was to discover that the news photographers were a regular feature and were always to be seen hovering in the street with their cameras, ready to take photographs of all who entered or left the premises.

I was approaching from the Old Brompton Road end, walking along the narrow pavement, glancing in the windows of the small but very expensive boutiques to my left and at the expensive cars parked to my left.

I heard the sound of anticipation before me. Cameras the size of building blocks had become raised in my direction. Two photographers fell to one knee to get an upward shot, others ran up steps to get a downward one, whilst others ran toward me to get a close-up picture. I did not know why, until I heard footsteps coming up fast behind me.

I ducked as I thought of the butcher as he approached Victor swinging his frozen turkey. I thought I was about to be assaulted. Turning and ready to defend myself, I came face to face with Diego Maradona. I did not know who he was and I did not know his name but this man, who had drawn so much attention was heading in the same direction as me. He too was going to the San Lorenzo. The cameras were for him. He sounded like a horse as he made his hurried way. Very powerful! It made me think that trouble may well be afoot, I could not help but think him as being wildly agitated.

Mara was so pleased to see me, she tearfully announced that she had so much to thank me for. I did not know quite what, but I allowed her to hug me in that Italian way, pinching hard my cheeks, pulling at my ears and playing mindfully with the knot I wore in my neck tie.

I was still feeling a little distant and dream-like but awake enough to fully realise that something very strange and highly meaningful was unfolding in my life.

After spinning me around a few times, brushing off my shoulders and straightening my tie again. Mara excused herself saying she would be back soon. She went up the stairs to the first floor where she had been summoned by the leader of the Palastinian people, Yassar Arafat. He ate upstairs accompanied by his auntarage of body guards and food tasters. They filled the dining area that was usually reserved for large parties and celebrating football clubs. The premiership trophy, the F A cup and the European trophies had been centre piece on several occasions.

Mara had left me in the bar with Peter Ustenoff, the great actor, film producer and raconteur and Ian Woosnum, a golfing star of the day. I knew of neither of them. I had no knowledge of fame or celebrity. In truth I did not know who our prime minister was. I had only rarely seen a television, had never been to a cinema since Victor and I once payed sixpence to watch Batman on a wet Saturday morning and I did not buy newspapers. I had spent much of life overseas.

When I asked my ship captain for advice in Singapore. I remember he asked me if there was anything else he might help me with and I remember asking him if he knew how

Arsenal were doing back home and that was the closest I ever got to world news.

My first experience of the San Lorenzo restaurant remains clear and most vivid in my mind, Peter Ustenoff taught me a great lesson that evening. He taught me the importance of speaking well. I'd always known this to be a precious skill, but listening to Peter, proved to be truly significant. I was mesmerised by his elegance, knowledge and enthusiasm for conversation. He did not know me from Adam but asked me many questions and took great interest in every answer I made. He wished to know about life in the East End. He picked up on my accent but then asked me about my view of the world. He told me that I must have very good karma.

This comment was the cause for me to think of Rinpoche. I wondered where Peter had become familiar with the word. The word Karma I knew to have come from the ancient Sanskrit, an early language of India. It translates into English as cause and effect. The ups and downs of life are said to be the result of earlier causes. Those who have a harmonious, happy life are said to have good karma. Perhaps Peter came from a part of Russia that bordered Tibet where cultures mixed to a degree. I knew there were Tibetan monasteries in Russia. I had thought I may visit them but I did not get there.

Peter saw things from a wider angle, his questions came from all and every direction. Often, I had to change my chain of thought. There was no sense in my trying to match his intellect. I conversed as best I was able.

He was certainly entertaining and he certainly made me think about the potential that our lives present. I asked him if he believed in miraculous events but he had no time to answer, his car had arrived and he left without a further word. I wonder if he had anything to say to the paparazzi.

Whilst talking, Diago Maradona had burst between us heading for the exit. He moved with such determined purpose that he left a draft in his wake just as a train leaves a draft as it thunders through a railway station. I am certain he was not in a good mood. He was searching for someone but this did not phase Peter at all. He remained completely undisturbed, paying no attention to the whirl wind that had just rushed through. This was the first and only time I was to meet Peter but I have not forgotten the experience for which I remain forever thankful.

Mara Bernie and I were to become great friends, stars from all over the world from stage, screen and sport would ask for her trusted assistance in matters of all kinds before arriving in London from their homes or activities overseas.

Daily, Mara would ask me to help in making arrangements with all sorts of things ranging from collecting an item from Harrods for an overseas visitor arriving in London after shop hours, to having a roulette table installed into the hotel suite of a visiting middle eastern prince. I once collected several shirts for Mike Tyson. They were wrapped and in a parcel. I wondered what neck size they were. This is how I met Mikes wife Robin Gibbons who was to take me to Wimbledon tennis.

Without any planning my life simply changed. I went to the theatre with Dora Brian. I was given regular tickets to the theatre by Tom Wilkinson, these things were always left with Mara and for some reason I was showered by many with enormous generosity. I still have a Styff teddy bear that was given me by Bianca Jagger. She had no reason to gift this to me but she did.

Mara insisted, that I always ate at San Lorenzo, she kept me close to hand, it seemed that I was on call but this was an absolute privilege and I was very thankful to her. She was a very strong, powerful and determined character with great integrity. She had a strong intuition and understood my wish to tread water. Without discussion or reason, dear Mara was set to support me as she believed I was once set to support her in a moment of need.

I had my favourite table and used it almost daily. It was in the far corner where I was able to sit, relax and observe. I would nod to David Frost and wave to Kate Moss bless her. There was a familiarity among regular diners.

During those months, my whole life had changed. I had no doubt I was on course for ordination and I was very thankful that I chose to bide my time and not return home to Vallance Road simply because I had a bed there.

I'd become particularly close with Goldie Hawn. Goldie in those days was such a big name in the movies. She came to London at the request of Mahomed El Fyad. He requested her to turn on the Christmas lights at Harrods. Goldie told me that she found my company refreshing would you believe. She felt compelled to constantly remind me to not waste a moment of my life, to take every opportunity and to never lose sight of my ultimate goal.

It seemed like she had a purpose to drill this into me. She often mentioned the subject as though it was her job to constantly remind me of this vital fact. I listened and appreciated her repeating herself. The best messages were always delivered with few words. It was short sentences that I found most informative and profound. Lectures did nothing for me.

I asked her if she thought I was easily led, that I could be side tracked, to which she laughed and said, I do hope not, she had such a cheeky, endearing smile. I wish for your dreams to come true. What a wonderful thing to say. I have so many memories of golden moments and several whilst in the company of Goldie Horne. We were once in a jeweller's shop.

The owner closed and locked his door to keep others out whilst he paid her uninterrupted personal attention. But maybe he was locking the door to make it awkward for us to leave prior to making a purchase. He wanted a sale rather than the company and an autograph. He reminded me of a jewellery dealer I once met when with Dad's mate, Izzy Isaacs. Izzy bought jewellery when he was financially flush and sold it when it when he was not. It was not rare to see Izzy either stomping or floating along Cable Street in Stepney. Floating and happy when buying. Grimacing and stomping when selling. Cable Street was known for the Jewish dealers. It was a Jewish area. Thinking of this caused me to think of Mr Wilson. I wondered if he still lived there.

It was not unusual for Goldie to be locked in. She was always treated as special. I would watch and always notice how everything would go over her head. She was never anything else other than endearing. Goldie had no need to say anything. Her smile said it all.

Dustin Hoffman was in London at the time, sporting a big grey beard. He was in London to play King Lear. I mention my knowing of Dustin as he was the most extraordinary man. If I were to add all the time together that I spent in his company, then I doubt it would exceed three or four hours but during this time I saw him change facial and bodily expressions depending upon the topic of our conversation. Dustin had the ability to take on a persona of another person to the extent that he actually looked like them.

He was extraordinary in this way. He could look old, and in an instant appear young. Female and in an instant male. I can honestly say that I have had the privilege of coming face to face with many characters that dwell within Dustin Hoffman. On one occasion, when he stood to leave my company, he leaned over our table to say cheerio for now. I looked up from my seat. It was a female face that I saw and Tootsie who spoke to me.

Where ever he went in London, he travelled by bus. I invited Dustin to join me for dinner at Mara's but he never did due to the hours he spent in theatre but may be another time. I enjoyed the easy company of this most humble man.

We did not meet at the San Lorenzo, we met at the Chelsea Farmers Market in Sydney Street. Despite the cold weather he liked to sit outside his favoured cafe where he would enjoy his morning cup of coffee with a cousant.

As wonderful as I found the company of my new-found friends, I think the most fascinating encounter, in terms of being odd or bazar, came when I met the Russian Baroness, Isabella Baronovska. If ever there was a living person that stepped straight out from the pages of a children's story book it would have been Isabella.

I first met her in a Chinese restaurant in Chine town. I would regularly pop in there for a light lunch prior to popping across the road and around the corner, to listen to a lunch time orchestral performance at St Martin's in the Field.

As I entered the restaurant, Isabella was sitting at a table alone in an otherwise empty room. It was not a large restaurant. It had twelve tables that I had counted a dozen times. I drew the line at counting the squares that formed the pattern of the table cloths. They were like large chess boards in one inch red and white squares. I did on one occasion count the squares that went from corner to corner and, then edge to edge but I resisted doing the mathematics.

She was the only customer there, she ate alone under the largest hat I had ever seen in my life. It was royal blue, as was her dress and the gloves that travelled to her elbows, but like all aristocrats, she was well colour coordinated with the deep blue off set by her single line pearl necklace and matching accessories.

I sat at my favoured table set in the far corner from where I had a clear view of her. I was fascinated by her demeaner. She had a red and watery eye that moved independently of the other. It reminded me of the whale that looked at me in the pacific, or rather like the eye of a chicken, red, round and not blinking. I did not know if she was studying me or not.

In her hand she held a silk handkerchief with which she constantly dried her wet and painful looking eye, it wept and flowed without ever slowing or relenting. She looked stern, the type of stern that took no nonsense, she looked uncompromising and very rude. I was not surprised at the manner with which she spoke to the waiter. She barked her needs toward him across the restaurant, even if he was out of sight in the kitchen, still she would bark. If he was close enough, she would poke him with her silver topped cane for attention, she viewed him as a minion and she treated him as such.

I wondered how she was able to get away with it. I could not help but to become more fascinated by her as I listened to her tone of voice as she passed orders that really were quite unacceptable. Then she asked me, in the tone of a commanding officer of an elite troop, what is it, that you find so amusing?

This was my opportunity to enter into conversation, I was intrigued and wished to discover who this lady was. Her English was from what you may call high school, there was no hint of her being Russian. She said, you may join me if you wish but this was not kindness, it was an order to which I immediately, and willingly obeyed.

We had a wonderful lunch. She was a real mystery and I found her to be highly entertaining. She called for her bill informing me that I will be paying for my own food, then sent the waiter outside to bring in her driver.

He was very smart in his chauffer's uniform, he had come into the restaurant to assist her out through the door. She refused to remove her hat and leaving the premises took some skill and manoeuvring. I think now, that it could have been a comedy scene from Only Fools and Horses. I wondered what Dell Boy would have made of her. Isabella charge like a raging bull through the exit door. She was no spring chicken but very strong. Speed and weight it seemed would ensure she went onto the street without losing her hat. If it had not been for her red eye, that never looked away from me, it would have been a comic scene.

During our meal I discovered who my new acquaintance was. She was related to the late Zhar of Russia and was smuggled out of the country as a child following his assassination. I heard all about the revolution and her view of it. After several years in China she was sent to school in Switzerland before purchasing a house on Chelsea's Chaney walk and remained in England as an exile.

I told Isabella about my interest in Tibetan Buddhism. At this point she reached into her ornate bag from which she removed an ornate, stone studied silver box. From the box she removed a rich, embossed calling card. This she passed to me with an order. I have a story of great interest to tell you she said. You will come to my home on Tuesday next, where you shall dine with me. You will arrive at 6pm. You will not be early and you shall most certainly not be late.

Mara smiled broadly when I told her the story as though she knew something but was not about to tell me her secret. She knew of the Baroness and had met her on occasion. You are privileged Mara informed me with a smile and a theatrical curtsey. She looked forward to hearing of my most unexpected dinner date.

The following Tuesday evening at exactly six o'clock, I pulled on the heavy cord that rang the interior brass bell. The chauffer, though now in a butler's uniform, immediately answered the door that must have been made from half an oak tree. It was thick, heavy, rich and expensive. In itself it would be a valuable antique. It was large enough to allow a horse and trap through. The hall way was a large expanse of black and white tiles. I did not have the time to count them but the large area caused me to think once again of a chess board. A metre high rook, a castle, a pawn would not have looked out of place as decorative pieces upon it.

In the centre of the hall, the Baroness, wearing her hat and with her eye red and running, sat at a beautiful black lacquered grand piano. She continued to play whist I stood and watched as she displayed body language to match the movement of the music. Over dinner she asked me if I liked Bach.

We sat at a large table that would seat eight with Isabella at one end and myself at the other. Between us were two candelabra that thankfully I was comfortably able to see across. We ate simply and though a vegetarian I politely, with a prayer, ate the pork she had served to me and though not a drinking man, I drank the wine she had served for me too.

Isabella told me that whilst in China as a child, she was the guest of a high regional official. During her eighth year there, a delegation of Tibetan monks arrived on horse-back. In the centre, on a fine mount was a child monk of high regard. He was a Rinpoche, a monk who had chosen to take rebirth for the benefit of sentient beings. He had seen our village in a dream and recognised a sister from his previous incarnation. He had travelled for several weeks to come and say hello to her. It was not unusual for high Lamas, particularly Rinpoche's to see the past, the present and the future in their dreams. Their mind was free of all obscuration's and therefore saw all three times in one clear light.

Without guidance and free of hesitation, young Rinpoche dismounted from his horse and walked directly to a small and very humble house where he introduced himself to an elderly Tibetan woman who lived and breathed to solely serve the poor of the area. They spoke for several hours and shared food together until finally they emerged to bow low and touch foreheads and he left.

Isabella said no more and made it clear in her indomitable way that she had nothing further to say except that she thought I should hear her story. She felt compelled to tell it me. She then informed me that it was seven forty-five and it was time for me to leave. I was bluntly informed we did not have a friendship and that it was unlikely that we would meet again and certainly not by arrangement. Within five minutes I was back on the doorstep. As the door was closed behind me, I heard the piano, I assumed she was playing Bach. It was two days later that Mara handed me a hand delivered letter. It was from Isabella and in it she told me to not put her story to me in print until after her death. She gave no explanation and gave no indication as to why. I silently agreed.

I did see her again on two separate occasions, both times she sat in the back of her old Austin Princess chauffer driven car. It was the model with the long bonnet and runner boards that ran from fore to aft. On both occasions she was wearing her elaborate hat and no doubt she would have her silk handkerchief in hand to dab and dry her red and very sore eye.

I wandered about our meeting and the significance, if any, of it. I thought of Mr Wilson, Grandpop, Mum, Peter the orphan and several others including my old boatswain and the Portuguese policemen. All had said something to me of meaning. All I saw as guiding angels in my life. Perhaps in the future I would look back and see Isabella in the same light but for now, I thought that she was merely a most fascinating interlude. Perhaps she was an example of how not to treat a fellow human being. Every person I knew had been in one way or another, a product of their environment, pets and wild animals too. Certainly, I believed the same could be said of Isabella.

I realised that if you go to Rome you will meet Italian people and if you go to San Lorenzo you will meet celebrities, stars of the cinema, politicians, there children and all that you would usually see in a newspaper. Many asked me what I did for a living, which was difficult to answer. Having been given all my needs, I did not need money as such, but without design I was living the high life at the insistence of others. I must have been a figure of interest.

Friends and acquaintances of Mara were giving me gifts for the kindness they said I'd given freely to them. I built a collection of 80 paintings, several of which I sold to George Melly. I would meet with George in Soho where often worse from wear through his drinking he would flamboyantly lift his hat and introduce me to his friends as his favourite art dealer.

The last time I saw George was at a Jazz evening in the Canasario Hotel in Wimbledon, where being held upright by the piano he sang 'It Ain't Nobody's Business But Mine.' I took a tip from George, he said if you don't want to keep telling people what you do for a living then become more flamboyant. Clothes explain it all.

I spoke to Mara about my manner of dress and as a result, and with George in mind, I went to Saville Row, where I was measured for a suit. I took the advice that George had given me but made certain to keep my choice of style and material between the two extremes of flamboyant and run of the mill. It was of a Gatsby style that I chose and I confess that once ordered I wondered if I would need spats.

The suit was to have a high waist line with which I would wear braces. The jacket was fitted to skilfully improve my body shape, double breasted with six buttons in all. The material was a beautiful Harris tweed which meant it would always retain its quality appearance whether pressed or not. It would eventually cost me £1500.

I must say that the wearing of my new suit made me feel rather self-conscious, if not pretentious to the extreme, but as George had promised, it acted like magic and Mara was very pleased with it too. She hugged me, squeezed my cheeks and brushed off my shoulders. The following day she took me with her to church and on the route back she stopped to buy me a cravat. Dear Myra was a devout catholic and went to church in the Old Brompton Road three times every day. Early morning, midday and early evening, I knew where to find her. She believed in prayer and said them often.

Her relationship with the church ran as deep as any ocean. It was through Mara that I met Mother Teresa, who visited her when she came to England with the intention to establish a rescue centre in Liverpool.

The suit helped me to fit into the environment and gave me confidence. I told Mara of my trips to the West End as a child and how I felt awkward because I was not dressed well, she laughed at my story of the Japanese uniforms and she told me like stories of her own from when she first came to London following her youth in Naples. Mara was an expert at putting others at their ease.

Prior to the suit I had been wearing cloths given me by my friend Jasvinda and his hairdresser, another George, who cut and styled the hair of many from stage and screen. Bless him, he regularly shaped my hair too and always insisted that I should not pay.

On three separate occasions I took female actors to George prior to their first auditions. He was so talented and the girls were so grateful. He asked for no reward other their success.

I was very grateful to the kindness and generosity of my two friends, indeed their kindness left me to look very smart and most prosperous but my new suit did make me feel to be less of a charity case, that caused me in turn to feel independent.

When out and about and sitting in the various coffee houses that I was drawn to frequent it became quite usual to say hello to strangers without the thought that they may think me weird.

It was not unusual for strangers to think I was Dudley Moore, others asked if I was Bernie Winters and others asked if I was

Roy Castle. I did not think that I resembled anyone of them but if others thought that I did, then I suppose I must have done.

With no plan. It just happened. I began to employ my new cloths to help others, to use them as a tool.

Chelsea was a hub of young play writes, musicians, artist and actors. Many came from far off places dreaming the dream of recognition of their talent. They dreamed they would meet those who would recognise their abilities and their career may take root. It was exhilarating to spend time with those who truly believed in their future. Driven by their self-belief they left family behind and put much at risk. I was able to identify with them. Their dream was different to my own but in other ways it was the same. We all had a vision and to realise it we had been willing to take a path.

Often, with limited means, they would share rooms and apartments with others. This helped them to afford high West End rents. Often, they would go without the basic necessities of life. They would scrimp and save to make ends meet, just so as to be in the right place whilst they waited for their moment. This was not unusual with those in the arts. Michael Caine is one example of a humble beginning.

Among my new acquaintances in London, were those who worked in television, in radio and in theatre. Some were producers, others technicians and others worked with scenery or sound effects. I began to collect contact details and where I felt appropriate, I made introductions. I had met many people during my life and I came to recognise what I called the serious player. I would help them along if I were able, just as so many had unselfishly helped me throughout my life. It was a wonderful prospect to introduce a young play wright to a radio producer or an artist to an art Gallery. If they found common ground and all got along, then all well and good.

Fiona Fullerton at this time was a trustee with the Royal Marsden cancer hospital. The trustees organised an art auction to raise funds. All my artist friends, without a single exception, donated a canvas for the cause. This brought them in touch with several celebrities and business people and I know commissions were later taken. I was delighted for all concerned. Everybody was happy.

I had time to fill. A return to the Himalayas was inevitable in my view. It was a question of when I would return rather than if. I was able to see Khyentse Rinpoche in my mind. I could see the Khempo and the majestic mountains behind them, like lions with white snow topped manes. All were clear and inviting and I had no doubt I would bow before their majesty once more.

But for now, in the interim, I would explore this present life style. I knew that I was living a life which meant very little in terms of what I considered to be my purpose. The time I was spending amongst the rich, the famous and the ambitious was really a confirmation that a life of renunciation as a monk would be a far preferable life for me. I was most grateful to have seen so much of life.

I had, through personal experience, been able to see that the difficult conditions of London's East End and other testing areas of this world had their definite drawbacks, but wealth, power, influence and fame was also empty, as these had their drawbacks too. Both ends of the spectrum were often made of unfulfilled dreams.

These thoughts were not of a selfish nature. I deliberately put time to one side to give me the opportunity to reflect upon these most important matters. Mr Wilson and Grandpop had suggested to me that the world would become my oyster. Was my life in London my oyster?

I did not think so. I was always looking beyond, for what I really sought. At what point would deep, rather than mild dissatisfaction set in? How long would it be before my present circumstances turned from tolerable to intolerable frustration?

Happiness, contentment, would be up lifting for others, just as a dour mood of disappointment would house the power to alter an atmosphere for the worse and bring others down. This is not on a gross conscience level but it does not make it less true. To live a life where-by all sentient beings and the environment benefit by my birth, then I must be a perfectly happy living example of the full human potential.

These were important matters to contemplate, as few people I had ever met were completely satisfied with their lives. Happy in general was the most they would expect. I was determined that this would not be me. I came to the conclusion that not every event in life makes us happy but it should not have the power to make us miserable either.

There was a general opinion that complete satisfaction was not possible. Occasional happiness and occasional dissatisfaction were an expectation and accepted as normal. Only in the East had I encountered those who had found unbridled fulfilment.

If there was to ever be peace in this world then all individuals must end their own inner conflicts. Rinpoche had mentioned of how we first control our negative emotions and then we expel them as we would a demon who had dwelt in our house. In this way outer mayhem will cease. I was determined to not become upset. I would remind myself of the so-called primitive societies I had met and not enter into a quarrel. I would give the victory to others and not seek the last word. I reasoned that peace could only arise within me when there are no further questions to answer. Only then would my mind lay at ease. I did not seek fame or recognition. These things are not necessarily healthy as they can set one up for a great fall. I sought spiritual realisation and that alone.

I had no experience of business but that did not matter. I did not plan to demand introduction fees or to indulge in contracts or to have an office. I looked for no percentage of a person's success or good fortune, so I naturally put no thought to such things. I simply wished to help dreams to come true. Therefore, stress or fear of failure held no power over me. Failure under these circumstances would not be an option.

My goal was to continue to engage in conversation with all and sundry, inspired by Peter Ustenof. I would see where this would lead me. Friendship always has its own rewards and I knew that my own future good fortune would come from living with good intentions.

A whole string of events began to unfold. They were wonderful times, I laughed with Barry Humphreys and split my sides with Ronnie Corbett. I went to the theatre with Dora Bryan and Dame Flora Robson.

I was learning so much from great men and women. I felt that I was attending the university of life, studying happiness, success and prosperity. My early interest in words was deepening. I was developing a much wider view of their significance, the timing and their delivery being of the utmost importance. I read the words of Luther King, Winston Churchill, Tony Benn and others.

I recalled the words of learned Lama's, the great spiritual masters of the Himalayas that I had the immense good fortune to have, the year before met. My chosen teacher, Dilgo Khyentse Rinpoche's words were now settling upon me like a mystical wonder, soft beautiful and glistening, just as they did when I was in His esteemed presence. There was no body language, no change of tone or particular emphasis, just a peaceful unbroken flow of words that encased me like the clear waters of the Caribbean.

It was at this time that I first met Ray Winstone with his cockney accent and confident stance. He caused me to recall the East End gangsters who spoke with a threatening and forceful edge to their tone. All who spoke with purpose had their style. The aim, to captivate their audience.

It was at this time that I first met with Jack Nicholson. Wow! What a guy. The moment I walked into his company I felt a queer sense of inadequacy. It was not an emotion I was familiar with, it made me oddly jittery and uncomfortable. It caused me to question 'what have I done with my life?' Jack had an air about him which indicated he had lived. That Jack Nicholson smile was created by a lot of living. Before he uttered a solitary word, I believed him to be the cheekiest person I had ever met. His charm and mischievous nature radiated from him like the heat from an open fire. He had an astonishing effect on me and I am certain on others too. His star qualities shone like a beacon. He was definitely born to fill the big screen.

What interested me most about his presence was the fact that he had no need to speak to convey a message. All his answers were conveyed by a strong energy, body language and facial expression.

He took me to the Ritz Hotel and introduced me to Marlon Brando. Marlon was in London with his children. At that time, he weighed 30 stone and did not leave his suit. The Ritz was always eventful.

This is where I met the head of the Greek Orthodox church, Archbishop Athenagorus. He was a giant of a man with a long square beard that hug below his chin the size of a carrier bag.

We sat in the restaurant and spoke of spiritual matters whilst, in my case, attempted the best that I was able, to sip coffee that was more like treacle than liquid. It was awful and would not swish in the tiny cup that it was served in. This was the Archbishops favourite tipple and when he offered me a refill, I chose to not be so impolite as to refuse. Like eating meat whilst dining with the Baroness Isabella. Rather than discuss dietry matters, I chose to listen instead. I wanted to hear of the Archbishops views on God and the afterlife.

An evening with Marlon was always entertaining. Robert Mitcham would drink his gin from a half pint glass, Joan Collins would stay a while, before returning to her rooms.

Adnan Cashoggy reportedly the richest man in the world would show his face if in London.

I mentioned that this was a highly significant time for me, life truly changed on meeting Jack. I always knew from somewhere inside that I would follow the spiritual path and continue with my quest of answering the most important questions of our existence, but for now the material life was manifesting around me and the prospects were tempting. I can say that knowing Jack almost led me astray.

I had a house in one of the most fashionable areas in London, a wardrobe that started in Saville row, friends who had achieved great success with life showing opportunities that went beyond a dream. It's strange looking back how events seem to take shape. I think of the Hollywood era and the sporting era, the comedy era. It's when new introductions appeared from the same field, Ronnie Corbett and Barry Humphries came at the same time, Jack Nicholson, Marlon Brando, Dustin Hoffman, like little pockets of sameness. It was what I call the royal period that brings back memories for different reasons.

It started with my friendship with Sir Loren Vanderpost, he became confidant to Prince Charles following the death of Lord Mountbatten. I spent many hours with Loren Vanderpost, he was an author, an explorer and had discovered many of the ancient artefacts that we know of today. He gave me a collection of his books, one of them being the story of how he discovered the Lost Tribe of the Kalahari Desert.

I was in his penthouse apartment when his phone rang. He listened, then nodded, then turned and politely asked me to leave without delay. I did as he asked, he was ushering me with some urgency. Leaving the door to his appointment wide open.

Loren stood with me at the down elevator, second passed in silence as we followed the lights of the ascending lifts, until the both doors pinged and opened. My lift was empty and waiting for me, when out from the other stepped 3 security men with Prince Charles in the centre of them. Sir Loren explained my presence, quickly said his goodbye and shooed me on my way. It was wonderful to see Prince Charles in person

Little did I know, that later in the day my friendship with Princess Diana was to begin. We met in the cloakroom of the San Lorenzo restaurant. I had no personal experience of the enlightened state of mind but I had spent much time in the company of enlightened beings and was able to quote with some elegance the views of the spiritually adept. Tales of the Himalayas were of great interest to the Princess and were to form the foundation of our friendship.

The Princess and I met on many occasions. The San Lorenzo was her favourite restaurant. She and Mara had a very close friendship. Mara was like a favourite aunt. I did not tell Diana that I had seen her husband at Chelsea Towers. It was not necessary and I had seen the newspaper headlines. Whatever was going on between them was not my business, so I left it at that.

I was in the San Lorenzo one evening when Di appeared and asked me to join her party on the first floor. It was a Royal affair. I was seated next to Sarah Ferguson and across the table from Prince Andrew. The room was filled by titled people and their friends, we were all sat along one extended table and everybody spoke at once. I did not know if they were celebrating or whether these events were common place but certainly the rich and privileged knew how to party in a riotous way. It was a boisterous evening and I was pleased to eventually excuse myself for some peace and quiet. I felt for Di, she sat in company though seemed to be alone. There was too much noise to chat. I winked at her and left.

It was an experience to join the company of such people but I knew I would not be doing it again. The paparatsi had a field day and I was pleased to have avoided the frenzy that later followed.

Throughout my time in London's West End, the most significant meeting was with Sandra, the daughter of a prominent business man of great wealth. Often, I would hear his name. Whether it was a big business take over or his interest in horse racing. He had many horses all trained in Lambourn.

Sandra was a sad case. She had no career and no interest but she did have an enormous financial yearly budget to survive on. Forty thousand pounds a year and nothing to do with our time can lead to many problem and Sandra it seemed found most of them. Her biggest problem being heroin and those who were very happy to take her money whilst keeping her supplied.

I had no experience of drugs or of drug addicts. So, when this scabby faced, skinny but no doubt underneath it all, a beautiful girl told me that she was finished with taking drugs then I believed her. We sat and chatted. Or more like, we sat while she chatted and I listened.

Why would I not believe Sandra, when she said she was about to change, big time, her life style? I had changed mine with fluency on occasion so others can change theirs too, that was my reasoning. Made sense to me. If you don't wish to carry on along a road then change roads. If you don't want to take drugs anymore then don't call your supplier. If you do not wish to drink anymore then it makes sense to not take another top off from the next bottle. My perception on these matters was so very limited. I showed no understanding. My views were harsh and lacked compassion. Little did I know the hold that these dreadful drugs have upon an addict, nor did I understand that dealers do not like to lose their customers either. If a dealer does not see you, then they will come and look for you, ever ready to keep you in line. Sandra was in a fix and I had no idea just how deep this heart wrenching dilemma went.

This dear and desperate girl approached me because she said she was drawn to do so. I had met a friend of hers when at Champney's health farm in Hertfordshire. Her friend had told her I may be able to help her kick her habit.

Sandra, when she spoke to me was overflowing with determination, inspiration and conviction. She was up on her toes and ready for her challenge. She wanted somebody to tell about her vision for her future and she chose me.

It was very disappointing to not see her for the next few months. I had heard stories of her being back on drugs. That she had been found close to death and been hospitalised. I had heard the stories of rehab and failure again. It was all so tragic.

Don't ask me why but I felt a true sense of responsibility towards this dear and lost girl. Why would I meet her if not to be of some positive use? I felt that I must step in and offer a helping hand. I had no idea as to the depth of the treacle she was wading through but unprepared and lacking in knowledge as I was, I sought the opportunity to help her.

It was not a sexual thing. I had no designs upon her. Nor was it financial benefit I sought. Her wealth did not enter my mind. I simply had met her and now I wanted to help. Having met her, what else would I wish to do? I wasn't going to stand by like others appeared to do, oblivious to her tragic circumstances. At the very least I could be a stable element in her life, someone who would always listen and make no judgements. She was a decade or more older than me but I saw her as a good kid. I liked her. Mind you I had always liked older women. Probably started with Mum's mate but I thought of Gloria too.

When I next saw Sandra, she was looking beautiful. She entered the café where I sat like Marilyn Monroe standing over the air shaft. She knew she looked beautiful and twirled and twisted to display her point. Hair freshly styled. Face clear and beaming. Her skeleton frame had hour glass flesh all over it and her patent shoes shone as did the glow all around her.

She had left rehab that very week for the umpteenth time and come searching for me. Sandra had called Mara asking of my whereabouts and eventually found me in China town drinking what must have been my tenth cup of coffee of the day. With Sandra it had been heavy drugs. With me it was coffee.

We spoke for only a few minutes before I stood to leave. Where are you going Sandra asked? I was about to order food. Let's go elsewhere I said. I knew how easily Sandra made new friends and I did not want her forming any bond in the café. It was owned by a Chinese gangster who always put my bill in the waste bin behind the till. I don't know why but he liked me and I did not wish for him to like Sandra too. She was still vulnerable. Despite her beautiful smile I could see fear in her eyes. The corners of her mouth showed her insecurity and deep sense of inadequacy. Her eyes though bright said please do not hurt me. Her fragile confidence was an act. She broke my heart. She was open to be abused in so many ways.

We ate in a noodle parlour. She spoke and I listened. The noodles were wonderful. Fried in a wok that filled the small premises with steam. The hiss from the stove sounded like a steam train pulling out of Paddington station but the smell of the food made me believe I could eat all day. The truth is I probably could have done. I had spent my morning in my favourite chair in front of my favourite painting within the National Portrait Gallery. I did this often. It was an old habit from my youth. National Portrait Gallery for two or three hours and then across the road to listen to the orchestra in St Martins in the Field. With food between the two. Perfect!

What am I going to do she asked me. About what I asked? I hadn't been listening but I had the gist of the conversation and heard myself saying.

Go to Kathmandu. Stay at Kopan monastery and spend the next few months with Lama Yeshe. If you do that, I said, then you will never again have a single twinge of desire for anything undesirable. Your life will change. You will have direction and reason. Therefore, you will have contentment.

I do not have a clue where my words arose from. My friendship with Lama Yeshe was by no means deep enough for me to go recommending or sending students to him. I knew well of his reputation and extraordinary ability to effect western lives for the better. There were stories of how students had lost their desire for abuse simply by keeping his company. I prayed a silent prayer of forgiveness, hoping Lama will forgive me should I ever meet him again.

When shall we go to Kopan Sandra asked? We? I said. Well I'm not going alone she said. Okay! Let's go as soon as we are able, we can book our flights today and apply for our visa's, then we shall have no excuse. Let's not procrastinate. It was in fact two week later due to visas and what have you before we were at Heathrow destined for Delhi and a flight on to Kathmandu. I'm going to come back a monk I told her. How a single moment can alter the flow of our lives!

Part 4

Back to the Himalayas.

I went to live with Sandra for the two weeks before we left London. Not as lovers or even a couple but because I wanted to be close to her and cause distractions when, or if necessary.

We shared a bed and slept well. I told her how very special she was. I truly wished to be the very best friend Sandra had ever had. How wonderful to play such a positive role in the life of another. I wanted her to trust in me and not think that I had any selfish motivations. I had no idea as to how events would pan out in the future but one thing was for certain. I wished for Sandra to live a long and productive life and for her to look back on this episode with great love and affection towards the time we spent together. I used these two weeks to help her re-establish the confidence she would have once had in herself. She was at present as fragile as fragile could possibly be. She was an egg shell under an elephant's foot. It was my job to not shatter her chances of growing her self-esteem by being like most other men she had ever met. I would not make decisions for her. We would share our ideas and make plans on an equal footing. We would share responsibility and I would ask for her advice. I would encourage her to take a lead. We will be equals on the same path.

We agreed between us to be intimate without the physical intimacy, not that we discussed it, you are either honourable are you are not. Sandra found it hilarious. We made fun of ourselves. She laughed raucously and teased me mercilessly at how difficult it was for me to resist the temptation she presented, but this jovial banter was to form the foundation of a very dear and cherished friendship. Nothing was hidden, everything was open. We spoke by actions and not words. Something I saw as being not merely meaningful but unquestionably sacred.

We went to the art galleries and the museums that I had become so familiar with. We went to the theatre too. We had a constant supply of tickets, always left for us in an envelope at San Lorenzo. Everybody was silently playing their part. Sandra had the most wonderful singing voice and sang show songs all the way home. We ate cheap food at cheap street outlets. We sat in taxi's with sticky fingers. At Mara's we sought inspiring company. I acted and spoke as though Sandra had never had a problem. As far as I was concerned there was no point or advantage of fearing or lingering in the past. We looked only to the future. No sense in looking back, we were not headed in that direction. Tomorrow was always going to be better.

It was wonderful to talk with people who had their experiences of India. Joanna Lumley was born there and told us several very funny stories, or perhaps the stories were not so funny, maybe it was the way she told them. There is no one so comical as an Englishman abroad. Joanna and Sandra burst into song *Mad Dogs and Englishmen*. These are fine memories. We did all we were able, to avoid those who were steeped in their present troubles and only wished to speak of their current miseries. There are some who will corner you but we would dance around them and make our excuses. The moment I saw any sign of tiredness in Sandra, I told her I was tiring and would she mind if we left for home. I didn't want her to become physically tired just in case tiredness led to her becoming mentally exhausted and prone to weaken over her resolve to remain drug free. So far was so good!

Apart from my caring for her wellbeing I also now had a large degree of other interest too. I had been in touch with Judge Mota Singh. Mota was a high court judge who sat mostly at Snaresbrook crown court and on occasion at Knightsbridge and the Old Bailey. I was introduced to him by his son Jasvinda who had been most kind to me and introduced me to George the hairdresser. The Singh's were a highly influential family, not just in England but across the world. I told him of our plans to visit India. Having listened, he insisted that he arrange for Sandra and I to stay with Indian dignitaries during our time there. We were in for a very special treat. It was of the utmost importance to me that we did not let Mota down. I did not wish to be in a position where-by I may have to cancel our plans due to a dip in Sandra's resolve.

I am certain from this, that you will understand the knife edge that I felt myself to be sitting upon. I had in confidence, informed Mota of Sandra's delicate position and told of the reason for our trip. He warned at some length of my lack of experience and the potential problems I may face but despite his general concerns his kindness and faith in my over-all intention shone through. There is no doubt that the late Judge Mota Singh was a true friend, not just to Sandra but to all he met. He was a wise and compassionate man. He once told me that English law was based upon mercy and where a strong resolve for change was clearly displayed, that genuine resolve should be supported.

Finally, the day of our departure arrived. My feelings of unease had been building over the previous twenty-four hours and reached their crescendo during the night. It was a very nervous time; until we arrived at Heathrow in good time for our flight. Mara had hired a driver to drop us off at the airport. This was her gift to us, always thoughtful, always wise and always knew what was best, so thankfully we had no tube trains to contend with. No luggage and no crowds, no drudge and no tiredness, only joy.

It had been an emotional goodbye the evening before and the comfort of Mara's hired Bentley brought all those emotions back. The luxury and deep comfort gave cause for me to think of the undiluted kindness displayed by those who I knew to be life-long friends. I had been saying my fare wells to so many friends whilst keeping one eye on Sandra. Not wanting her out of my sight even for one moment had placed me on edge. Friends asked me if I was distracted and the truth is that I was, I was badly distracted, I was split into two, my attention was both here and there at the same time. I was like a mother, watching the cooking pots and the children at the same time.

I wanted to follow Sandra to the loo, even be in the stall with her. I knew she was struggling. Mara told me to be understanding. She took me to a corner and reminded me, that at home, Sandra had the knowledge, that should she need heroin then she can buy it. When overseas in a place such as India, what would she do if she went into spasms? Sandra was scared! She told me that I must allow her space, that I had taken on a responsibility and it was no small matter. But despite her reservations, Mara remained supportive, encouraging and always optimistic. Space I thought! Jun and the bears! Not too close and not too far! The perfect space between the two extremes!

It was not an easy time for either of us. I knew, due to her fear of dependency, Sandra was collapsing. Her face was like granite. The room was warm but she was cold. Her smile had gone. Her mind was elsewhere. She sat with her knees clamped together. She stood and then sat again whilst all the time she was playing with her finger nails and looking everywhere but at me. I spent the evening close to the door. One thing was for certain. Sandra was not going to flee. Not now. She had done so well. And, whether she believed me or not, I wanted the best for her. Jasvinda had a message for us from his father. Did we wish for tickets to the test match in Delhi? We both laughed. Mota was cricket mad and kept a box at Lords. I took this opportunity to give Jasvinda my Gatsby suit. He had always admired it and I wished for him to have it.

Sandra became a completely different person when we arrived at Heathrow. She was light and very excited. The fear had left her eyes. Her mouth showed that she felt no doubts, no fear. The sunshine, that was her glow, showed pure joy. The unfettered joy you see on the face of a child at a special moment in his or her life. Sandra was beautiful! I was delighted to have her on my arm.

We danced a fox trot in the passenger lounge. It started as an embrace, then became a movement, and then Sandra took the lead and moved me at her will. We received great applause and another couple joined us. Sandra was so very happy. She was a good dancer too. I wondered about her past. Had she been trained in the arts? She smiled and asked "are you alright? She had trodden on my foot. "I'm fine" I replied. "Are thee? She looked at me and said "why the accent?" I had a thought of my old ship mate Harry. "Where is he now" Sandra asked and I told her I had no idea, but did not think he was stuck up a mountain. Then our flight was called.

The flight to Delhi was uneventful. Good food, first class seats and plenty of smiles along with silent eye contact that spoke on our behalf. Apart from visits to the loo and holding food utensils, Sandra held by hand throughout the whole flight. She kept squeezing and at one point, during a movie, asked if we may ever get married. My thoughts were more on what I was going to say to Lama Yeshe when we eventually reached Kopan. "Hello Lama. I have a surprise for you. Can I leave Sandra in your good hands until she has no further thoughts of drug addiction?" Mum had mentioned pot holes. Perhaps this is one. Honesty it is said is always the best policy. I had no absolute proof of this and felt certain there would be exceptions to the rule but not on this occasion, I will tell Lama that the words simply poured out of my mouth. "Marriage" I said! "What brought that to mind?" "Well I'm a few years older than you" Sandra said "and I think I may need a carer." I told her that I would always care about her. Marriage or not! Friendship is friendship eh! "Now tell me about your time at sea" she said

On our arrival in India, as Mota had promised, we saw our names among all those held out on hand written cards. Cars were waiting it seemed for all the passengers that flew with us. "I hope the car has air conditioning" Sandra said. "Are we sure we wish to stay with a family? Shall we cancel and book a hotel?" Let us keep our arrangements for now, I suggested, I wanted to avoid the romance that hung in the air and of course to honour Mota's kindness. Too much holiday atmosphere I knew to be a potent force to make mistakes and I knew how important it was for the long term to resist the temptations that we were both feeling. I loved Sandra, of that there is no mistake but it was better for her to discover her own future path and not in any way be dependent, in the long term, upon me. To overcome and to gain true confidence in herself she had to stand on her own feet and know the luxury of independence. I thought ahead to the years that were to come. I did my very best to have vision. The type of vision I believed all leaders should have. When Sandra and I eventually looked back at this episode in our lives, I wanted to us to recognise how truly blessed we were, to have crossed paths at such a perfect moment. Sandra told me years later that she believed in divine intervention and is thankful that we did not stain our immense good fortune with the blind element of lust. Then with a cheeky grin and her tongue in her cheek, she asked again if we may ever get married. She knew that comment would make me laugh. I had developed, as I have mentioned, a deep affection for Sandra and it's true to say that I adored her. I liked to look at her, she was a picture. I liked the scent of her natural perfume and I melted every time she came close to me;

she had a killer smile and beautiful hair that reminded me of both hay and honey at once, she was truly a living sunshine.

Our driver was obviously a servant and bowed more times than I could count. He bowed with every word he said. He bowed as he took our luggage and bowed when he finally placed it in the back of a brand-new people carrier. We drove for forty minutes until we finally entered through security gates on which there were three guards. The house was a mansion and there to greet us in the extreme heat was our host, his wife and a line of five servants. All but our host bowed continuously. It was all very formal. They were determined to give us undiluted Indian hospitality. Sandra asked about the food we would receive. "Indian I suppose" I replied. "Why do you ask? Do you think we may get a pizza takeaway I joked?" Then with a smile and grimace she asked me if I had noted how many times the driver had farted. "Twelve times" I said. After eleven I was hoping there would be another. I never did like odd numbers, "and he sniffed and spat six times," I said. Her last words on the subject were. *"Okay Sherlock!"* You should have been a detective." If only she knew my history of the compulsion to count, I thought. I hoped they did not place me in a room too high, it may have a balcony and I may have to resist the temptation to jump.

It was our plan to stay in Delhi for only a couple of days before flying into Nepal and Kathmandu. But Sandra had surprisingly settled in and became very close to Anshika, the wife of our host. Anshika was beautiful with classical Indian features. Prior to marriage she had been a news correspondent for Jee TV and now she was taking great delight in sharing her wardrobe with Sandra, an equally beautiful women willing to immerse herself in a brand-new culture.

Sandra had come alive and truly I believe her experience here in India had completely taken away any thought of drugs and the wanting of them. Long may it last. I thought that we could return to London after just our short stay and she would not return to her former life. It was wonderful to witness the joy, the undiluted happiness that radiated from these two ladies. They giggled and danced like the reunion of sisters. They even meditated together, along with the whole house hold in the family's shrine room that housed life size statues of Guru Nanak and Guru Goben Singh, the first and the last of the ten Sikh gurus. Sandra was in her heaven and had made a new and very precious friend. The girls spoke about their friendship and how they should be certain to stay in touch in.

Four days into our stay I was beginning to have thoughts of moving on and decided to talk to Sandra about this later in the day, but I soon changed my mind when Anshika introduced us to an astrologer. He was a wonderful little man of great knowledge. The whole household bowed in his presence. Every time I looked at him, I thought of Mahatma Gandhi but thought it inappropriate to say so. I had met men like him before, silent, unexcitable, youthful in movement yet ageless.

Master Jun had told me that our thinking mind creates a wall that shuts us off from being able to see the ultimate truth of clarity, this being because our thinking is based on our present perceptions and more often than not these were poor views. I decided to settle in and use my time by observing our star reading friend.

Though very clean and very smart in his white outfit with baggy trousers and loose shirt he was bare footed. His legs were barely thicker than his staff, a wonderful knotted stick polished to a smooth shine by years of daily handling and oiled by the sweat of his hands. It was obvious from the stories I was told that he had become a legend in his life time. Having predicted the ups and downs in life of all who had met him, he wandered from place to place and was welcomed in every port of call. It was from him that I first heard it said, that not every birth was to be celebrated. I felt a certainty that one day I would investigate these words. I had been brought up to rejoice at the prospect of a new arrival, believing that all would be well for the child, but perhaps I was wrong. Perhaps it was all written in the stars, for better or for worst.

I was fascinated by this little old man who weighed no more than I guessed a sparrow. I sat and watched him. His discipline and simple needs were a wonderful thing to witness. He reminded me of the Khempo, though they were not the same they were similar, like two separate peas from the same pod. They were from different traditions and different cultures but both were silent and content in their own way. The thought of the Khenpo brought back memories of Taiwan.

I thought of the many tea shops that were to be found throughout Taipai. It was in Maokong that I first tasted bubble tea. Made with locally grown leaves and very milky, it was served chilled with tapioca floating in it. The tea was sweet and drank through a straw. I loved this tea and would always drink it whilst eating pineapple cake. One dreamy thought led to another and before I was aware of it, I relived a moment, when I sat by the lake of the *Sun and the Moon*. With a mist hovering over it at head height, with no ripple upon it, with the silent stillness that surrounded it, I found it to be the most peaceful place on earth. It was like a charcoal drawing. The only movement came from a stalk that stood in its shallow edge, or maybe it was a heron.

The old man was quiet and still, his needs were basic and close to zero. I knew by all I had witnessed that I was in the right place or at least in the right country heading in the right direction. We were getting closer to what I called Khempo land. I thought of my old friend Victor, of Master Jun and Master Wu Chi. Would they be surprised at my present circumstances? What would Mum and Dad say? I did not have to wonder about Grandpop. I could see him smiling. As ever, he remained very much with me, then a new thought arose in my mind. I wondered if I would meet once again with Peter, my old ship mate, the orphan from Southampton who was the first person to mention the Himalayas to me. I wondered about living angels, those among us who do not necessarily think a great deal of themselves, often they lack in self-esteem but none the less they inadvertently give direction and pause for thought to others. Peter had lived through great emotional trauma and discovered a life when the odds were stacked against him. He told me once that he often wished that he had not been born, but I had good reason to celebrate his birth. I would always be grateful to dear Peter, he mentioned the Himalayas, the monks and the nuns and I heard his words load and clear, I got the message. He awakened a familiar feeling, a vision within me. I had faith that his unwitting kindness would in future bring him great good fortune. No doubt the old astrologer would play his part too. Perhaps we were here to meet him. He would fill Sandra with great optimism.

My thoughts were broken by the gleeful approach of Sandra as she half ran and half skipped across the dust to where I sat under one of the Banyan trees, the trunks of which supported immense canopies around the enclosed compound. I had been watching her. She had been in deep conversation with our new friend, she had opened her palms to him and he had read them. No doubt I was about to hear all the details.

I'm definitely going to stay with Lama Yeshi Sandra told me. Wow! I thought this could be sticky. "Let's wait and see I said, trying my best to sound optimistic without sounding certain.

We've yet to make the request" I said. He knew everything about me Sandra went on to say. He said I was here in India to rest and recover from trauma that had its causes from events of many lives ago. I am about to start a new life of charity she said. He sounded so certain, he told me that a dark period in my life was behind me, that I would one day be grateful to the difficulties of the past as those times would become the foundation of my future, it's from where I will draw purpose. Do you think I should believe him? Bless her heart. She was so beautiful. The sun had brought out the gold in her shoulder length hay and honey hair. It looked highlighted by the Gods. Like a golden harvest. She was adorable. So innocent. So pure and no longer lonely. I saw with clarity now, that she had abandonment issues and I knew that though we would soon part I must never abandon her. I will love her for always. We would always have our friendship.

It was eight days before we left Delhi and the wonderful hospitality we had been so generously afforded. It was not easy for Sandra to say farewell to Anshika. She had formed an attachment. They would meet again. Of that I felt certain. Waving to the congregation from our now moving people bus, we inched at crawling pace along the pot holed, dust covered driveway, past the giant trees and under their immense canopies. Soon the house was out of sight as we drove through the security gates with smiles, salutes and more waves and broad smiles from the security guards. We were not off to

Delhi airport. We were being driven to Amritsar. The home of the Golden Temple that stood at the centre of the Sikh world. Sandra was ecstatic. We were to stay with one of Anshika's cousins. I truly believed that Sandra's old life and old habits were long behind her. She was a different person to the one I first met in London. How did I meet her I wondered? Was Sandra an angel, just like Peter? She just appeared out from the blue, just as Mara had done. Perhaps that's how things happen, so I won't think about it I thought, but I will be forever grateful to her and forever thankful for her birth. My whole life had been a series of events that appeared through perfect timing. I remembered that feeling, that I had years back, when I had been in the East End of London. I thought I was in storage waiting for my life to begin. I'm certain there is a great deal of truth in this. Here I am now, still in perfect harmony with unfolding events. The first chapter on life began in the East End. The second at sea. The third with Mara and now the fourth episode is where it all starts again.

I had known a time when money was tight. Mum and Dad had witnessed and lived through some testing years. Many families lived in a financial straight jacket. Circumstances had tied their hands behind their back and restraints left them with little if any wriggle room. We did not feel poor as such. We made do by watching pennies. We lived in the knowledge that diligent and an optimistic outlook would see us through. I had also seen wealth. The world of absolute abundance. Life with and among the rich, the privileged, the famous and some who were infamous. The lesson here was to realise that both rich and poor are actually, in so many ways, the same. Both held the potential to be a trap. Both can be restricting. Lives can be easily ruined by wealth as can lives be enhanced by a more austere existence. The vital element is in the mind, wisdom and compassion, whether we are rich or poor. When released from Robin Island, Nelson Mandela stated, that if he did not use the remainder of his life for the benefit of others, then he may just as well still be in prison. Mother Teresa, who I was most fortunate to meet through dear Myra knew no bounds to generosity and would have lived the same life with or without financial support. There are multiple examples of this. Most of those who show great generosity are not rich or famous, they are to be found in each and every community. Like living angels, selfless beings that live in every corner of the world where they silently offer great kindness, comfort and understanding. I had no difficulty in renouncing the world so to concentrate on spiritual understanding. I believed then, as I believe now, that no depth of understanding is beyond our human comprehension and I was going to realise the peaceful nature of my own mind. Why would I not if the potential is there? All I required was enough to sustain myself. *A comfortable space between the two extremes of rich and poor.*

How wonderful it was to share this trip with an angel? Dear Sandra! Fast asleep beside me. Truly kind and truly loving. So soft, so full of sweet perfume. She did not snore. She slept sound like a baby but the driver did fart about once a mile. Another one hundred and forty farts to my calculations would see us to our destination. I will contact Mota Singh and thank him for all he had done to make our trip so comfortable. "He will wish to know why we did not go to the test match" Sandra had said. Also, I will ask him to make arrangement for us to enter Bhutan. This small kingdom of blissful existence was my personal destination. I wished to see Rinpoche. I prayed He would be there when we arrived, but I paid no more thought to it. As always, I believed that all would pan out in perfect fashion.

We chose to visit Amritsar as we had been invited to do so. We could have said no but why would we? It was polite to follow the wish of our host in Delhi. They were so proud of the world capital of Sikhism. Whenever the holy place was mentioned, heads bowed in respect and beautiful, blank and distant expressions crossed the faces of our hosts, like clouds dispersing to reveal the warmth of the sun. A refusal to visit Amritsar would have felt like an insult to our new and selfless friends and apart from not wishing to be negative I wanted to keep Sandra happy too. I did not want her to have anything on her mind other than joy. It also gave me more time to consider what I was going to say to Lama Yeshe. If he was there at Kopan monastery! It was essential that no apple carts were turned over. Especially Sandra's. This was her opportunity and so far, so good. Lots to look forward to.

Sandra woke from her slumber and snuggled up closer. Her head on my chest and her arm rapped lazily round my waist. I was damp from the heat her body generated. We were stuck in a traffic lock. Lorry, van and car horns blasted. Scooter and motor cycle horns tooted, a cow stared at us through the window and our driver did a load fart. India eh! I gave thanks for the air conditioning. Whilst reaching for her camera and rolling her head in an attempt to loosen her stiff neck, Sandra asked if we may stay in a hotel." Just one night." Then go meet our new host the following day but we were now in Amritsar and it made sense to not cause our driver any anxiety by changing plans. I heard Sandra's plea, she wished for some space to relax a little. I hoped our schedule was not going to wear her down. Soon we were faced with another set of security gates. New host waiting and more servants bowing. There were even more banyan trees.

"You don't seem your normal jolly self" Sandra said. "Too much rice" I replied with a smile. "Constipation!" She laughed heartily. "I thought you were walking funny." She thought it hilarious. It was great to see her so free and feeling easy but I thought I was having a baby and sat in a great deal of discomfort that only added to Sandra's sense of humour, she could barely speak without a titter and splutter, she apologised for her seeming lack of sympathy but she still laughed. "No more rice for me for a while" I said. Even a simple statement like that caused her to enter into a raucous belly laugh. She fell back in her seat and threw her legs in the air in a display of great hilarity. "It's the way you say these things" she said.

Our new host were just as friendly as our last. They wanted to know all about my friendship with Mota Singh. "A very important man" our host said as he rolled his head from left to right. "He is very high in our society" he told me, "very influential." Then he added with great pride and with his chest out, that Mota lived in the next house to Roger Hunt, the world champion formula one racing driver. I did not tell him that Roger was a rather noisy neighbour and that Mota wished that Roger lived a little further away. How funny, that the mention of Roger Hunt was at the top of our new host mention list. I told him that Mota preferred cricket to motor racing and that he would always attend Lords for the test matches when India were on tour. I asked him if he knew that Mota had been the Mayor of Mombasa in East Africa at the time of independence, that he eventually left through fear for his family's safety. He brought his wife Sworen, along with his children to England where he was to qualify as a high court judge. I thought, but did not say, that had I known him during my time in Africa, then perhaps he would have rescued me from the stench of the police cell and got me out of custody quicker than the Captain had and without fifteen pounds being given to a corrupt police officer. We spoke at length about the achievements of Mota Singh. He was an extraordinary man. I began to gather a clear picture as to the esteem in which Indians held him. But whilst we were talking, Mota had been talking too. Our host suggested we freshen up for dinner. "Then you can tell my wife all about your friendship with Princess Diana" he said. Sandra's mouth fell open. "You did not tell me about this. How do you know Di?" she asked. But why would I tell her. I had no reason to do so? I had taken Mara's advice and said nothing to anybody. I was once offered several thousand pounds for this story, The East End Boy and the Lonely Princess. I could visualise the horror of our friendship in print, twisted, distorted and shaped to sell copy. The money was offered by a journalist writing for a German magazine and of course I refused to accept his offer. Just to be with the journalist made me feel nauseous. Truly there was lust, greed and a willingness to betray in his eyes. I could not quite believe that he would think I would be complicit in his treacherous plan. He reminded me of Uryer Heep. He with the sweaty fish like hands. I do not remember the reporter as being particularly sweaty, or that his hands were particularly fish like, but I do remember thinking of Charles Dickens and his rather unsavoury fictional character. It was exactly this image that he unconsciously radiated and the image that I consciously picked up.

He did not understand the meaning of friendship. He had no concept of honour. He lived in a world where treachery was all too common. When he approached me, he was drawling, his chin was wet. It was like spending five minutes with a twelve stone, six feet tall lizard. Myra had warned me of the press and that I should be on my guard. You never know who you are talking to she would say but she had no need to press this wisdom home. I had from my young years been brought up to understand the potential devastation of a loose tongue. I have always found it quite remarkable how memories have the ability to come back vividly to life. I could see the nod of understanding my old headmaster offered, when I informed him that I did not know of my friend Vicky's whereabouts when he played truant to find his father. I am certain that nobody likes a trouble maker. I wondered why Anshika had not mentioned Di, as Mota would surely have told them for our present host to be aware, but no matter, perhaps Anshika thought it to be none of her business, which made me like her even more.

For Sandra the next few days were wonderful. Servants taught her Indian dance. She helped in the kitchen, learning how to mix and fry an array of colourful spices and herbs that were stored in large jars along a wooden shelf that was shiny from constant use over a very long period of time, like a church pew that has been sat on for one hundred years, but then the whole house was rather like that. Well used. Shiny and clean. Ancient and worn with the constant and all-pervading aroma of sandalwood incense that burnt from the large brass bowl that stood at the foot of the stairs in the centre of the hallway. It was a large bowl too, certainly large enough for a small child to splash about in. I wondered who had made it and how old it was? It had Indian figures and Indian scenes tapped by hammer into it. It was a piece of art that I am certain was treasured by the family. Sandra later said that her memories of the house were of prayer, well wishes, kindness, cooking and that giant incense bowl.

I told Sandra that I had seen our driver. The one that had driven us to Amritsar, the same one that had picked us up from Delhi airport. I also pointed out that his car is still here too. "I know she said." "He is taking us to Dharamsala."

It was at this point that I felt my mood, for the first time in years start to alter in a most uncomfortable way. It was not a feeling I liked. It brought a bad taste to my mouth. Maybe it was the sun. Might be the sun and the constipation. It was probably a whole mixture of things but the questions did not help either. For the first time in my life I was following someone else's timetable. This maybe a good thing Sandra suggested. She told me not to be so grumpy and with a smile suggested, that I would feel better once I had a poo. Very funny eh!

She was right. We were in no rush. Our visa's could go on for ever if we wished. Life was fantastic. Sandra was doing so well. Not once had she mentioned any longing. Not once had she even looked like flagging or losing her grip. The truth was that Sandra was the best company ever, she was paying all our bills and I should be, not only grateful, but privileged to be in such a position. Weeks later, a lady told Sandra and I, that her husband was always miserable. We listened with a sympathetic ear. Then I heard Sandra ask, with a broad smile on her face and one eye on me, if there may be any possibility of him being constipated!

Dharamsala was much the same in terms of our accommodation. We stayed in the most beautiful house that over looked one of the finest scenes we had ever seen in our lives. It would be wrong of us to say that the Himalayas held the greatest views in the world. Sandra and I were always spell bound by what we saw but others may prefer the harbours of the Mediterranean for instance. The terracotta tiles and the white villas of Tuscany, but for us, it was the dramatic that we revelled in. We often stopped to study the artistry of nature, of how the elements shaped the land scape. I told Sandra of the waves we rode at sea. Of how they rolled ferociously toward us, taller than Trump Tower, as wide as Brighton sea front and as powerful as nature could ever manifest. We loved it!

Our host was a very busy man. We felt we had visited at the wrong time. We sensed we were an inconvenience. The kindness and generosity were the same but the personal contact was sparse. This gave Sandra and I the opportunity to visit McLeod Ganj alone. It was a wonderful feeling to be free.

We called in on my friend Dolma and asked after the welfare of Lhamo. Dolma was so pleased to see us and with a smile told us that Lhamo had left that morning to buy a new tyre for his jeep. He had three further punctures since last seeing me. She made us chai tea and offered us food, then showed Sandra a group photograph we had taken on my previous visit. The photo was not square. It was lopsided. It was taken by an inexperienced passer-by but now stood on Dolma's shrine. She told Sandra that she prayed for my happiness every day.

We stayed that night at the Tibetan Hotel and the following morning decided that we would go collect our luggage in Dharamsala and settle into Mcleod Ganj for the duration of our stay. Sandra was delighted at this decision. The girls were so happy. Dolma came with us. Sandra making yet another solid friend was perfect. To see the girls genuinely laugh as they did, was a wonderful sight to see. They laughed at the simple things, the bumps in the road, the hooting and the tooting of the vehicles and the monkeys that ran alongside us.

We made no fuss at the home of our host. We thanked them for their hospitality and explained our situation. All was understood and no bad feelings were felt. We parted good friends but I am certain with some degree of relief on both sides. Years later Mota was invited to America by Hilary Clinton. She was seeking advice on how best to gain the votes of the Sikhs that had settled in the United States. Mota told me that our host in Dharamsala was an aid in this matter. It made me smile to think that the short stay we had within his home would one day have an effect on American politics.

Sandra was completely taken by the humble nature of Dolma. She went to great lengths to explain, as best she was able, what she thought of this beautiful Tibetan girl. Sandra thought Dolma to be remarkable. She found the whole culture to be remarkable. The people are so strong she said and yet so gentle. They have no home but yet they are at home within themselves. They have no excess and yet they have everything. They have every reason to be sad but yet they display only contentment. I would sit and observe the manner in which Sandra sat and observed the manner of the Tibetan people. She was inspired at the manner with which they were able to let go of the past. How they were able to flow with change and accept the nature of impermanence. Sandra decided to study the nature of non-attachment and asked many questions of Dolma on this subject. But Dolma was unable to help as she did not know what attachment meant. Hanging on to things, even a thought, was a very strange concept to Dolma. "Why do you do that?" she would ask.

Dolma led Sandra to the Dalai Lama's office and told the monk on reception that a friend of Princess Diana was in town and would like to speak with his Holiness. The monk told her that the Dalai Lama was not in India, He was in Europe. Then the monk asked. "Who is the Princess Diana?" "She's not as well known as Mota Singh" Sandra said with a side glance showing humour. From interest Sandra asked the monk if he had heard of Mahomed Ali, but he said he had not.

It was four weeks later that Sandra and I arrived in Nepal. We went directly to see Sangmo at the café. Lhamo entered with us and joined us for a meal. The children brought their school homework to the table and Sandra helped with their English pronunciations. Immediately they became great friends. The youngsters told Sandra about Lama Yeshe and told her they will take her to Kopan and introduce her, just as they had done me. Sangmo was proud of his children and Sandra was enchanted.

This time Sandra chose our hotel. We were not in London, Paris or New York but the best available was still more than adequate. Whilst I was testing the bed, Sandra came out from the on-suite bathroom. "You're really in trouble now" she said with a cheeky smile on her face, her eyes alive with humour. "Why? " "What's wrong" I said expecting a sexual advance. "The on suite is completely tiled" she said. You will be counting tiles every time you enter. There must be several hundred of them. They will drive you mad. I was pleased at this news. It was another opportunity to break the habit.

Sandra was right. There were hundreds of tiles. Try as I might to ignore them, I was compelled to count how many climbed the walls from floor to ceiling and how many across the walls from side to side. I then did my multifurcation's and was happy with the total whether it be right or wrong. "This has to stop" I said to Sandra. "This habit, that I thought I had overcome, will drive me mad one day."

Still laughing and still smiling, Sandra called room service. Still teasing, she asked me if I would like to order by numbers. We were tired and decided to shower, stay in and relax. We had a balcony that looked out to great views in the distance but we kept the door closed. Too much hooting and tooting from the chaotic road below. We settled happily with the air conditioning on full blast knowing that the mosquitos were kept outside.

We spent the evening talking. Sandra told me that she was doing well but she had her moments when she felt weak and vulnerable. It was not always easy for her to keep her resistance in place. Goodness me. She tore my heart out. I wished I had a magic wand or the ability to take her recovery upon my own shoulders but of course this could not be. This was her battle and all I could do was to be her friend. We decided it best to not talk about the struggle but to talk about the victory. This perked her up. "Yes! let's be positive. My past is history and it's not like that now." She took on a revitalised air of optimism. She became more energised and I wondered if we should have gone out.

Over the following three weeks. Using our hotel as a base. Our home in Nepal. We travelled across the small mountain kingdom, from Solukumbu and the base camp for Everest, through to Pockera and the base camp for Anapurna. We travelled in comfort. A brand-new jeep. A driver who did not trump and air conditioning all the way. I think we were avoiding Kopan.

"How about a day relaxing tomorrow and then to Kopan" I said when in the shower calling through to Sandra, who was sitting in front of the mirror adjusting her single string pearl necklace.

"Yes! Fine" she said! But I could hear, this was said with trepidation. Her voice was a reluctant whisper with an edge of croak. I put on my bath robe and found Sandra out on the balcony. She seemed to have aged ten years since I had seen her twenty minutes earlier. Her right hand was up to her mouth, the first finger was scratching at the skin around her thumb nail, her knees were clamped together and she avoided my eye. She was troubled. This is the moment that Mara had warned of. "What did Sun Tzu say in the *Art of War?*" *Divide opposing forces into manageable units, only that way will you be victorious*. "Three things" I said. First, let's eat in the worse restaurant in Kathmandu. Some place that we will never forget. We've been to the best, now let's search out the very worse. Beforehand we can go to the market and choose an outfit for each other. Something we have no choice but to wear, no matter how outrageous. And thirdly, "Let's not set anything in stone" I said. "We came here with Kopan in mind but you may not like the idea of staying, you may like to stay with me. It's daft to make a business out of a good time. Let's enjoy ourselves." Let us go as tourist and whist their we can investigate. We can do our *Sherlock* thing. "We can take one step at a time" and then I said what I had been trying not to say since leaving London. "You know I love you and I will do whatever it takes to protect you." That was it! Floods of tears and much to be explained. It was the children who saved the day. I phoned their father as they wished to stay that night with us at the hotel. We asked them to come quickly. We were going to eat in the worst place and wear the most colourful cloths and they had to choose both.

Kopan was a wonderful sight. It was truly a blessing to lay our eyes upon. It had developed further since my earlier visit. I could see that much work had been done. Sandra had not been prepared for such a wonderous, beautiful sight and just stopped, half in and half out of our taxi. "Wow! Some rehab" she said. Her tone made me smile broadly. Come, let's us take you inside, called the children excitedly. "Let's have a great day" I whispered to Sandra. And as I said this, the sounds of the horns, symbols, drums and conk shells filled the air as though to welcome us. There were monks and nuns and visitors everywhere. It was a very busy place. But very peaceful! I was pleased I was not wearing the pink baggies that I had worn the evening before. There was no pressure on Sandra. We were merely here because a visit had been decided upon. We retained our hotel room. Our luggage was still there. Safe and sound on the top floor where the best views were available. We had left items of clothing drying on the balcony so Sandra new we would return. We had plenty of time and I was hoping that slowly, not too fast, Sandra would get used to the idea of staying a while. Hopefully it would be her suggestion but I was starting to have my reservations. I could not imagine, even for a single moment, that I would leave her here all alone. I did not believe that she would advocate this either. It was not for her and I could not foresee my waving cheerio to her from the rear window of a tuk tuk. It was not going to happen. I did not believe that she would see herself as being in recovery. I thought she was more likely to see herself as alone, vulnerable and abandoned. I believed that within twenty-four hours she would be on a plane to London. I thought it better that she should see herself as being recovered and stick with me. It was better for Sandra to discover something meaningful to occupy herself. In that way her transition would be seamless, natural and organic.

Our day went fabulously well. The children obeyed their father and stayed close to Sandra. One hanging around her waist and one hugging her leg. We made friends with a girl from Newcastle who spent the whole day with us, she thought the children were ours by adoption, she was enchanted by the love that was in the air. I spotted Lama Zopa who was inseparable from Lama Yeshe, so I knew the later would be around somewhere. This gave me the opportunity to wander off and see how the ground lays before any introductions were made. It was wonderful to see Zopa. I told him I was here with a friend. I did not mention our original reason for our visit. I knew Sandra would not be staying. She may return on another occasion and maybe one day she might spend time here but it would be nothing to do with recovery. It would be because she chose to for other reasons. Perhaps she may return for old time sake.

Julie, our new Geordie friend, along with the children, were giving Sandra a guided tour and telling her all she would like to know. I caught up with them in the food hall, where Sandra told me that she was taking Julie back to our hotel with us. "She needs things" Sandra told me, "so I shall take her shopping tomorrow in Kathmandu. I will not be staying here" she then announced. "Not yet anyway. I'm going with you to Bhutan. I do not feel ready for a life as a Buddhist" she said. "I do not think I could bare it, there would be too much time to think and for now I need distractions. It's too early for me to face myself." "Good" I said, "I'm pleased." In fact, I was delighted.

I got along well with Julie. She was a good sort. A school teacher who had some months earlier lost her mother following a long illness. They lived together, Julie being unmarried she had taken the loss of her mother badly. She came out to Nepal to gain a bit of space and some understanding of life and death. She had taken Lay Buddhist vows and become a student of Zopa Rinpoche. She said that this one decision alone had changed her life. She coped well with communal living but was quite open when she suggested to me that Sandra may not do so. I nodded. I thought she was right. Julie was very bright and never whinged. Her strength and intelligence were obvious and her effect on Sandra was very positive. Already, after only one day she had inspired Sandra to look into aid work. This was Julie's aim. She was planning to teach English in schools in and around Kathmandu. Sandra had no working history. She had been to university and could have qualified in so many areas but the only thing she really knew about were horses. The children went home to Mum and Dad, Julie went to bed early and Sandra and I spoke that evening about how her life as a drug addict may prove to be a major ingredient for her to have a meaningful future. She had experienced much during these desperate years and learnt much. Anshika's astrologer back in Delhi had predicted this. Her father had wished her to become a lawyer. If this had transpired, then she would not have met Anshika, and Julie, who offered her an altruistic life. A truly worth-while reason to live. Further to this, she and I would not have met, and that would have been a shame!

Sandra had ridden during her teen years and had fond memories of the horses she kept at the family's country home in Hertfordshire. "There was a time that I would dream of the

Olympics" she said in a dreamy far away comment. I thought this to be a healthy sign. She rarely if ever spoke about the past. Her drug addiction had started early in her life and had put pay to any career she may have entered. "I wonder if there is a racing stable in Nepal" she said? I told her of the Tibetans and their horse-riding skills and of the festivals I had attended in Ladakh and particularly in Bhutan. Let's make certain we attend another one we agreed. This was a very exciting prospect.

The girls went shopping and I went wandering. Independence for Sandra was a good thing to encourage. They returned from the markets having, it seemed, bought half the wares that had at one time been on display and I gave Julie a pair of pink baggies. "They have only been worn once" I told her. Sandra said "yes, I will show you the photographs." The traders must have been delighted but all had a good time, Sandra, Julie and all who met them. They had enjoyed lunch out and treated several monks to refreshments that were out and about too. Everybody was very happy and had a wonderful time. Over dinner that evening we decided that we would enjoy one more day in Kathmandu and then head for Bhutan. Sandra went to see Sangmo to organise our transport. We had decided to travel via Delhi. Sandra had bought gifts for our first host and all the servants and she wanted to introduce Julie to Anshika. How could I argue? It is difficult to argue in the face of such generosity and we were in no great hurry. There was no need for a watch or a timetable. Why change the habit of a life time? Let things flow. That was our moto. In truth, I too was grateful for distractions. I was not ready to bring our time together to an end. There would be a right time and we had not reached that moment yet. Our time at Kopan had revealed many things and one of them was that Sandra still needed solid companionship. It was my responsibility to be a responsible friend. This trip was not all about me and my own personal goals. Sandra and her welfare must always remain the priority. If I shifted the focus to my own personal wishes, then I would be taking advantage of her and I had no intention to do that. Sangmo introduced us to a driver. This time it was a cousin, also named Sangmo, would you believe. The children were heartbroken to hear we were leaving Kathmandu. They begged us to return. So touched was Sandra that she put our leaving back for two days. This gave her the opportunity to spend time with the little ones. "Her tiny angels" she affectionately called them. The children had insisted that they take Sandra and Julie to meet their aunty who lived some way from the city. "You will have to keep to the path" said their father "and no wandering off." If I had known that their aunty was a hermit and lived in a hut that clung precariously to a mountain side, then I would have gone along too. Both Sandra and Julie told me of the events of the day. So impressed were they, that they both spoke at once. They were so excited. The children were familiar with the narrow path that led to the hut. Twice a week, Sangmo would send them off with food for their aunty, though Julie believed that the elderly lady who sat spinning her prayer wheel and mumbling her mantras, was more likely to be a grandmother. "There were monkeys all along our way" said Julie. "Sandra and I felt that they were our guides" she said. "The children recognised individuals and spoke to them like they were old friends." The primates sat on low branches and watched us pass through. "It was really like something from a children's fairy tale." "The scenery as we climbed higher and higher was stunning." The old lady had lived alone for several years. She had lost her husband and raised her children and now she wished to recite one hundred thousand mantras. The final moment, before we finally left Kathmandu, the children poured three cups of tea and told Sandra, Julie and I that they would keep them for our return. This is an old Tibetan custom. Sandra left Sangmo with an envelope. She asked him to accept it and to be certain that the children's aunty had all her needs. I have no idea how much money she gifted, she did not say and I did not ask but I knew Sandra would be more than generous, she always was.

Our visit to Kopan and meeting Julie had made Sandra more assertive. I first noted this as we left the monastery. She had answered the one question that had been troubling her. The question being, whether she would stay or not. Now that the weight that burdened her had been removed, she was able to lighten up again. To witness events such as these, gave me great pause for thought. How terrible drugs are. How many young, kind and generous individuals such as Sandra were swamped by addiction? How many lives were spoilt by this addiction? I wished I had the power to rid the world of such horror.

Dolma was delighted to see us arrive once more at the Tibetan Hotel, she was fast becoming a sister. Our driver was to stay with us for the duration and she made him very comfortable. We were beginning to become a large party. We ate together, laughed together and went to the Dalia Lama's temple together. It was wonderful to see the street traders and stall holders. They all knew Dolma and remembered Sandra and I. Julie was having the time of her life. Her constant smile had become a feature. The Dalia Lama was now in residence. Sandra approached the office of His Holiness and once again requested an audience. To her delight, the monk at the reception desk remembered her. Not because he remembered her mentioning Princess Diana and not due to his wish to please Mota Singh, but because he remembered Sandra. Who on earth could ever forget such a beautiful honey haired girl? To our delight, Sandra skipped across the forecourt where many monks sat in Debate. "His Holiness will see us tomorrow morning at ten o'clock" she said. Julie nearly folded in two before leaping into the air like a Jack in the box. "What should we wear" she asked. I suggested pink baggies but Sandra said no by punching me on the arm.

Meeting the Dalia Lama was to say the least, a very special experience. Once gathered in the small room, Dolma approached Him first. Her reverence was something to behold. In tears and sobbing, she fell before Him whilst whispering *"Your Holiness."* She quivered and shook as though a light and loving electricity was humming within her. The Dalia Lama helped her to her feet, insisting that He wanted no ceremony. He turned His smile towards us. Sandra and then Julie approached next and simultaneously burst into an uncontrolled torrent of tears. I stood behind them and watched as their shoulders heaved, before I too felt the emotion arise to a point where there was no holding back. I was choked and could not speak. My nose ran uncontrollably and I wiped it on my sleeve. What else could I do? If I had known I was going to collapse, then I would have taken a tissue. I have been very fortunate, to have met His Holiness on several occasions over the years and He has always remembered me. On each occasion I have had questions to ask, then found that once in His company, there are no questions at all. I am not going to attempt to explain what it is to be in the company of the Dalia Lama. There is much written on this subject and thousands of people across the world have been in His presence in one form or another. I will only state here, that I have been privileged to have come face to face with wisdom and compassion in their indomitable pure form. This experience was a perfect note on which to leave McLeod Ganj.

We ate a hearty meal that evening and, in the morning, Dolma gave me such a loving and meaningful hug. It was a hug that put a seal on our affection for ever. I have never forgotten the heartfulness of that moment. I knew I had found a most beautiful and loving sister. Again, she stood in prayer alongside our jeep. She prayed once more, for all those in transit to reach their destination without hindrance. Working in the hotel trade, I suspected that Dolma would say this prayer several times a week, if not several times a day. Dolma wished for all living beings to find happiness before her. Her thoughts and prayers were not limited to friends and family, they were all inclusive. She thought of animals too. *May all those who hibernate wake in the sun.*

Anshika was delighted to hear of our meeting with the Dalia Lama and ordered tea to be made whilst she sat and listened to the rest of our news. She was delighted to welcome Julie too and did so without mention. Also, she was delighted to learn that Julie had been a school teacher. She was eager to take the girls off to visit a Delhi school that she supported. Indian tea in Indian weather is always refreshing and most welcome but it still was not Taiwanese bubble tea but I did not say so. The girls spent much time over the next few days discussing their good fortune to have met, and of the potential that may develop because of it. I spent my time sitting under my chosen Bangyan tree. A servant had brought me a wicker chair and a wicker table. She also kept me furnished with cold drinks for which I was most grateful. Anshika gave me the use of a straw hat and I sat and read a Dharma teaching. A book Sandra had bought for us in the shop at the Dalia Lama's temple. "Don't run off with it" she said in humour. "I want to read it too." It was a teaching on non-attachment. I wondered where Anshika had bought the hat. They were common in England. A white straw trilby with a red, yellow and blue band. They were mainly worn by older men in the summer. They had replaced handkerchiefs knotted at the corners. Perhaps they made them in India. Many things in England were made in India and many of our words had their roots here too. Bungalow and pyjamas are Indian words, bandana is another example. Still I was fascinated by language.

Sandra had told me, when on route to Bhutan, that she had much food for thought. "I can see a purpose to my life forming" she said. She was taking in all she heard but was not about to make any promise of financial assistance until she had considered all aspects and gained a clear view of how a plan would work. How wonderful! I thought. Sandra had good sense in her blood and it was coming to the fore. The business side of Sandra's character was showing. "Any fool can part with money" she said. Then continued to tell me of the vision that Anshika had put forward. Anshika was determined that all children in India would receive an adequate education, she was very clear on this point but was well aware of the struggle that would lay ahead if she were to achieve her goal. There were many obstacles to overcome in India, political and otherwise. The cast system being one of them, corruption in high places being another. Sandra, I believed was more taken by Julie's more simple ideas for Nepal. "Plant a small seed" Sandra had said "and see how it grows." I listened with great interest, thinking Sandra would have made a superb lawyer. I also believed that Dolma had a greater influence over Sandra than I had realised. Meanwhile in London, Mota Singh was presiding over a lengthy and complicated fraud trial which was his speciality, but like a true hero he had dealt with all our travelling affairs. He told us to stay put until we received our cover letter, to and from the highest authority. He told us that he would add Julie to the paper work having received all her passport details sent to him at his request. Nothing was too much for Mota Singh. Sandra spoke to Mota on the telephone, telling him that the fee cancellation was not a problem. She was happy to cover all cost. "No need" said Mota in his usual cheerful way, as he then proceeded to inform her, with great pride, of what he had organised on our behalf. A look of wonderment slowly crossed Sandra's face. This I could not help but notice as the wonderment developed into the most mischievous smile, a smile that soon turned to a look of sheer open-mouthed astonishment. "What has he said?" I ask her! "Don't get upset when I tell you." She quickly added. "Tell me, what?" I said with some urgency. "Mota wants for us to enjoy the highest privilege in Bhutan" She said. "He knows what this trip means to us, so he has made arrangements of the highest order. You will not believe this!" "The nation is expecting a visit from a close friend of Princess Diana. We must expect a royal reception." Goodness me! This was typical of our dear friend. "His going the extra mile again" I said. I thought of a few words to express myself but I stayed silent. Some Anglo-Saxon words are not appropriate. Our journey to Bhutan was full of anticipation. Enjoying the outstanding scenery, enjoying the scorching weather and enjoying the company. No punctures in our tyres and much singing. Sandra gave us a rendition of *It's a Beautiful World and Amazing Grace!* How fitting with the spectacular scenery in the back ground. I thought of the shows we had seen in London, she could have starred in them, she had a wonderful voice. How talented this girl is, I thought. There was much jovial conversation as we discussed what maybe awaiting us. Julie was thrilled. "What an adventure" she said. "I cannot believe what is happening." She wished her mother was with us. "Perhaps she is" both Sandra and I said at the same time. I thought Grandpop was with me but I did not say so.

We had no difficulty in entering Bhutan. The necessary paper work from Mota had arrived at Anshika's. All was in place with all our fees either paid or wavered. There was no sign of a special reception. We were treated with great curtesy, just as all tourist are. Bhutan is a wonderful place. I adore it. I could hardly believe that I was back in this beautiful country. I could do little else other than to appreciate my immense good fortune. I had so very much to be thankful to Sandra for, and of course, to Mota Singh and all my dear friends that had contributed to this moment. Truly, I felt blessed. In one quite moment, I felt a smooth but very light nectar run down my body. It had a honey quality to it and a consistency that slowly made its way down from head to foot. Events on a personal level were proving, as always, to be perfect. I prayed now that this would also apply to Sandra's long-term good health. I saw no reason why it should not. Her complete recovery would certainly turn events into a living fairy tale. Sandra would become a living example of the magic and mystery of the East. Then I thought of Dolma and altered my thoughts. *May all living beings enjoy long term good health.* I could feel the merit of this thought. The nectar flowed again.

During our final dinner in Delhi, Sandra had strongly suggested that Anshika should come to London at some point in the future. Sandra did not wish to dismiss involvement in the charity work that the family generously put their name to, but she wanted time, and wanted to cement relationships. The idea of a visit to London excited Julie too, so all three were now on fire with wonderful thoughts of shopping in Oxford Street and walking in Hyde Park. My father used to speak at Speakers Corner I thought but did not say. "I will take you to San Lorenzo" Sandra said. It was following this conversation that Sandra mentioned her plan, that had just appeared to mind, that she was going to sell her house in Flood Street. "The house has some unhappy memories" she said. "When I return to London, I wish to return to a new address. A new home. A new start." Later that evening Sandra mentioned just how important she felt it to be, to change her whole environment. She told me of when she had left rehab with great optimism, but all that positivity slipped away when she returned to old and familiar ground. Old and familiar ground brought back old and familiar ways. This I believed made excellent sense. "How can I sell and buy property from here" Sandra asked? I suggested she ask Mara to represent her. "She will take her time and will find the perfect home for you. Mara has great foresight and will find you the perfect property. Let her know your requirements, bedrooms, office, library etc and leave it with her. We can stay here until all is done." Would she be able to deal with all the finances" she asked? "Then bring in Mota Singh" I said. "He will tell the agents about Princess Di and everything will be perfect." Sandra smiled her smile at me, then picked up the phone and eventually was put through to London. Mara answered the phone after only three rings. "I know the perfect house for you" she said. "It's in Knightsbridge. I will send you the details. I am certain I can deal with this. The present owners will be delighted. Between us we can organise all the details." Sandra was delighted and after a long conversation that I thought may go on all night, she handed me the phone. It was wonderful to hear Mara's voice. She was very emotional and wished us every happiness. *May all living beings be so fortunate I thought.*

We travelled for another five hours before we eventually reached our pre-booked hotel in Thimphu, Bhuton's capital. The only difficulty we had, was in the leaving of our friends behind. We had to make many promises to return. After an endless stream of bows, hugs and tears we had finally hit the road. The servants this time followed the car beyond the security gates and out onto the road. All peering through the windows. All smiling broadly and all wearing items bought for them by Sandra in Kathmandu. It was a happy yet sorrowful day. The essence of our friends stayed with us like a perfume that never lost its scent. Years later Sandra told me of how that experience had assisted in her recovery. "I have never lost that sense of warmth and genuine generosity" she told me. In truth, neither had I. All these years later I could hear across the phone lines that she was deeply thankful. I could feel her emotions as they choked her voice and filled her eyes. Have you seen Dolma, she would always ask?

That first night in Thimphu was in itself a great release. It brought with it a great sense of freedom. There was no expectation placed upon us, we could do as we pleased. No chains of a timetable. Just air, space and freedom. China lay to our north. The mountains between us were immense. The highest peaks rose to over 23, 000 feet. It was not difficult to realise why this was the region of the enlightened. Every aspect of our view was a direct reflection of the spacious mind. Who on earth, I wondered, could ever be unhappy in a place such as this? I was back to sleeping with Sandra's head on my chest as she slept as sound as a child might, following a full day in play. She was beautiful!

I had one of those nights where I did not know whether I had slept or not, just as I did on the night before I joined the Rhodesia Castle. I was awake early with thoughts of the Liverpudlians arising in mind. I smiled as I thought, *may all living beings find the causes for happiness.* I must have sensed that there was about to be a knock on the door. I thought it was Julie as we had left the door unlocked for her to enter, when and if she wished, I called for her to enter. To my surprise a young lady entered. She looked beautiful in full national dress. Chestnut coloured skin and cheeks as round and as red as tiny cricket balls. She was very nervous. I could not see her teeth. Her mouth was closed tight like a tiny zipped purse. Her red full lips matched her cheeks. I felt sorry for her. She was embarrassed and wished to flee as soon as she was able. Seeing us still in bed, with Sandra slowly emerging from her sleep with little grunts and moans, our guest turned her back to us and faced the wall. She shuffled with tiny steps backwards towards the bed. From over her shoulder, she was shaking a letter, as if it was a fan. I could not reach it and wondering what it might be, I suggested she leave it on the table that stood in front of the window, next to the balcony door. "While you are there" I asked. "Would you be very kind and open the balcony door for us?" Miming the action with a point and twist of my wrist. It seemed a good idea to let the day in. "Why not?" It was going to be a very hot one. To my surprise, the young lady, in all her finery, signalled that I must accept the letter by hand. She had no intention of leaving it on a table, even though our table was clearly in our room. On one elbow and stretching across Sandra I accepted the letter. With her task completed, our guest bowed toward the wall and with great urgency proceeded to head for the door. Before stepping out onto the landing she stopped once more and bent low with her forehead on her finger tips. Both hands were clasped together, palm to palm. Then she was gone. I got up from bed and strolled across the room to open the balcony door. Air! How wonderful! Sandra, fully awake now, opened the letter, no envelope but folded well and tied with a silken ribbon. "Wow wee" said Sandra. That smile was on her face again but this time her eyes were as wide as I have ever seen them and her jaw was so wide open. I wondered just how wide the human mouth could stretch. This is an invitation from the Queen. She requests that we join her for dinner. She has asked us to pack our luggage. Three servants will collect our bags. Rooms are being prepared for all three of us at her residence. "Three servants" I said. "One each" Sandra said with merriment.

The king of Bhutan is historically known as the Druk Gyalpo. This translates to the *Thunder Dragon King*. What else would we expect? It is the land of Magic and mystery, particularly with Bhutan's close connection with Tibet. *The Land of the Snows*. The history of these country's is overflowing with mysticism. With great humour, Sandra said that locals do not climb mountains here, they fly over them. She could not wait to see what was in store for us. "Don't tell me we are guest of the king and queen" said Julie over breakfast. "This really is unreal." "It's a fairy story." I smiled and told both girls that the Royal family do not live in the Royal Palace, that they now lived in Samteling Palace that was known as a cottage. The original palace had been occupied for several years by the late Gayum Angay Phuntsho Choden Wangchuk, a mother in law of an earlier King, Jigme Singye Wangchuk who abdicated the throne in 2006 in favour of his son Jigme Khesar Namgyal Wangchuk. Gayum Angay had taken ordination as a Buddhist nun following the birth of her last child and lived there until her passing. It was now used as a welcoming centre, banquet hall and art school, where monks and nuns were instructed in the ancient art of Thanka painting.

I was particularly happy at the latest turn of events, as it was the present Kings mother who had invited Dilgo Khyentse Rinpoche to take refuge in Bhutan following the brutal occupation of Tibet by the Chinese communist.

Many Tibetans left the Land of Snow, some for their own safety and that of their family. Others left at the direct request from His Holiness the 14th Dalia Lama. Khyentse Rinpoche was one among the later. Renowned throughout Tibet as a great and learned Lama, the Bhutanese Queen, with great devotion offered Rinpoche a house for retreat in the 1970's. Rinpoche accepted the generosity of her majesty Ashi Kesang Choeden Wangchuk and moved in. He spent part of every year there and became the main spiritual teacher to the Royal family.

The house is in kyichu near to Kyichu monastery where Rinpoche played a large part during annual festivals. It was my prayer to meet this great man again. a few years earlier when I had decided he would be my heart felt spiritual teacher; I had sworn to return again. At that time, he had told me that I had requested ordination too quickly. I should go home and experience further life, maybe become a father. I wondered what he would say this time. I had taken his advice. What else would I do? After all, Rinpoche was my teacher. I wondered what he may say at my fresh request to become a monk when I arrived at Kyichu with the Queen. I could see his smile in my mind's eye. Rinpoche radiated loving kindness.

We were all back to our hotel in good time before the royal servants arrived to escort us to the Palace along with our luggage. We had been for an early morning walk, a peaceful stroll. A lazy amber. Every road, every pathway, every home and every business had the most wonderful views. Mountains, valleys and distant forest, all covered by a vast and boundless sky. All was quiet. All was still. All was picture book Bhutan. There is so much beauty in the world but to my mind, so much is diluted by noise, by traffic, by pollution, by rushing and by stressful pursuit. We watched the street dogs as they lazed in the middle of paths or on the edge of roadways. People approached them with food that they accepted without movement. Signs of gratitude were not necessary. All thought the same. *May all living beings have food to eat.* Everybody was happy, we had eaten a breakfast in a rickety café. Sandra and Julie had a pot of tea and I had more than one coffee. We gave the street dogs toast. Sandra asked them if they wanted jam on it. They did not answer but she put jam on just the same. Julie looked thoughtful. I asked her what was on her mind? "When we are not so busy, we have far more time for others" she said. Zopa had told her, that she would not find true happiness until she put the welfare of all sentient beings before her own. I asked her if she could feel a nectar run over her when she had such thoughts?

Our next meal was to be a Royal feast. We were collected by three hansom men. All strong, all with pony tails, all wearing a chuba and all in Gengus Khan fur boots. The forest that stretched along both sides of the road were dense. We looked at the mountains in the back ground and listened to tales of the wild animals that passed through there, particularly the mountain lions. There were stories of their magnificence to kept us occupied. Bhutan is so beautiful. I thought I had seen every shade of green prior to my going there but green takes on a new bright, rich hue as the light lays so very peacefully across the vast and Holy valleys. The peace is palpable. It's in the air. It's something so real. It's something that is felt in the very marrow of your bones. Spiritually it is something that can be fed from.

Again, following a long drive, we were met by the whole household. King, Queen, son and daughter and servants. All bowed. All were respectful in the Himalayan way and all were delighted to greet us. Servants took our bags to our rooms. The young girl that brought the letter to our hotel was among them but still she would not look at us. Bless her heart! She was very shy. It was her who led us to our rooms. We took our time to freshen up, shower and change cloths. There was enough time to sit and relax, all looked forward to a late dinner. Sandra was delightful and looked forward to chatting with the Queen, she had the ability to make whoever she met to feel comfortable, she had a wide knowledge and showed inexhaustible interest in the life and views of others. She was not the same person that I had come to know in London, all her insecurities from Kathmandu had melted from view and I prayed, would never return. We were uncertain as to protocol but decided to go down stairs. We felt free to do so and did not wait for an invitation. Our rooms were on the second floor. No lifts but no need for one. The stairs were not steep, they declined at a steady flow. We floated to the ground floor. Our eyes were drawn by the furniture. All ancient and all traditional in the Bhutanese and Chinese style. It was stunning, so beautiful and like everything else in this unique country, it exuded a peace that was a direct reflection of Bhutan. The whole palace was quiet and seemed to be in a state of deep meditation.

Dinner was the most auspicious experience. All our wishes were met. Julie was offered a teaching opportunity within the royal household. Sandra was granted any wish she desired and I was told that the queen wished to take the three of us to meet Her dharma teacher, Dilgo Khyentse Rinpoche. In addition to this, we were introduced to an elderly man servant who was to tend tirelessly to our every need. The food was wonderful, hot, spicy and plentiful. Julie asked if there was ever any crime in Bhutan. The Queen told us that there was one prison in the country. "At present there are three men held in it. They were caught peddling tobacco." She said!

Sandra, Julie and I were all getting used to happiness as a daily condition. It was not a happiness that caused us to laugh all day long. It was a meeting of the outer and inner conditions being the same. It was a long time since we had seen misery. In fact, we had not heard any negative conversation since we had left London.

Sandra had told Julie to decide what she would truly like to do. "I will be your patron" she told her, "even cover the cost if you would like to set up your own school with the royal family blessings. Perhaps we may link it to the children's school in Kathmandu. You could perhaps travel between the two. It would not cost much as the buildings are already here." Julie was shy but also ecstatic at the opportunity, she had no idea as to who Sandra was, or of her history, but assumed, she might be royal too as she witnessed the smiling manner that Sandra slid down her chair when the queen asked about Princess Diana and asked us why the princess did not come visit Bhutan too. The King wanted to know if James Hunt would have come to Bhutan one day. Words travel fast eh! I wondered how it was that the *Thunder Lion King* had become interested in motor racing. Actually, I wondered how he even knew about motor racing but I suppose Kings know everything, just as an East End mum knew everything too. Centuries ago, when Tibet was totally isolated. The king had heard word of the Buddha teachings in India. He wished to bring peace to his land and sent emissaries to India to bring the teachings back. How had he heard of Padmasamhava? How did he know where to find him? But he did. Perhaps that is the power of a king, maybe he has a minister of outside events, I thought.

The following day the queen escorted us on a full tour of Bhutan. Nobody knew how long this would take. We all took a bag with us. A change of clothes, some toiletries and a tooth brush. We had no security with us. There was no sense or expectation of danger. There was no feeling in the mind *of 'us and them'*. This was shown clearly when our clean but simple jeep dropped the king off in Thimpu, where he would spend the day drinking coffee and playing drafts with his friends. He did not look like a King as he trotted across the road wearing his gardening trousers, a waist coat and a battered old trilby hat. He wore these above a pair of boots that turned up at the toe as would a shoe if it were two sizes too large. He reminded me of my old boatswain in his boots bought from the too big shop. I mentioned to Sandra that he could be a character in the children's pop-up book, along with the Baroness Isabella.

Meanwhile, the three girls and I, along with Samtem the man servant, hit the tracks. The queen wished to introduce her quest to her people. "There are three different peoples, that make up the Bhutanese population" she told us. The first we met were Bon, they practised the earliest and most ancient religion of the region, the Bon tradition. The Bon actually pre dates Buddhism but was blended centuries ago with the forming of the Nyingma school of Tibetan Buddhism, which is a mix of the two. They built their homes on stilts and farmed large areas in the North. Each family had their own land allotted to them by the Dragon King. Some call it a feudal system but it does not matter what name they gave to it as everybody was happy and did not expect to be any other way.

It was peace that reigned rather than philosophical disputes. The only cause of concern was the growing Chinese interest in the region. They had already suggested that they would finance a new road that would run across the top of Bhutan, following the trail of the ancient silk route. It will be good for trade they had said but the king would not hear of it as Snow lions are rare and he knew that at least two of these beautiful wild cats lived in that part of the kingdom.

The next people we visited were the Buddhist. Their whole culture was built around their admiration of the spiritual giants, the victorious ones, the great conquerors of ignorance. They devoted themselves to seeking enlightenment by taking on the persona of the deities. To be amongst them was the most extraordinary experience. Truly it was a Buddha land. The peace was beyond anything that we may imagine. We did our best to walk in silence. Even the sound of a foot fall, we felt to disturb the peace. I had felt the same silence around the Khempo. It was the same experience. He had blended with something beyond comprehension and something beyond comprehension had blended with Him. A sense of having melted into the universe was calculable. These people lived in complete harmony with the land and environment. They understood the value of the medicinal plants. Everybody played their part in daily life. Some were weavers, others were planters and others were taking care of the livestock. Just as I had experienced in Japan, all worked in silence. The only sounds were the light tapping of a tool or the mumbling of a mantra.

It was suggested that we did not visit the third of Bhutan's people. Sandra, Julie and I were content with this decision as the day had been long. The third group were the Hindu's, they lived on the border with India. Three religions lived peacefully within one harmonious kingdom. How wonderful was this! It had been over twelve hundred years since there had been a war in this country. No wonder that the atmosphere was pure. It was not just the mountain air. It was human attitude too. During this wonderful day Samden told me, he had in his rooms at the palace, a complete block print of the epic poem of king Gesar of Ling. It was centuries old and had been passed down through generations of his family. This was wonderful news. It was printed in the ancient language of Sanskrit but none the less he was very happy for us to sit with it. I had first read of the existence of this epic poem some years earlier and had been most fortunate to have found abridged versions of it in several different libraries. It is reputed to be the longest poem ever written. It told the story of King Gesar of Ling and His search for enlightenment. I used one story to develop and improve my patience. The story tells of how the King rode upon His magnificent pure white stallion, Khyang Go Kharka. They travelled through a narrow valley. Demons who wished to place obstacles in the Kings path, rolled a boulder to block their progress. Undeterred, the King spent the next several lifetimes, stroking the boulder with a feather until it finally yielded and He continued on His way towards ultimate understanding. These stories are told to children in a society that believes in constant rebirth. What was it that Lama Yeshe had said to me? *"No old age, no sickness and no death."*

Few words were spoken upon our return journey apart from an explanation from time to time in regard to the landscape, wild life and fauna. All were respected, all were preserved and all were happy. Strangely I spent much of the trip in silence. Tomorrow we were to go visit Khyentse Rinpoche at his residence. I was very emotional and I set Sandra off too. She held my hand. She understood the profundity that I felt. She felt it too! This was also the day that Sandra received a message from London. The purchase of her new home had been completed. But Sandra had no plan to immediately leave for London. She was going to stay in Kathmandu with Julie as her companion. They were going to spend time with the children and go visit their aunty again.

Conclusion

There is no other species on earth as fortunate as a human being. We have the luxury, the mental faculties, to change our mind, to seek a life style that holds undiluted merit, therefore immovable happiness is ours to be found.

Through meditation, contemplation and daily spiritual practise, it is truly possible to develop our true human qualities of wisdom and compassion. The happiness I speak of is not the unstable nature of transitory pleasure, but an installed inner peace that is able to cope, whatever the circumstances before us.

There is no greater blessing for our mother, than for the birth of her child, to be of immense benefit to sentient beings and our environment. Her future will bare natural rewards. Our dreams and our wishes for her joy, will manifest in a future life.

***

I have been a monk now, for something approaching thirty years. I still do not know the time, I still have no watch and I have no thought as to the date. All will happen in its own time and if not in this lifetime, then in the next, or maybe the one to follow, or maybe the one after that, but certainly sometime in the future. It's all a simple matter, of planting a seed through pure intentions, and then to display patience until the conditions gather and our wishes manifest. This is not magic, sorcery or wishful thinking, *it is the way of things.*

Through my investigations I am satisfied that life does not end at one death, *there is always a future.* There is always a moment before and always a moment to follow. Our mind, I have discovered to be a mental continuum, that has no beginning, nor does it have an end. From it will manifest countless forms. The nature of these forms is completely dependent on the state and condition of our mind.

But I am not going to turn this final part to this book into a lecture. I would however urge all those who show interest in the subject of spiritual awareness, to investigate the nature of existence for themselves. To be a spiritual Sherlock Holmes, to properly employ their mental faculties. To hunt down those ultimate realisations that dwell within every one of us without exception. It is this that matters. It is this that our lives are for. It is this that ends our suffering across time and space. Spiritual realisations are not limited to one single lifetime, they support us throughout eternity.

***

Sandra and Julie stayed with me for the two months prior to my ordination. The Dalia Lama and Trungpa Rinpoche were also present. My head had been shaved, apart from a small tuft on the crown. This was to be cut by Rinpoche at the ceremony.

This was the time of the horse festival. Sandra was able to witness the horsemanship. She was enthralled.

Mara and Mota have both passed from this life. I have sworn to be kind to every sentient being, just in case it is them reborn. If there is no limit to potential, then I believe they may re appear once more in my life. There is no harm done if I am wrong about this. It's healthy for my own future to be kind whatever to all living beings.

***

May all living beings, without a single exception, find the causes for their happiness and rest in the peaceful nature of the vast expanse.

***

Acknowledgements

There is far too much to be grateful for. I would even wish to thank the air made available for me to breath.

But I think of my son Alec, his partner Charlotte and their child, Rome.

I think of Terry, a wonderful example to so many, always willing to help and give of herself to those who struggle.

I think of Dorothy, who got me started, in writing this book

Jain, a constant source of encouragement, who wrote for me, the introduction

And to all my friends that have played their part in my life

I say Thank You to you all.

***

Printed in Great Britain
by Amazon